Parties, Elections, and Policy Reforms in Western Europe

Social pacts – policy agreements between governments, labor unions and sometimes employer organizations – began to emerge in many countries in the 1980s. The most common explanations for social pacts tend to focus on economic factors, influenced by industrial relations institutions such as highly coordinated collective bargaining. This book presents, and tests, an alternative and complementary explanation highlighting the electoral calculations made by political parties in choosing pacts.

Using a dataset covering 16 European countries for the years 1980–2006, as well as eight in-depth country case studies, the authors argue that governments' choice of social pacts or legislation is less influenced by economic problems, but is strongly influenced by electoral competition. Social pacts will be attractive when party leaders perceive them to be helpful in reducing the potential electoral costs of economic adjustment and wage restraint policies. Alternatively, parties may forgo negotiations with social partners and seek to impose such policies unilaterally if they believe that approach will yield electoral gain or minimize electoral costs.

By combining the separate literatures on political economy and party politics, the book sheds new light on the dynamics of social pacts in Western Europe. This book will be of interest to students and scholars of political science, economics, political economy, European Studies and comparative politics.

Kerstin Hamann is Professor of Political Science at the University of Central Florida. She is the co-editor of *Institutions and Democratic Development* and *Assessment in Political Science*.

John Kelly is Professor of Industrial Relations, Birkbeck College, University of London, UK. His books include *Union Organization and Activity and Rethinking Industrial Relations* (both published by Routledge).

Routledge research in comparative politics

Parties, Elections, and Policy Reforms in Western Europe

Voting for social pacts

Kerstin Hamann and John Kelly

Routledge
Taylor & Francis Group

LONDON AND NEW YORK

First published 2011
by Routledge
2 Park Square, Milton Park, Abingdon, Oxon, OX14 4RN

Simultaneously published in the USA and Canada
by Routledge
270 Madison Avenue, New York, NY 10016

Routledge is an imprint of the Taylor & Francis Group, an informa business

© 2011 Kerstin Hamann and John Kelly

Typeset in Garamond by Glyph International Ltd
Printed and bound in Great Britain by CPI Antony Rowe, Chippenham,
Wiltshire

British Library Cataloguing in Publication Data
A catalogue record for this book is available from the British Library

Library of Congress Cataloging in Publication Data
Hamann, Kerstin.
Parties, elections, and policy reforms in western Europe : voting for social
pacts / Kerstin Hamann and John Kelly.
    p. cm. – (Routledge research in comparative politics ; 36)
Includes bibliographical references and index.
1. Europe, Western–Politics and government–1989– 2. Consensus (Social
sciences)–Europe, Western. 3. Political parties–Europe, Western.
4. Elections–Europe, Western. I. Kelly, John. II. Title.
JN94.A58H36 2010
306.2094–dc22   2009052927

ISBN 13: 978-0-415-58195-0 (hbk)
ISBN 10: 0-415-58195-8 (hbk)

ISBN 13: 978-0-203-84865-4 (ebk)
ISBN 10: 0-203-84865-9 (ebk)

Meinen Eltern
K. H.

To my mother
J. K.

Contents

Tables

Figures

Preface and acknowledgments

This book is the product of several years of collaboration and many discussions about the relationship between governments and trade unions. Our interest in explaining the recurrence of social pacts to reform welfare, labor market, and incomes policy across Western Europe was sparked by our different perspectives on pacts because of our backgrounds in Political Science and Industrial Relations, respectively. It was a small next step to combine these differences in perspective to construct an explanation that takes a political science lens to explain social pacts, and which grants unions a prominent role even in countries where much of their strength has been eroded over the last two decades or so. Social pacts, in our view, are worth studying because they form part of a political process that results in social welfare, labor market, and wage policies that are an integral part of the political economies of Western European countries and elsewhere. Who participates in these decision-making processes matters because it relates to whose interests are represented and thus ultimately concerns the quality of democracy. Therefore, it is important to understand the conditions that lead governments to offer pacts to unions and sometimes employers, as it is equally important to analyze the conditions that lead governments to prefer reforming crucial policy areas through legislation. We hope that our research makes a contribution to the debate on these issues and hopefully sparks debates that further our knowledge of the democratic processes in Western European countries.

While the book is the result of a collaborative effort between the authors, the network of collaboration is so much wider and includes many colleagues who made invaluable contributions that facilitated our work and improved the book through discussions at conferences where our ideas and findings were presented. Colleagues were also involved informally, by reading and commenting on portions of the manuscript, or by assisting with our research. In particular, we owe a debt of gratitude to Alexia Katsanidou, who was employed as a Research Assistant on the project and did invaluable work on the quantitative data that form the core of Chapter 4. We would also like to gratefully acknowledge funding from the British Economic and Social Research Council (RES-000-22-2149). Our sincere thanks also to Racine Altif and Kerri Milita, who provided outstanding research assistance.

For discussing and commenting on our ideas, we are indebted to Karen Anderson, Sabina Avdagic, Lucio Baccaro, William Claggett, Jimmy Donaghey, Kevin Featherstone, Marion Frenz, Anke Hassel, Seth Jolly, Oscar Molina, Laura Morales, Hutch Pollock, Ida Regalia, Martin Rhodes, Barbara Sgouraki-Kinsey, Paul Teague, Jelle Visser, Mark Wickham-Jones, Bruce Wilson, as well as three anonymous referees.

Kerstin Hamann, Orlando and John Kelly, London

Note

A much shorter, and early, version of a small section of some of the material on Ireland and Austria (around 6 pages) appeared in *Comparative Political Studies*, 40(8), 2007.

1 Introduction

The puzzle of social pacts

Social pacts are standing out as a prevalent mode of welfare, labor market, and wage reform since the early 1980s in Western Europe. Between 1980 and 2006, 110 pacts covered a total of 145 issues within these three domains in 16 Western European countries (EU15 plus Norway). In addition, trade unions (and sometimes employers) also rejected a sizeable number (47) of pacts that governments had offered, resulting in a total of 157 pact offers extended by governments to unions and employers. Unsurprisingly, given this empirical prominence, social pacts have become the subject of a growing body of scholarly research.[1] While much of this research addresses the question of why pacts emerged just when corporatism was perceived as declining, so far our understanding of this phenomenon remains patchy. Consider the following: Ireland has a continuous history of social pacts from 1987 despite the fact that as a liberal market economy it does not appear to possess the preconditions for effective tripartism; in Austria, with a long history of tripartism, agreements were repudiated by governments after 1999 as they opted instead for union exclusion and legislation; in Italy, successive governments have oscillated between a preference for pacts and a preference for legislation; and even in Scandinavia, where strong unions would seem to make some form of union involvement in policymaking highly probable, Danish and Swedish governments have at times opted for legislation while excluding unions. So far we do not have an encompassing explanation for why some governments sometimes prefer reforms through pacts, but at other times would rather legislate; why countries that have similar economic and industrial relations institutions or patterns of economic performance nonetheless vary significantly in the predominance of pacts; and why countries with strong histories of corporatism or union inclusion in policymaking occasionally abandon these paths and opt for legislation as their preferred mode of reform.

This book advances our understanding of the ways in which governments choose to implement reform policies by focusing on electoral pressures on governing parties. We show that governments' preferences for reforming contested policy areas through pacts or legislation correspond to pressures governments are exposed to in the electoral arena. Governing parties' reform strategies for potentially unpopular policies respond to those pressures as they attempt to maintain electoral competitiveness. As such, social pacts are not merely responses to economic pressures, but are politically constructed.

The argument in brief

While building and expanding on the insights produced by existing research on the origins of social pacts, we also depart from this literature in two important ways. First, we take issue with the common assumption in this body of research that governments are primarily economic managers responding to economic pressures. Instead we develop and test the argument that governments and the political parties they are comprised of are also, and perhaps primarily, political actors, interested in promoting their electoral fortunes. To do so, they strategically and selectively employ social pacts when it seems that these might be electorally advantageous instead of passing potentially unpopular reforms via legislative procedure. We assume that political parties are concerned with winning votes and oftentimes office, both of which are usually necessary to pursue specific policy agendas (see Strøm and Müller 1999). Thus, when engaging in policy reforms, governments are conscious of the potential electoral consequences of their policies. Second, we depart from existing studies, most of which center their analysis only on pacts, by reasoning that governments have a choice in how they pursue reforms. They can either opt for social pacts, negotiated with either or both of the social partners, or they can use the legislative route towards policy reform. We thus understand pacts as an alternative to legislation, and therefore assume that variation in pacts within and across countries is best understood when compared with governments' resort to legislation. As we discuss in Chapter 2, in corporatist countries with highly coordinated or centralized collective bargaining institutions, governments presumably do not need to choose between pacts and legislation because existing institutions will deliver wage moderation. Yet both pacts and legislation are still found even in highly corporatist countries such as Belgium, Finland, and the Netherlands on both wage and non-wage issues, suggesting that social pacts exist independently of corporatist institutions. Our focus on governments' strategies as an attempt to bolster their electoral fortunes reflects the fact that we are primarily interested in governments' motivation to *offer* pacts rather than unions' willingness to *sign* pacts. In other words, we are less concerned here with whether governments succeed in working out deals with unions and employers and pact offers are accepted by the social partners or not, a question that is certainly interesting and important but distinct from our analytical focus. Hence, we use pact offers rather than signed pacts as the object of study in our analysis throughout the book unless otherwise stated.

To develop and test our argument we combine several literatures that have until now existed largely along separate lines: the political economy literature on state intervention in the economy, which has explored the economic and institutional logic of government negotiations with the social partners; and the economic voting, welfare reform, and party politics literatures, which have explored the changing behavior of voters and parties and the ways in which parties implement contentious issues such as welfare reform. By combining insights from these literatures we construct a comprehensive explanation for the emergence and persistence of social pacts in Western Europe while simultaneously accounting for variation in the occurrence of social pacts across countries as well as within countries over time. We build our reasoning on the assumption that many government proposals to target welfare state cuts, attempt to limit wage growth, or reform labor markets, are potentially unpopular with the electorate. We further assume that parties forge social pacts not only to deal with economic problems but also in response to electoral calculations. Social pacts will be attractive when party leaders perceive them to be helpful in reducing the potential electoral costs of unpopular economic adjustment and wage restraint policies. Alternatively, parties may forgo negotiations with social partners and seek to impose such policies unilaterally if it appears probably that this approach may yield electoral gain or minimize electoral costs.

Research design and data

We define a social pact as a national agreement between government and unions, and sometimes employers, intended to regulate wages or reform welfare or labor markets.[2] Thus, we exclude bipartite agreements between unions and employers that are concluded without government participation even if the government has encouraged the social partners to sign such an agreement. We therefore exclude the famous 1982 Wassenaar agreement between unions and employers – although the government had threatened the social partners with legislation, it was not actually involved in the negotiations.[3] We also exclude the 1977 Moncloa Pacts at the outset of democracy in Spain because they were signed between political parties and did not directly involve the social partners in the negotiations.

To test our core propositions, we follow Tarrow's (2004) advice to embrace both quantitative and qualitative methods. Thus, our research design embraces two methods of data collection and analysis. We first employ quantitative analysis of a pooled time-series dataset of social pact offers and legislation and a series of variables related to electoral factors across 16 West European countries for the time period 1980–2006. Multivariate analysis allows us to establish associations between variables and assess the general validity of our core argument for all cases. However, it is also important to explore the causal mechanisms underlying our hypotheses to establish whether variables related to electoral pressures really are salient for the political actors at the heart of our argument. We thus supplement our quantitative analysis with qualitative case studies exploring eight countries. Such cases can also uncover the conditions under which our argument has more or less validity and illustrate the contextual conditions that modify the operation of our central variables.

Our database spans the years 1980–2006, beginning when pacts first began to emerge and covering over a quarter of a century of continued pacts. This timeframe is also long enough to allow us to test rival hypotheses extant in the literature. The dataset comprises all pact offers in the EU15 countries (Austria, Belgium, Denmark, Finland, France, Germany, Greece, Ireland, Luxembourg, Netherlands, Portugal, Spain, Sweden, and the United Kingdom) as well as Norway. We included Norway in common with many other studies in West European comparative political economy and comparative politics (e.g. Fajertag and Pochet 2000; Huber and Stephens 2001; Immergut *et al.* 2007; Iversen 2005; Katzenstein 1985; Mares 2006; Müller and Strøm 2003; Swank 2002). Several of these studies also include Switzerland, the other major West European country outside the EU. However, as two of our main data sources on social pacts, the *European Industrial Relations Review* and the *European Industrial Relations Observatory*, do not provide any data at all on Switzerland, we decided to omit this case to ensure consistency and comparability of data across all cases.

Given our theoretical focus on governments' motivation to offer pacts rather than the success of pact negotiations, we recorded not only formal, signed pacts, but also instances of social pact offers that were not signed because they were rejected by unions, employers, or both. Our data comprise wage pacts and interventions covering other labor market reforms – such as work-time, training, and industrial relations institutions – in addition to welfare state reforms, including pension reforms. The focus on wages (and, to a much lesser extent, on welfare) prevalent in the existing literature makes sense as much of the existing research has been based on the assumption that pacts are motivated by European Monetary Union (EMU). However, if we consider the possibility that pacts may be driven by factors other than EMU, there is no reason to restrict the scope of pacts to wages and wage-related issues.

The premise of our argument is that pacts may prove to be an electorally attractive way for governments to implement unpopular reforms. However, we acknowledge that not all welfare reforms are unpopular. For instance, when particular aspects of welfare policies have become delegitimized or publicly criticized, as was the case with aspects of unemployment benefits in Denmark and Sweden, voters might largely support rather than oppose welfare reforms (Klitgaard 2007). Where our sources indicated that unions agreed on proposed reforms we did not include those in our database. However, given the absence of systematic survey data on the popularity of specific reforms, we are aware that we were probably unable to identify all the reforms that had widespread support in the electorate. We thus erred on the side of caution and included all reforms unless there were clear indicators that they enjoyed union or popular support. The comparative country chapters will discuss some of these cases in more detail.

Measuring the incidence of legislative intervention in these areas is not straightforward for two reasons: In the areas of welfare and labor markets governments frequently enact minor adjustments of benefit levels through administrative reforms of benefit rules. In other words, many legislative initiatives reflect administrative routine rather than a strategic choice to exclude the social partners. It therefore makes little sense to include all of these diverse initiatives under the rubric of legislative reform, as distinct from social pacts. Moreover, many pieces of recent labor market legislation have reflected the need to comply with EU Directives on issues such as work time. Although the legal enactment of EU-driven labor market reforms could in theory be preceded by a social pact, the content of most Directives provides relatively little scope for national discretion and hence for significant negotiation and amendment by the social partners. Thus, we expect that for those instances, pacts are not really a viable alternative to legislation. Our data collection nonetheless provided evidence of a substantial number of legislative interventions. (A detailed description of sources for all our variables is contained in Appendix 1.)

Case selection for qualitative analysis

The selection of cases for our qualitative analysis was driven by a concern to represent a variety of economic institutions, broadly following the Varieties of Capitalism and welfare regimes frameworks. The Varieties of Capitalism literature has clearly identified two types of capitalism, the "liberal market economies" (LMEs) comprising the UK and Ireland, and the "coordinated market economies" (CMEs) typified by Germany and including many other members of the EU15 (Hall and Soskice 2001a). A third, theoretically less well developed category is the Mediterranean or "mixed" cluster, which includes Southern European countries (see also Molina and Rhodes 2007a).[4] The literature on welfare regimes, in turn, has identified three slightly different clusters of West European countries: liberal regimes such as the UK; Christian–Democratic (variously also labeled corporatist or conservative) regimes in continental Europe and the Benelux countries; and the social democratic regimes of Scandinavia. The Southern European welfare states are not generally grouped into a separate category; Esping-Andersen (1990) and Huber and Stephens (2001), for example, group Italy and France together with the conservative regimes of continental Western Europe (Austria, Belgium, Germany), but the younger democracies in Southern Europe (Spain, Portugal, Greece) are excluded from the analysis.

The organization of the qualitative chapters is based on a combination of these typologies because the major types of capitalism covary with several political, social welfare, and industrial relations institutions (see Iversen 2006: 616), which means we can control more easily for those factors in our country case comparisons. Specifically, we point to four main factors. First, some institutional arrangements may appear more favorable towards concertation and consensus building than others. For example, it could be expected that the institutions of the CMEs, which emphasize coordination between economic actors through non-market mechanisms, are more likely to facilitate social pacts than are LMEs with their more market-driven arrangements emphasizing competition (Hall and Soskice 2001b: 8–9). At the same time, the high levels of industrial conflict and the existence of centralized trade union confederations in the Southern European economies have been reasoned to provide powerful incentives for governments to engage in concertation (Molina and Rhodes 2007a). Second, as demonstrated in Chapter 2, while wages form part of many social pacts, a large proportion of social pacts contain components other than wage agreements, such as welfare state reforms or labor regulations. For example, since the 1970s some Southern European governments have begun to construct new systems of labor regulations after their transition to democracy. Theoretically, it makes sense to expect the issues and contents of pacts to be different in different varieties of capitalism and welfare regimes. Pierson (2001: 432), for example, points to the "numerous linkages ... between liberal welfare state arrangements and the liberal or 'disorganized' model of capitalism." Likewise the welfare reform agendas in the social democratic welfare states of Scandinavia may differ from the issues that are paramount in the Christian Democratic welfare states of Germany and the Benelux countries. Third, it is not just the economic institutions, but also political and industrial relations institutions, that tend to cluster in the different models of capitalism. For example, overall, employer and labor organizations tend to be weakest in the LMEs, somewhat stronger in Southern Europe and in the conservative welfare states such as Germany, and very strong in the social democratic countries. This means it is potentially more difficult for governments to seek negotiated reforms with unions and/ or employer organizations in the LMEs (see Pierson 2001: 433).

Lastly, the welfare states in LMEs tend to be smaller in comparison to the social democratic or conservative welfare states, leading to lower expectations in the general population of expansive benefits, and less hostility to reforms and welfare cuts compared to voters in other welfare regimes (Pierson 2001: 433).[5] To illustrate, in the mid-1990s, over 57 percent of the electorate in Sweden received social benefits, just over half the electorate in Germany did so, but less than one-third of the electorate in the United States received benefits (Pierson 2001: 413). Similarly, Svallfors (1997) compares countries grouped into four types of welfare systems and overall identifies some differences across regime types with respect to attitudes to redistribution and income differences, while Linos and West (2003) find differences in the social bases of public support for the welfare state across regime types. Swank (2001: 213) also expects broader political support for welfare spending in universal systems compared to corporatist and liberal systems and refers to the likelihood that the median voter benefits from universal welfare benefits. Brooks and Manza (2007: 41–2) illustrate that despite substantial within-regime type variation, popular preferences for the level of welfare differences vary across types of welfare regimes, with support highest in the Christian Democratic countries, fairly closely followed by Social Democratic regimes, with liberal regimes a distant third (data for 1996).[6] In sum, research indicates – albeit inconsistently – that macroeconomic institutions, captured in the Varieties of Capitalism and welfare regime typologies, could potentially have an important bearing on the way governments seek to reform welfare systems, labor markets, and wage bargaining outcomes.

We thus establish a fourfold typology of regime types based on economic institutions and welfare regimes and consisting of the Scandinavian social-democratic group, the continental European Christian Democratic regimes, the liberal market and welfare regimes (UK and Ireland), and the Mediterranean "mixed" group. Within each of these four types, we selected two countries to explore variation across cases as well as within cases. Specifically, Chapters 5 and 6 each contrast a matched pair of countries exhibiting sharp divergence in the use of pacts and legislation. Chapter 5 focuses on the only liberal market economies in Western Europe: Ireland, where pacts have been prevalent, and the UK, where pacts have been absent. Chapter 6 covers two of the Scandinavian economies, Sweden and Finland, because pacts have been common in the latter country but much less frequent, and more problematic, in the former. We decided not to include Norway because its oil revenues have helped protect the economy to some extent from the problems found elsewhere in Scandinavia (Arter 1999a: 188; Nygård 2006: 358). Moreover, union density in Norway is significantly lower than in the other Nordic countries, in part because it never adopted the Ghent system of union involvement in unemployment insurance (Western 1997: 58–9). The Danish economy certainly experienced severe economic problems, but this happened in the early 1980s rather than the early 1990s and therefore sets the Danish case apart from Finland and Sweden (Green-Pedersen 2002: 44–5).

Chapters 7 and 8, on the other hand, are set up to investigate variation within similar countries over time: the oscillating patterns of pacts and legislation in Spain and Italy (Chapter 7) and the turn away from tripartism in Germany and Austria (Chapter 8). Our choice of the Mediterranean economies is based on the apparent similarities in the existence of cycles of pacts and legislation in Spain and Italy. Given this similarity, the logic of our argument is that the same explanatory variables should be at work in both countries. We do not discuss France in depth because it is not uniformly situated as a Mediterranean country in either the VoC literature or in the welfare regime literature (see, for example, Amable 2003; Esping-Andersen 1990; Hancké *et al.* 2007a; Huber and Stephens 2001). We excluded Greece and Portugal largely because of the scarcity of extensive secondary data. While Spain and Italy have both witnessed substantial numbers of social pacts, Germany and particularly Austria in sharp contrast both experienced a decline in tripartism and an increased resort to legislation. These two cases thus serve as test cases for our argument: if our explanation, grounded in electoral factors, has validity, it should also be able to accommodate cases in which tripartism has been declining as well as those in which it has become prevalent. Certainly, other cases in the continental conservative welfare state category have not experienced a similar decline in tripartism, and we thus do not claim that Germany and Austria serve as representative examples of this category. For example, pact offers have been extended quite frequently in Belgium and the Netherlands, although they are less common in Luxembourg. We have also aimed to maximize national variation in the incidence of pacts and legislation; thus, our cases include some countries that have featured numerous pacts (Ireland, Finland, Spain, Italy) and those that overall have displayed considerably less enthusiasm for reform through pacts (UK, Sweden, Germany, Austria). Again, an encompassing explanation should be able to account not just for cases with a high frequency of pact offers, but also for those cases that display far less recourse to pacts. If our electoral explanation holds, it must be able to accommodate these very different cases and account for differences between countries as well as variations within countries over time.

A roadmap for the book

The sequence of the book chapters mirrors the development of our basic assumptions and reasoning. Chapter 2 provides an overview and critical appraisal of the literature that has addressed the reasons why social pacts have become so prominent in Western Europe. We point to the insights gained from this literature and identify some weaknesses – in part based on the empirical evidence we have gathered – that leave the emergence and persistence of pacts, on the whole, still unresolved. Chapter 3 develops the argument that governments are political actors and need to respond to potential electoral backlash emanating from welfare, wage, and labor market reforms in a changing electoral context shaped by increasing electoral volatility. We base our reasoning on the literatures on economic voting and welfare state reform and conclude that governments may choose social pacts or legislation as ways to minimize the potential electoral costs of these reforms. Chapter 4 builds on the previous two chapters and develops specific arguments and hypotheses concerning the conditions under which governments might prefer pacts or legislation. The chapter then proceeds to test these hypotheses through multivariate analysis against our data from 16 countries for 27 years (1980–2006). The next four chapters (5–8) provide a qualitative analysis of social pact offers in four pairs of countries: Ireland and the UK (Chapter 5), Sweden and Finland (Chapter 6), Spain and Italy (Chapter 7), and Germany and Austria (Chapter 8). The Conclusion in Chapter 9 reviews our findings, reassesses our argument, extends our findings to cases not covered in the qualitative analysis, and points to implications for further research.

2 The institutional political economy of social pacts

A critical appraisal

Since the early 1980s, governments in almost all Western European countries have sought to boost national economic competitiveness by regulating wages, deregulating labor markets, and reforming welfare systems. In some countries these policies have been pursued through national-level bipartite agreements with unions or tripartite agreements with unions and employers. Commonly referred to as social pacts, these agreements emerged in the 1980s and 1990s in a range of countries with very different welfare regimes, industrial relations systems, and corporatist structures, such as Finland, Ireland, Italy, and the Netherlands (Fajertag and Pochet 2000).

The most common explanation for the emergence of social pacts conceptualizes them primarily as governmental responses to the 1992 Maastricht criteria for European Monetary Union (EMU), although sometimes the Maastricht criteria themselves are regarded as a response to increasing global competitiveness (e.g. Hancké 2002; Hancké and Rhodes 2005; Hassel 2003, 2006; Marginson and Sisson 2004; Pochet 2002; Pochet and Fajertag 2000). As industrial relations institutions are also ascribed an important role we can aptly label this approach "institutional political economy." However, we find that this explanation is both empirically and theoretically wanting. Empirically, we identify a series of unanswered questions in existing studies concerning the timing, contents, and institutional conditions of pacts. With respect to theoretical frameworks, it is true that governments strive to meet economic objectives such as the EMU criteria. However, exactly *how* governments attempt to meet these objectives is subject to other constraints, including their desire to perform well in elections. Much of the existing literature assumes a causal relationship between economic pressures and social pacts, while the role of governments as political rather than economic actors who exert choice over strategies is largely neglected.

In this chapter we first outline the main approaches to the reemergence of social pacts, looking in turn at explanations grounded in political economy, institutional analysis (including varieties of capitalism), and bargaining power. We also briefly assess the literature concerning the persistence, or institutionalization, of pacts over time. We then critically appraise the literature on theoretical, methodological, and empirical grounds, where we refer to empirical evidence drawn from the database we constructed for this project. We develop our own argument more fully in the next chapter.

Approaches to the emergence of social pacts

The literature on social pacts since the late 1990s was initially focused almost entirely on one question: If the conditions for tripartite (or bipartite) corporatist agreements had largely disappeared in the recessions of the 1980s, then why did these agreements apparently reemerge in the 1990s? Analysts turned to the corporatist literature of the 1970s (see, for example, Schmitter and Lehmbruch 1979) and noted two conditions that were identified as central influences on governmental interest in policy negotiations with unions. The first one was the control of governments by social democratic parties sympathetic to labor interests; the second one was trade union power, often reflected in high levels of union density and militancy and in some cases reinforced by relatively tight labor markets (Baccaro 2003; Molina and Rhodes 2002). These conditions began to unravel throughout Western Europe in the 1980s. Neoliberal conservative parties were electorally successful, most obviously in the UK. Trade union density and strike rates began to decline sharply from the early 1980s in most, though not all, West European countries as unemployment climbed steeply. Unemployment across the EU was just 5.0 percent in 1976 but had mounted to 8.1 percent in 1981, peaking at 10.5 percent in 1986. After falling to 8.1 percent in the late 1980s, it rose again to reach a new postwar high of 11.3 percent by 1994 (OECD June 1990; June 2007). Yet despite the gradual disappearance of the conditions for what was called "neo-corporatism" or "social concertation," it seemed that some form of concertation, in the form of social pacts, was actually reemerging (Hancké and Rhodes 2005; Molina and Rhodes 2002: 317).

The new social pacts are policy agreements between governments, labor unions and sometimes employer organizations to regulate wages, labor markets and/or welfare systems. Although on the surface, these agreements seemed to bear some resemblance to the neo-corporatist arrangements of the 1970s, several features make them notable and distinct: They are signed in countries that often do not conform to the characteristics usually identified with neo-corporatism, such as the presence of leftist governments and strong and centralized social partners. Instead, the new wave of pacts has often involved centrist or conservative governments and unions whose power is weakening. Consequently the balance of outcomes from the new social pacts, described by Rhodes (2001) as "competitive corporatism," is likely to be less favorable to labor compared to the agreements of the 1970s. Rueda (2007) challenges the link between social democratic governments and labor-friendly policies by drawing on dual labor market theory. He argues that labor markets in the advanced capitalist countries are increasingly divided between a well-protected core of (often unionized) "insiders" and a more vulnerable periphery of "outsiders" subject to less secure employment and more frequent spells of unemployment. Social democratic parties, he argues, increasingly reflect the interests of insiders in employment protection but will be no more concerned with social pacts to create employment than other political parties. As the literature acknowledges, these differences between neo-corporatism and the social pacts since the 1980s require an explanation that departs from the approaches used to analyze the earlier corporatist agreements.

Political economy

The most common accounts of social pacts since the 1980s suggest they reemerged as centralized mechanisms of governments' attempts to control wages in response to two sets of forces. First, the 1992 Maastricht Treaty laid down economic ceilings in readiness for European Monetary Union in 1999. These comprised tight limits on public debt (no more than 60 percent of GDP) and annual public borrowing (no more than 3 percent of GDP), and stipulated target inflation and interest rates close to the lowest rates in the EU (see Jones *et al.* 1998; Pochet and Fajertag 2000). Wage restraint was one obvious tool for governments to meet these targets. Wage moderation would help stimulate labor demand and retention and by thus reducing the level of unemployment, would cut public spending on unemployment benefits. In the public sector, which still comprised approximately 20 percent of the EU labor force in the early 1990s, wage moderation would help restrain the growth of public spending on labor intensive public services. As economies were affected by cost push inflation, wage moderation should also ease infla-tionary pressures (Ahlquist 2008; Hancké 2002: 132; Hassel 2003: 722; Keune 2008; Pochet and Fajertag 2000: 9; Traxler 2000: 401, 406). Second, the drive to Monetary Union itself has been understood as a response to global competitive pressures affecting European industry. Wages may often constitute a small proportion of total production costs, but they tend to be the cost item that is most easily manipulated; hence the emphasis in many social pacts on the rate of wage increase (Pochet and Fajertag 2000: 18; Rhodes 2001: 174).

Although wage regulation has been a central theme in much of the litera-ture, some analysts have observed the presence of other issues in social pact agreements, especially welfare spending (Brandl and Traxler 2005; Casey and Gold 2000; Ebbinghaus and Hassel 2000; Hassel 2009; Mares 2006). However, this is consistent with the role of EMU as a driving force behind social pacts because controls on welfare spending should also assist the restraint of public spending and borrowing. Evidence from Hassel (2003) on the timing of social pacts 1980–99 suggests that the majority – 21 out of 27 in 13 countries – occurred during the Maastricht period 1992–98, a fact consistent with the theoretical emphasis on EMU. Calmfors *et al.* (2001) list 37 social pacts and national agreements from 14 countries between 1980 and 2000 and similarly conclude that most of the pacts and agreements fall within the Maastricht period.

The role of institutions

A slightly different approach to explaining the emergence of social pacts downplays the role of the EMU and Maastricht criteria and lays more stress on both pre-EMU competitive pressures and on institutions, in particular wage bargaining institutions (e.g. Hassel 2006; Rhodes 2001; van Waarden and Lehmbruch 2003). An influential institutionalist theory in comparative political economy is the "Varieties of Capitalism" approach (e.g. Hall and Soskice 2001b; Hancké *et al.* 2007b). If the economic institutions central to the theory do in fact structure the relationships between actors and vary systematically across types of capitalism, we should also expect the incidence of social pact offers to show similar cross-national variation. Consequently it might be expected that social pacts would be more prevalent in the Coordinated Market Economies rather than the Liberal Market Economies because the former possess the institutional preconditions for social pacts, especially highly coordinated and centralized actors and bargaining institutions. Traxler and Brandl (2009) show that the incidence of wage pacts in 14 West European countries between 1980 and 2003 was positively associated with centralized (multi-employer) bargaining.

Hassel (2006) perhaps provides the most articulated institutional account of the incidence of social pacts. In her view governments resort to social pacts in order to regulate wages and are most likely to do so where the wage expectations of union leaders and members are "sticky," that is, relatively unresponsive to fluctuations in unemployment, even where independent central banks operate tight monetary policies (Franzese and Hall 2000). Wage stickiness is influenced by four industrial relations institutions. First, a low degree of coordination among the social partners in collective bargaining means that moderate wage settlements are not necessarily transmitted across bargaining units. In contrast, highly coordinated bargaining systems that are also highly centralized are, Hassel suggests, sufficiently sensitive to market pressures and monetary policy that pacts are redundant; the same is true for highly decentralized bargaining systems. It is systems with moderate degrees of coordination and centralization that are most likely to display social pacts (but see Hancké 2002: 131–8, who argues pacts emerge in the most centralized bargaining systems). The second factor influencing wage expectations is the presence of militant union factions that may hinder consensus on wage moderation (see also Baccaro and Lim 2007 for a similar argument); third are regulations, laws or bargaining agreements that index wages to the cost of living; and fourth is a bargaining system in which the "wage leaders" – the most influential bargaining units – are sheltered from the global economy, most commonly because of their location in the public sector. Taken together these variables influence the degree of responsiveness of the wage bargaining system. Highly responsive systems, as in Germany, Austria, and Sweden, require relatively low degrees of government intervention, whereas less responsive systems, as in Portugal and the UK, require significantly more government intervention (Hassel 2006: 183–4). Government intervention is shown to be positively associated with bargaining coordination throughout this whole period and with bargaining centralization in the 1970s, but not in subsequent decades (Hassel 2006: 83).

In addition Hassel contends that political institutions also matter and draws on Lijphart's (1999) distinction between the Westminster and consensus models of government. In the former, majoritarian systems, single-party governments enjoying large majorities in the legislature are less susceptible to influence by the social partners and therefore see less need to sign social pacts compared to their counterparts in coalition governments in consensus, proportional representation (PR) systems, especially where the party system is highly fragmented (Hassel 2006: 130–1; Ebbinghaus and Hassel 2000). Social pacts signed in PR systems may prove more expensive than unilateral legislation since the government needs to make concessions to the social partners. In line with this expectation Iversen (2007) illustrates that economic "shocks" elicit higher levels of government spending in countries with proportional representation compared to majoritarian systems. Hassel (2006: 144–6) also argues that left-wing dominated cabinets display higher levels of intervention than non-left wing cabinets in the 1990s, although not in the 1980s.

Hassel's institutional political economy focus offers several advantages over the more simplistic argument that EMU has stimulated a reemergence of social pacts. Consistent with the widely accepted proposition that "institutions matter," it offers a rich and multi-causal explanation for the differential incidence of wage pacts that emphasizes the way actors' behavior is shaped by their institutional environment. Empirically, it is certainly the case that wage pacts have been conspicuous by their absence from the UK with its majoritarian political system as well as from France, a country that scores very low on both bargaining centralization and coordination (OECD 2004).

Bargaining power

While it is generally accepted that economic and industrial relations institutions exert *some* influence over the governmental decision to offer a pact to the social partners, some researchers have suggested that within the parameters of these institutions governments retain a significant degree of strategic choice. If that is the case, the analytical challenge is to identify the factors that influence the choices of governments as they search for ways to moderate wage growth or restrain welfare spending. According to the core argument in this perspective the strategic choice by governments to offer pacts, and by unions and employers to accept them, is heavily influenced by perceptions of relative power. Consequently, variations in the offer and acceptance of social pacts both across countries and within countries over time are thought to reflect concomitant variations in the relative power of the social actors. We can distinguish two variants of this approach in the literature: first the hypothesis of "governmental weakness," and second, the "power imbalance" model.

According to the first argument, social pact offers by governments and their acceptance by unions reflect "governmental weakness" (Baccaro and Lim 2007; Baccaro and Simoni 2008; Vis 2009; see also Regini and Regalia 1997). Examining the cases of Austria, Ireland, Italy, South Korea, and the UK, Baccaro and Simoni (2008) note that the first of a long line of social pacts in Ireland was offered by a minority government shortly after its election in 1987. Similarly, the disintegration of the main political parties in Italy – Christian Democrats and Socialists – in the wake of the investigations of political corruption beginning in 1992 severely reduced the legitimacy of all the political parties and thereby weakened their capacity to govern effectively. In the particular case of pension reforms, one of the reforming governments was a technocratic administration that lacked a popular mandate while the other was a fragile coalition government forced to resign less than 12 months after its pension reform. Trade unions in both countries had been losing members at a dramatic rate as rising unemployment, among other factors, eliminated unionized jobs in manufacturing industry. In the face of deteriorating economic conditions and pressures for potentially unpopular economic reforms, it was government weakness in the presence of "moderate" trade unions that propelled governments to offer, and unions to accept, negotiated reform through social pacts.

In contrast Avdagic *et al.* (2005; Avdagic 2006, 2010; see also Meardi 2006; Molina 2005, 2006) propose that it is not governmental weakness that leads governments to offer (and unions to accept) social pacts, but a relative *imbalance* of power in favor of government. A strong government facing a weaker union confederation is most likely to result in a successful social pact. This is because governmental strength allows it to threaten credibly that it will break off negotiations while a weaker union movement has no other feasible option but to seek agreement. Where both government and union believe that a balance of power exists (they are equally strong or equally weak), breaking off negotiations will appear as a potentially attractive option if negotiations proceed badly. A preliminary test of the model on five countries – Italy, Netherlands, Poland, Slovenia, and Spain – reported very encouraging results with the outcomes of 14 out of 19 attempts at pact negotiation successfully predicted (Avdagic 2006: 11). Yet, Park (2009) reports rather different results for his comparison of four cases: social pacts were more likely where union movements were strong, i.e. united (Finland and Ireland) but less likely where union movements were weakened by interconfederal rivalry (Belgium and the Netherlands at certain periods).

Overall, these approaches enrich our knowledge of social pacts. Their strength lies primarily in the fact that by linking social pacts to the balance of power between the social partners they may be able to account for both cross-national and cross-temporal variation in social pact offers and acceptances.

Persistence of social pacts

Institutional analysis has also been at the core of research explaining the persistence of pacts within a country, that is, the repeated emergence of pacts. According to Marginson and Sisson (2004) social pacts are likely to persist where they have been integrated into (or "articulated with") collective bargaining arrangements at sector and corporate levels, as in Italy or Ireland (see Rhodes 2003). In Ireland, for example, pacts appear to have become institutionalized and the social partners now expect to negotiate a fresh pact each time the existing pact expires (Teague and Donaghey 2009). In other countries, however, such as Greece, pacts have been offered from time to time but have clearly not taken root the same way. One argument advanced in the literature is that through a social process of repeated interaction and learning the social partners have come to see the benefits of social pacts (Baccaro 2002a, b; Compston 2002; Culpepper 2002; Donaghey and Teague 2005). According to Natali and Pochet (2009) the institutionalization of social pacts also depends on a cross-party political consensus: where this has occurred, as in Ireland and Spain, pacts will be repeated, but where parties are divided, as in Italy and Portugal, the incidence of pacts will fluctuate over time (see also Anthonsen and Lindvall 2009 for similar findings on Switzerland and Italy). It is not clear, however, how we can conceptualize and measure "learning" and "shared understandings" independently of their putative outcomes. Consequently, the argument is prone to circularity: the repetition of social pacts through time simultaneously measures both the dependent variable (institutionalization of social pacts) and the independent variable (learning and shared understandings). Moreover, it is unclear precisely why, and under what conditions, some actors in some countries "learn" to appreciate the benefits from pact negotiations and outcomes while actors in other countries do not.

In sum, the pacts literature has noted an association between the emergence of social pacts in the 1990s and the attempts by many governments to comply with the Maastricht criteria for monetary union. Consequently, many of the new social pacts have sought to regulate wage increases. By identifying the role of industrial relations institutions the literature has also identified a potentially important source of cross-national variation in the incidence of social pacts.

Approaches to social pacts: a critical appraisal

These diverse strands of the pacts literature have raised important questions and advanced interesting arguments and explanations; yet, several key questions remain open. Theoretically, the role of the government as a political actor engaged both in the economic and political arena and the ensuing motivations for engaging in pacts has been largely neglected (although see Ahlquist 2008 and Vis 2009 for exceptions). We will pursue this question in the next chapter. For the remainder of this chapter, we will outline several shortcomings in the extant literature that become apparent when some of the major arguments and findings are evaluated against a comprehensive dataset of pacts. We thus assess the explanatory power of some of the major arguments against empirical data drawn from 16 countries (EU 15 plus Norway) from 1980 until 2006. As stated in Chapter 1, we define a social pact as a bipartite (government and unions) or tripartite (government, unions and employers) national-level agreement intended to regulate wage and/or non-wage issues.[1]

We find three major issues to be problematic in the existing literature. First, many of the arguments proposed in existing studies are tested against data and cases that are limited in scope and do not hold when examined against a broader range of cases. This is in part caused by the EMU focus of some of the work, which delineates the time period under study as well as the issues included in social pacts. Second, much of the existing research cannot satisfactorily explain variation both within countries over time and across countries. Third, much of the literature lacks a well-defined theory of government choice that can identify the circumstances under which governments are more or less likely to offer social pacts. We will now revisit the literature in light of these three shortcomings.

Limitations of case selection

Some of the problems related to limited data stem from the theoretical focus of much of the earlier literature on EMU. First, if we look at the occurrence of signed social pacts over time (as distinct from all pact offers), it becomes apparent that social pacts were signed in several countries long before the EMU criteria were devised and have continued to be signed since monetary union was created in January 1999. These facts are not evident in much of the work concentrating on the EMU period, but an encompassing explanation of social pacts must also be able to account for them outside the EMU period. Confining our attention for the moment only to wage and welfare pacts offered between 1980 and 1991 we find a substantial number of pre-EMU pacts – 29 in all covering 38 issues – many of which are excluded from several analyses: Hassel (2003b), for example, notes just five pacts between 1980 and 1991 (see also Calmfors *et al.* 2001; Rhodes 2001). Similarly, our data indicate an equally substantial number of social pacts (40 agreements covering 53 issues) that postdate EMU (see Table 2.1).

The total number of pacts per year was certainly higher during the 1990s compared to the 1980s, but the incidence of social pacts in the post-Maastricht years was only slightly reduced from the 1990s figure (Table 2.1). If EMU was the principal determinant of social pacts it is difficult to explain why so many pacts have pre- and postdated the period of the Maastricht criteria for EMU and why the rate of signed social pacts has declined only a little in recent years. In addition it is also worth noting that social pacts are

Table 2.1 Pre-EMU, EMU, and post-EMU agreed social pacts in Western Europe, 1980–2006

Country	Pre-EMU pacts 1980–91	EMU pacts 1992–98	Post-EMU pacts 1999–2006	Total pacts 1980–2006
Austria	0	0	1	1
Belgium	2	5	6	13
Denmark	1	2	1	4
Finland	3	5	4	12
France	0	0	2	2
Germany	0	0	1	1
Greece	1	1	0	2
Ireland	3	2	3	8
Italy	3	9	2	14
Luxembourg	0	1	1	2
Netherlands	3	2	4	9
Norway	2	2	3	7
Portugal	5	3	6	14
Spain	3	9	6	18
Sweden	3	0	0	3
UK	0	0	0	0
Total pacts	29	41	40	110
Pacts per year	2.42	5.86	5.00	4.07

Source: Hamann-Kelly dataset.

not confined to Western Europe. A succession of pacts (the Prices and Incomes Accords) was also signed in Australia from as early as 1983 and several labor market pacts were signed in South Korea and Japan in the late 1990s (Ahlquist 2007; Lee and Lee 2004; Suzuki 2004). Clearly the EMU requirements cannot provide a convincing reason for the social pacts that have been offered and signed outside Western Europe and they cannot therefore constitute the only determinant of pacts (see also Avdagic 2010; Natali and Pochet 2009).

The second limitation of the cases that inform much of the dominant literature is the concentration of these studies on just a few issues covered in pacts, namely wages and sometimes welfare (see, for example, Traxler and Brandl 2009). However, a substantial number of pacts have dealt with issues of labor market reform, which appear to have only a tenuous connection to the Maastricht criteria. The reform of collective bargaining structures, changes in employment protection laws, and adjustments to working time have all been the subject of social pacts, especially but not exclusively, in Southern Europe. Table 2.2 displays information on the content of the social pacts. Because some pacts have covered multiple issues, the total number of issues (145) is greater than the total number of pact offers (110).

Table 2.2 Issues in agreed social pacts in Western Europe, 1980–2006

Issue	Pre-EMU 1980–89 (% of 29 pacts)	EMU 1992–98 (% of 41 pacts)	Post-EMU 1999–2006 (% of 40 pacts)	Total 1980–2006 (% of 110 pacts)
Wages	22 (76%)	18 (44%)	15 (38%)	55 (50%)
Labor market	11 (38%)	21 (51%)	19 (48%)	51 (46%)
Welfare	5 (17%)	15 (37%)	19 (48%)	39 (35%)
Total issues (per year)	38 (3.17)	54 (7.71)	53 (6.63)	145

Source: Hamann-Kelly dataset.

Table 2.2 evinces that social pacts have dealt with labor market reforms almost as much as wage regulation and a significant, though smaller, number has addressed welfare and pension reform. In fact, a remarkable 50 percent of all social pacts (55 out of 110) have no wage component at all, a fact that calls into question the widespread assumption in the literature that social pacts are primarily a mechanism for moderating wage settlements.

Finally, the findings of much of the existing literature are limited by country case selection (although Avdagic 2010, Ahlquist 2008, Hassel 2006, and Baccaro and Simoni 2008 analyze a relatively large number of cases). Narrative case studies of individual countries, or small sets of countries, are useful for developing and formulating hypotheses, e.g. Anthonsen and Lindvall (2009) on Denmark, Italy, Netherlands, and Switzerland; Baccaro and Lim (2007) on Ireland, Italy, and South Korea; Ferrera and Gualmini (2004) on Italy; Jochem (2003) on Denmark and Norway; Meardi (2006) on Italy and Poland; Molina Romo (2005) on Italy and Spain; Royo (2002) on Portugal and Spain; Teague and Donaghey (2009) on Ireland; Visser and Hemerijck (1997) on the Netherlands; and Zambarloukou (2006) on Greece; or the cases in Becker and Schwartz (2005); Fajertag and Pochet (2000); Katz *et al.* (2004); and Pochet (2002). Selected case studies are less useful, however, to assess the validity of hypotheses more generally.

To illustrate, findings on the role of industrial relations institutions in the genesis of social pacts are problematic. For example, Ireland has experienced 20 years of continuous social pacts since 1987 despite the fact that its levels of bargaining centralization and coordination in the 1980s were no more than modest, according to OECD (2004) data. Conversely the Austrian pension reforms of 2001–02 could have been implemented through some form of concertation, which is deeply institutionalized in the Austrian political process and high levels of bargaining coordination and centralization prevail in that country (see OECD June 2004; Siaroff 1999). Yet, the reforms were implemented unilaterally with virtually no attempt to consult the social partners (see Chapter 8). Cases like these pose significant problems for institutionalist accounts and findings based on a small number of cases cannot easily be generalized.

Limitations in explaining variation

The second problem in the literature is that economic and institutional variables alone are not able to account for the striking degree of variation in the occurrence of social pacts both across and within countries. Certainly, some governments in the 1990s signed wage pacts in order to deal with problems of high inflation or high public deficits, for example in Belgium, Ireland, and Italy. But other governments did not respond to similar problems with wage pacts, for example Austria, Spain, and the UK, although pacts were offered on other, non-wage issues in Spain. Conversely, some governments offered and signed wage pacts in the 1990s despite running low deficits and experiencing low inflation, including the Netherlands and Finland. Institutional theory also runs into difficulty: according to one line of argument, countries with well developed corporatist institutions, including highly coordinated collective bargaining structures, have a greater capacity to agree and implement social pacts compared to countries with weaker corporatist structures or more decentralized bargaining (Hancké 2002). In contrast, Hassel (2006) states that strong and weak corporatist economies would feel little need for social pacts and such arrangements would therefore be concentrated in the middle-range corporatist countries. In fact, Table 2.3 illustrates there is no consistent relationship between corporatism and pacts. Many pacts have been

Table 2.3 Corporatism and agreed social pact offers in Western Europe

Country	Corporatism score late 1980s–mid-1990s	Social pacts 1980–2006
Austria	4.6	1
Norway	4.6	7
Sweden	4.6	3
Finland	4.3	12
Denmark	4.1	4
Germany	4.1	1
Luxembourg	4.1	2
Netherlands	4.0	9
Belgium	3.7	13
Italy	2.9	14
Ireland	2.5	8
Portugal	2.4	14
France	2.3	2
Spain	1.9	18
UK	1.9	0
Greece	1.8	2
Median	3.85	2.5
Mean	3.4	6.9

Sources: Corporatism scores calculated from Siaroff (1999, Tables 4c and 4d); pacts from Hamann-Kelly dataset.

signed in countries ranked high (Finland), moderate (Belgium, Italy) and low (Portugal, Spain) on corporatism while only few pacts were signed in a similar range of countries: high (Austria, Sweden), moderate (Germany, Luxembourg), and low (Greece, UK).

Within-country variation stands out as equally enigmatic: pacts have appeared, disappeared, and reappeared in Italy since the early 1980s in cycles that do not seem to be related to the Maastricht economic indicators. For instance, pacts were repudiated by the 1984–87 Craxi government despite concomitant rises in unemployment and in the public deficit and in Spain, pacts were common in the early 1980s, declined in the late 1980s, and reemerged in the 1990s (see Chapter 7; Hamann 2001). Gauging the impact of economic conditions on governments for offering social pacts systematically, we draw on our database of pact offers 1980–2006, containing both accepted and rejected pacts in the 1990s. We developed a multiple regression model on pact offers with three economic and two institutional independent variables: government deficit, inflation, unemployment, union density, and bargaining coordination (measured annually). Neither the equation itself nor any of the individual variables predicted the incidence of pact offers by government to unions (see also Avdagic 2010 for a similar finding).[2]

In addition, the institutional political economy approach appears ill equipped to probe into significant within-country variation in the incidence of wage pacts over time. Industrial relations institutions do occasionally undergo radical change – the best known examples include the radical decentralization of collective bargaining in the UK under Margaret Thatcher's governments and, almost simultaneously, the equally radical centralization and increased coordination of collective bargaining in Ireland (see Howell 2005 on the UK and Wallace *et al.* 2004 on Ireland). But time series data on bargaining coordination 1973–97 highlights that these institutions have proved remarkably resilient in most countries and that the British and Irish experiences are quite unusual (Calmfors *et al.* 2001: 73–4). Such stable institutions cannot therefore account for significant fluctuations within countries over time. Neither the "simple" political economy nor the more sophisticated institutionalist political economy approaches thus lend themselves to explain variation over time within country cases.

Theoretical limitations

Another limitation of much of the political economy literature is that it is devoid of a theory of government choice. That is, much of the literature is based on the assumption that government actions are determined by macroeconomic goals; the more sophisticated analyses also include the constraints and incentives provided by institutions to explain and predict the likelihood of governments to offer pacts to unions. Consequently, governments are not seen as exerting strategic choices in their decision of how best to achieve their

Table 2.4 Pacts and legislative initiatives on wages, labor market, and welfare reforms in Western Europe, 1980–2006

	Wages (N)	Wages (%)	Labor market (N)	Labor market (%)	Welfare (N)	Welfare (%)	Totals (N)
Pacts	55	75.3	51	65.4	39	52.0	145
Legislation	18	24.7	27	34.6	36	48.0	81
Totals	73	100.0	78	100.0	75	100	

Source: Hamann-Kelly dataset.

stated goals. Yet, many governments that wish to implement economic or welfare reforms have an alternative to union inclusion in negotiations on a social pact: they can act unilaterally and pass legislation to freeze wage rises, change benefit levels, or reduce levels of employment protection. This assumption is borne out by our data. Table 2.4 hints that while Western European governments have generally preferred to intervene in industrial relations and labor markets through social pacts, a substantial minority of governments has pursued reform unilaterally through legislation, but the reasons for these choices are not addressed in the social pacts literature. The use of legislation in preference to social pacts is especially pronounced for welfare issues, a fact that again highlights the problems that may be introduced through an exclusive focus on wage pacts.

The literature on bargaining power leaves open the question as to whether mutual weakness or power imbalance best predicts social pact offers. This literature had produced conflicting theoretical rationales and its empirical findings remain inconclusive. Negrelli (2000) has criticized the "mutual weakness" hypothesis, pointing out that social pacts have been signed both by "strong" unions, in Italy for example in the 1980s, as well as by "weak" unions (in the Netherlands). He argues that while the balance of power is important in accounting for pact offers by governments (and acceptances by unions), its effects are likely to be highly variable and therefore indeterminate. Using data from 14 countries Avdagic (2010) demonstrates that "weak" governments are neither necessary nor sufficient to generate social pacts and such tripartite initiatives are found in the presence of both strong and weak governments. If we consider only pacts on pension reform, the topic addressed by Baccaro and Simoni (2008) in relation to Austria and Italy, our own data include cases of minority administrations signing pacts on pension reform – in Denmark and Spain, for example. On the other hand, majority governments in Western Europe have also proposed and agreed pension pacts between 1980 and 2006, e.g. Belgium 2005, Finland 1995 and 2002, France 2003, and the Netherlands 1992 (Hamann and Kelly 2007b).

In contrast, the "power imbalance" hypothesis is weakened by the very cases that lend support to the "governmental weakness" hypothesis, namely pacts offered and signed by minority governments. Avdagic (2006: 10) points out that assessing governmental power is complex for the same reasons set out by Strøm (1990): for instance, she argues the leaders of seemingly powerful, majority administrations – as in Spain in the mid-1980s – may perceive themselves to be vulnerable to adverse public opinion in the wake of unpopular reforms. Conversely the "minority" Irish administration of 1987–89 was strengthened by its opponent's declaration that it would support the government's economic program and not seek to bring it down with a vote of confidence (Hamann and Kelly 2007a). Within this approach, however, it is not obvious why strong governments, however defined, should be at all interested in social pacts.

Overall, the claims of the strategic choice and power literature are theoretically plausible but have found very mixed empirical support. It is reasonable to assume that social pact offers reflect governmental strategic choices and that such choices reflect the power of governments relative to the social partners. However, it has proved difficult to move from that general argument to testable propositions supported by evidence from a large set of cases.

Conclusion

Each of the approaches we have reviewed can legitimately claim to offer some insights into one or more questions about the reemergence of social pacts in Western Europe since the early 1980s. The political economy approach based around the Maastricht requirements for monetary union is supported by the significant rise in the number of wage pacts from the 1980s into the 1990s. On the other hand, it is not clear why pacts have persisted since 1999; why only half the social pacts deal with wages as distinct from a variety of non-wage issues; and how we are to account for the significant variations within and between countries. Institutionalist approaches have also found difficulty in offering explanations for some of the observed cross-national variation by reference to industrial relations institutions. In addition, variation within countries has not been fully explained. The literature on bargaining power and strategic choice has moved in the direction of trying to model government choice but there is still considerable disagreement as to whether it is governmental weakness or strength (or either, under different circumstances) that generates pact offers to unions.

Moreover, one problem common to these approaches is the absence of a well developed model of the behavior of political parties in government. While we acknowledge that governments are in part economic actors, responsible for a variety of economic policies and macroeconomic outcomes, we argue in the next chapter that our understanding of social pacts will be considerably enhanced by recognizing that governing parties are also political actors, motivated to gain votes, remain or return to office, and influence policy (Strøm and Müller 1999). We also argue that governments can choose whether to include unions in policymaking through social pacts or to exclude them and legislate reforms unilaterally. The pacts literature has concentrated almost entirely on explaining the incidence of pacts, whereas we believe it is more fruitful to conceptualize pacts as an alternative to legislation. That is, we conceive a particular policy reform issue rather than social pacts as the appropriate unit of analysis to understand government motivations to engage in pacts. As we will illustrate throughout the remainder of this book, social pacts are just one way in which governments can tackle reform policies, and we cannot fully understand why and when they resort to social pacts unless we also understand when and why they prefer the legislatsive route. The following chapter lays out our theoretical reasoning for looking at electoral factors as the driving force behind government choice.

3 The political logic
of social pacts

Governments may be motivated to resort to social pacts in response to economic problems. However, as the previous chapter illustrates, economic problems by themselves hold little explanatory power for the occurrence of social pacts. Consequently, our analysis focuses on governments and political parties and their role in initiating or facilitating social pacts on wage, welfare, and labor market reforms in response to electoral pressures. Governments can, and frequently do, choose an alternative path to adjustment by using legislative procedure that excludes unions and employers. Why, then, do governments sometimes prefer negotiations with unions and employers to parliamentary procedure? This question is particularly interesting as pacts are not necessarily without cost for governments. Negotiations imply some compromising on the part of the government, meaning governments move away from their ideal policy position. They can also be lengthy, and failed negotiations can cast a negative light on all actors involved – including the governing party or parties. Negotiations with non-parliamentary actors can raise questions of democratic legitimacy and the democratic process in the minds of the voters. Yet, governments across Western Europe have regularly initiated social pacts since the 1980s.

To account for the reemergence of pacts, we introduce an explicitly political perspective by tapping into the literature on party competition and voting behavior. Parties and governments can use pacts strategically as a way to attract or retain voters given multiple pressures on governments. Many voters expect a continuation or expansion of their welfare benefits and improvements in living standards while governments wish to downsize welfare states and restrain wages in the face of changing demographics and fiscal demands. Governments are thus confronted with a dilemma, which is to meet these economic demands while maintaining or enhancing their chances for electoral success. Pacts can be used as one strategy in which governing parties respond to this dilemma because they can lend legitimacy to unpopular policies – and to the governing parties implementing them – by including the social partners, thus broadening the support coalition.

In constructing a conceptual framework to examine the political logic of social pacts and legislation we draw on several literatures concerning the behavior of political parties and voters. After setting out briefly our basic assumptions we proceed to elaborate our reasoning in more detail. First, we assume that parties, in or out of office, are continually involved in choosing trade-offs among their sometimes competing goals of vote seeking, office seeking, and policy seeking (Strøm 1990). In other words, governments are not just concerned with implementing policies in response to economic problems, as much of the pacts literature has implied, but also with their electoral performance. Second, whilst all parties face trade-offs, these are likely to manifest themselves in different ways for social democratic, Christian Democratic, and conservative parties (especially those with a strong neoliberal economic program), in part because of their differing electoral bases. Third, voters hold the government responsible for the economy so that the type of economic policies pursued by governments can have a significant impact on their success in seeking votes and office. These three assumptions need to be complemented by the recognition of changes in the behavior of voters and parties since the 1970s. Therefore, fourth, we acknowledge a decline among European electorates over the past 30 years or so in the willingness to vote (electoral turnout) and in the level of attachment to a particular party (partisan identification), coupled with an increased willingness to switch votes between elections (electoral volatility). These changes in voter behavior are also connected with the emergence of new political parties, such as regionalist, green, or far-right parties. The combined effect of these changes in the electoral landscape is that parties have faced more uncertainty and more pressure at the same time as they have pursued potentially unpopular policies. Therefore, we suggest that social pact offers are one strategy governing parties have devised to guard their electoral fortunes while implementing unpopular economic and welfare policies. Alternatively, in circumstances where governing parties anticipate electoral gains from legislation rather than pacts – for example, when voters have expressed dissatisfaction with tripartite bargaining – they were more likely to pursue reform through legislation without previous consultation with unions (and sometimes employers) instead.

Taking these basic assumptions as a starting point, we develop our argument in more detail by drawing on the literature on economic voting, which supports our idea that voters' electoral choices are in part motivated by economic factors. Next, we expand on these insights by linking them to conclusions expounded in the literature on welfare reforms, and in particular, the dilemmas welfare reform presents for different party families. We then examine the prevalence of social pacts since the 1980s through a lens of changing voting behavior and party systems, which heightened parties' uncertainty concerning electoral outcomes and increased the need to devise strategies to minimize electoral punishment for reform policies. Finally we proceed to set out our argument that social pact offers (or sometimes legislation) may be perceived as such an electoral strategy.

Voters, the economy, and government accountability

Strøm (1990) states that political parties care about policies, office, and votes. Much of the existing literature on pacts has primarily centered on the policy aspect. That is, scholars have focused on governments' desires to meet economic policy demands – in this case, frequently those imposed by external constraints, such as globalization pressures or EMU criteria. In contrast, the interest of politicians to get themselves or their party (re)elected has received less attention by the pacts literature. Obviously, policy and reelection interests are linked: if the policies that are implemented are widely unpopular, ineffective, or even disastrous, it will diminish the chances of the governing party to get reelected.[1] On the other hand, if the policies are successful and viewed favorably by a large number of voters, the chances of reelection are heightened. This poses a dilemma for parties that are committed to pass unpopular policies and yet want to be reelected.[2] Implementing monetarist policies, including wage restraint and restrictive welfare state policies, may constitute one such situation where governments perceive the need for unpopular reform, yet want to minimize potential electoral repercussions.

Our interpretation thus introduces an explicitly political perspective that complements those studies that view pacts primarily as a way of regulating the macroeconomy. The previous chapter has established the lack of an overall correlation between pact offers and the scale of economic problems, such as the government deficit. This reflects that fact that pacts have been used in countries with levels of deficit well above the EU average, such as Belgium, Ireland, and Italy, but have been absent from other high-deficit countries such as Austria, Denmark, and Sweden, perhaps because governments also have the option of taking recourse to legislation rather than negotiating pacts when economic pressures demand reforms. Consequently, we look at the role pact offers have played in the electoral calculations of political parties. Some literature has linked pacts to electoral considerations, though not in a systematic fashion. For example, Hassel and Ebbinghaus (2000: 65–6) refer to the potential electoral costs associated with the implementation of unpopular economic policies, illustrated by the 1995 French general strike protesting pension reform. Ahlquist (2008) demonstrates that wage pacts in Western Europe were more likely if an election was imminent. Analysts of welfare state reform have acknowledged the "high political costs associated with retrenchment initiatives" and the fact that "efforts to dismantle the welfare state have exacted a high political price" (Pierson 1994: 180–1), without, however, linking these reforms directly to the way in which they were initiated – pacts or legislation. Despite these studies, the pacts literature overall is characterized by a paucity of systematic analyses of the political dynamics behind different adjustment strategies.

Our understanding of governments as economic policymakers that are also concerned with elections echoes interpretations establishing that voters hold governments accountable. Specifically, voters hold governments accountable, or at least responsible, for economic policies and consequently engage in "economic voting."[3] Numerous studies have established that the economy matters to voters without, however, coming to a consensus on exactly how it matters, and under what circumstances. One general conclusion is that economic voting is contingent on numerous factors. For instance, some analyses demonstrate that the type of party matters for how voters react: leftist governments are penalized for poor employment records while rightist parties are punished more heavily for high inflation (e.g. Powell and Whitten 1993). Alternatively, the "issue priority model" hypothesizes the opposite: since leftist parties are perceived as most apt to curb unemployment and conservative parties as best at stemming inflation, it would be irrational for voters to punish leftist government for poor employment records and conservative governments for high inflation (Anderson 1995: 353). Other studies identify which aspects of the economy matter to voters, whether it is the overall state of the economy ("sociotropic" concerns) or an individual voter's personal economic wellbeing ("egotropic" or "pocketbook" concerns). A related, yet unresolved issue is whether voters are prospective (the vote is based on their expectations of what will happen in the future) or retrospective (the vote is based on the evaluation of economic performance in the past).[4]

To explain some of the differences in patterns of economic voting behavior across countries, other research has included institutional factors, such as party systems and types of governments. Overall, the findings suggest that when voters can clearly ascribe responsibility for economic policies and performance to a specific party (most likely, in single-party majority governments), they are more likely to engage in economic voting than in cases where responsibility is less clear (coalition governments). For example, Powell and Whitten (1993) find that it is easier for voters to identify who is responsible for policies in majoritarian governments – often found in countries with majoritarian institutions – compared to coalition governments. More generally, the "clarity of responsibility" hypothesis delivers evidence for the importance of institutional arrangements to shape the effects of the economy on voting behavior (see also Cheibub and Przeworski 1999: 230). Findings of this literature indicate that the macroeconomy has a larger effect on voting for "single- as opposed to multiparty government, majority as opposed to minority government, high as opposed to low structural cohesion of parties, and the absence of strong bicameral opposition" (Hibbs 2006: 579). Vote loss from one election to another is consequently highest for single-party majority governments, lowest for unsupported minority governments (which actually tend to gain votes when in government), with coalition governments in-between (Powell and Whitten 1993: 402–3). Yet, at the same time, Manin *et al.* (1999: 47) point out that while majoritarian institutions create governments that are more accountable, they also "generate governments that are farther from voters in policy space." Consequently, the effect of the type of governments and the relations between policies and popular preferences remains unclear, but regardless, voters allocate blame even when the ruling parties are further away from the voters' preferred policy position.

Looking at public support in opinion polls rather than election data, Anderson (1995: 375) analyzes the effect of the economy on voting intentions by disaggregating governing coalitions into their constituent parties. In a comparative study, he finds "no significant economic effects on support for the Social Democrats when they form single-party majority governments" for the Danish case, while support for coalition governments follows the logic of issue saliency with conservative parties gaining support when inflation rises and losing support when unemployment goes up, with the reverse being true for center-left parties. Furthermore, the parliamentary and the cabinet strength of the party of the prime minister matters as "bigger targets engendered stronger effects" (Anderson 2000: 164). That is, if the prime minister's party has a larger share of the parliamentary seats and/or of cabinet positions, the party faces stronger effects of the state of the economy on popularity than those with smaller policy responsibility. Finally, party system factors matter for economic voting: Economic effects are stronger in party systems where "fewer viable alternatives to the incumbent government" are present (Anderson 2000: 164–6).

Despite these differences in theoretical assumptions, cases, data, methodologies, and conclusions, the literature agrees that on a general level, voters' electoral choices are at least to some extent motivated by economic issues and that "the mass public holds the incumbent government accountable for the state of the economy" (Anderson 1995: 352). This is true even when voters diverge from the retrospective voting model and employ different ways of holding the government responsible, for instance by exonerating the government for poor economic performance due to external pressures (see Stokes 2001). In sum, while the economic voting literature is inconclusive as to *how* the economy influences voting decisions both theoretically and empirically, most studies concur that "it is clear that the economy is linked to the voter via the Responsibility Hypothesis. The voter observes the economy, judges its performance, and alters his or her vote accordingly" (Lewis-Beck and Paldam 2000: 119).[5]

Although economic voting research generally employs macroeconomic indicators, especially inflation, unemployment, and economic growth, we suggest that other economic policies, such as cutbacks in welfare benefits or wages, or labor market reforms, may also be salient for voters and influence their choice in elections. Research has established that voters react to welfare state performance (see, for example, Kumlin 2007a; 2007b). While changes in welfare schemes may be the means to an end – macroeconomic stability – for governments, they affect voters directly, and many voters are hostile to attempts at reducing their welfare benefits. That is, the type of policies adopted and the way in which they are pursued are likely to have significant electoral repercussions. To echo Pierson (1996: 177), "frontal assaults on the welfare state carry tremendous electoral risks," even if the ways in which economic performance and voting are linked are highly contingent (Anderson 2007), and pacts may be one method governments turn to in their attempt to minimize potential electoral punishment while engaging in potentially unpopular reforms.

Voters, welfare states, and political parties

Governments of all ideologies face the dilemma of the simultaneous need to meet economic targets, sometimes externally imposed, and selling their policies to an electoral market. For many governments, this means that they have to explain to voters why they are scaling down welfare states in order to obtain macroeconomic stability and balanced budgets. Voters, however, while desiring low unemployment and low inflation, are by and large also interested in keeping their benefits and wages and having favorable labor market conditions (shorter workweek, better employment protection).[6] This dilemma of combining economic adjustment measures to achieve positive economic outcomes while continuing to appeal to voters exists not just for leftist parties but also for conservative and Christian-Democratic ones. Especially for Western European countries, the implementation of monetarist policies might turn out to be problematic for parties of all ideologies due to the expectations of entitlements built up in the electorate. Survey data underscore that, by and large, citizens in Western Europe are opposed to retrenchment policies, especially for those programs, such as health care and pensions, that affect large segments of the population rather than small groups; in addition, interest groups representing those population segments, such as unions or retired people, are also likely to protest cutbacks for their clientele (Kitschelt 2001: 270–1; Ross 2000a; see also Edlund 2007; Pierson 1994, 1996; Rothstein 2000). Swank (2001: 213) summarizes findings that indicate that median voters are more likely to support universal benefits, which they are more likely to expect benefits from, than means-tested benefits. Rhodes (1996: 307) concludes that the electorates' preference for a "fat" rather than a "lean" welfare state in Western Europe "makes anything other than tinkering very difficult." Similar to Pierson (1994), he asserts that the reason for governments' difficulties in retrenchment are of a political nature, and more specifically, have to do with voters' preferences and parties' concerns about electoral outcomes. Weiss (2003: 15) finds that heightened global competition has increased many voters' economic insecurity, leading to renewed demands for social protection. Thus, widespread opposition to retrenchment policies makes their adoption and implementation politically and electorally difficult, and governments both of the left and the right will jeopardize their electoral fortunes if they push through a policy agenda of wage restraint (which also affects the middle class) and cuts in welfare state benefits (see Hassel and Ebbinghaus 2000). In contrast, where welfare states or specific welfare programs become broadly delegitimized, reform makes electoral sense for governments (see Klitgaard 2007).

Beyond these problems confronting all political parties regardless of ideology, different types of parties face specific issues. The comparative literature proposes that partisanship continues to matter for welfare policies, even though perhaps, as Huber and Stephens (2001) contend, less so than during the development of the welfare state (see Iversen 2006: 606), and some of the literature on social pacts has referred to the ideology of the governing party without, however, linking this feature systematically to an analysis of pacts (Hassel 2006; Rhodes 2003: 148).

If social-democratic parties embrace more market liberalization in an effort to adjust national economies to growing global competition, they might get elected into office, but then lose votes subsequently as many of the party's core supporters are disappointed with austerity policies. On the other hand, if social-democratic parties defend traditional pro-welfare state, expansionary policies, they might have to remain in opposition as they either lose credibility with voters or they are not considered credible coalition partners for centrist or center-right parties (Kitschelt 1999: 322–4). Ross (2000a) states that sometimes, leftist parties are more committed and better equipped to implement drastic cutbacks in welfare states because they need to heighten their economic credibility with business. Furthermore, they have more credibility with voters, who trust their commitment to the welfare state, making legitimization through pacts redundant. In these scenarios, it might make sense for leftist parties to reform via legislation rather than through offering pacts to unions.

Conservative parties, for their part, face a problem as orthodox neoliberalism no longer appears as a viable solution even for governments of the right (see Rhodes 2001). For one, it is national governments that were responsible for meeting EMU criteria, and market forces alone cannot guarantee that these criteria can be met. Second, the political and electoral problems of welfare state retrenchment face all governments, including conservative ones, in advanced industrialized democracies given widespread popular support for welfare programs (Pierson 1994). In addition, conservative parties in government should not be expected to implement far-reaching welfare state retrenchment since voters would be "skeptical of its motives" and the government would find it "extremely difficult to pursue a justification strategy of blame avoidance" (Green-Pedersen 2002: 37) due to the parties' historically small role in building and defending the welfare state (see also Ross 2000a). However, if public opinion becomes more critical of welfare states, conservative parties may find an electoral advantage in advocating, and legislating, a cut in welfare programs (see Pierson 1994: 147).[7] In general, however, the electoral cost of conservative parties engaging in welfare cuts through legislation is likely to be high.

Christian Democratic parties, on the other hand, need to address the problems of increasing secularization of West European societies and the reduction of their mediation function in ameliorating class conflict. In responding to such conflict they now have fewer macroeconomic tools and resources available.

Workforce demographics are changing, and at the same time new parties of the liberal and extreme right are gathering support at the expense of both Christian Democratic and conservative rivals (van Kersbergen 1999). With respect to cuts in welfare programs, Christian Democratic parties committed to retrenchment are expected to be able to implement cutbacks in welfare, especially if the parties govern in conjunction with leftist parties. Christian Democratic parties possess more credibility of commitment to the welfare state than conservative parties due to their reputation for "societal accommodation and pragmatism" (Green-Pedersen 2002: 38–9). Therefore, it is not just the party ideology, but also the party system configuration and patterns of competition between major parties that matters in the analysis of party reform programs and the method of implementation, whether through pacts or legislation (Green-Pedersen 2002; Kitschelt 2001).

Changing voting behavior and changing party systems

Governments do not only face the need to implement new policies that contract rather than expand wages and the welfare state, they also have to do so in a context of changing voting behavior and new dynamics of electoral competition, evidenced by increasing volatility and the emergence and rising popularity of new parties. Thus, parties can no longer count on the support of a stable core part of the electorate that votes in the party's favor with little attention to the actual policies implemented. Consequently, they need to develop new strategies to retain a large share of their traditional voters while also attracting new voters from beyond their core electorate. Pacts, or in some circumstances, legislation, can therefore be used as one electoral strategy available to political parties in government in the face of pressures for adjustment policies.

In fact, social pacts (re)emerged at about the same time as massive shifts in electoral behavior and party systems in Western Europe occurred. The reasons for, and results of, these changes in voting behavior are manifold. For one, voters' electoral choices were based on factors different from the ones that had determined voting behavior in the postwar period up until about the 1970s. In particular, Lipset and Rokkan (1967) observed that the cleavage structures of the 1960s, based predominantly around class and religion, still reflected those of the 1920s. Hence, the parties and party systems, organized around these "frozen" cleavages, were likewise characterized by continuity or "freezing." Since the 1970s the significance of these cleavages for voter behavior has declined and parties and party systems have thus begun to "unfreeze" and entered a "state of flux" (Dalton 2002: 134; see also Mair 2001).

The "unfreezing" of the party landscape is caused by a wide range of factors, including changing demographics, rising educational levels, the growing importance of mass media, the rise of new issues, and softening class lines as an outgrowth of changing employment and production patterns. These factors in turn have affected voting behavior, electoral outcomes, and party systems (see Dalton 2000; Dalton and Wattenberg 2000; Luther and Deschouwer 1999: 250; Poguntke 2004). Class voting and partisan identification declined in almost all West European countries, resulting in voters' "dealignment" from established parties (see Dalton 2006: Chapters 8, 9; Dalton *et al.* 2000; Gallagher *et al.* 2006: 289, 294). Declining partisan attachment across a large number of advanced industrialized countries has thus occurred in response to "changes in the nature of contemporary electorates that might be identified with the modernization process of advanced industrialized societies" (Dalton 2000: 29).

As a result, while electoral volatility was relatively low in the postwar period until the 1970s and parties could, by and large, assume a relatively stable share of core voters to support them, electoral volatility has since increased. Mean aggregate electoral volatility in 16 EU countries increased from 7.4 percent in the 1960s to 11.8 percent for the 2000–04 period (Gallagher *et al.* 2006: 294). Survey data at the individual level lend support to claims of rising electoral volatility at the aggregate level. For example, while only 20 percent of Dutch respondents professed in 1971 they would sometimes vote for a different party, over two-thirds did so in 1991; similar patterns can be found in other countries (Dalton *et al.* 2000: 44–6). Parallel, "dealignment" from established parties is mirrored by electoral support for new parties (Dalton *et al.* 2000) and voters who are switching party support have become more likely to vote for a new party that did not previously exist: A comparison of 16 Western European democracies establishes that the mean aggregate electoral support for new parties increased from 4.4 percent in the 1960s to 27.4 percent for the 2000–04 period (Gallagher *et al.* 2006: 292). Moreover, voters make their decisions later on in the campaign process and base their decisions more on short-term issues (Dalton *et al.* 2000: 48), again heightening parties' uncertainties about electoral outcomes.

Volatility has also been facilitated by the fact that the character and internal organization of many dominant parties has been changing away from an emphasis on party membership to periodic support during election time. While "mass parties" established durable links to voters through their emphasis on membership, this model of party organization has been in decline since the 1960s (Scarrow 2000). Party membership data indicate that only four West European countries – Germany, Belgium, Ireland, and Switzerland – experienced absolute membership increases since the 1960s, most of which were small (Scarrow 2000: 89). Looking at "membership density" – the ratio of a party's membership to its electorate – from 1960 to 1989, Poguntke (2005a: 58) finds that density declined in ten Western European countries and increased in only one, Ireland.[8] That is, the percentage of party members to voters has been steadily declining for many parties in Western Europe, and voters are less closely tied to "their" party and therefore more prone to switch their electoral support.[9]

Parties may be less likely to count on a relatively fixed share of votes not only because traditional social cleavages are weakening but also because of a concomitant decline in the influence of secondary organizations that tend to mobilize voters and channel their votes towards a specific party. For instance, the decline of class cleavages in many countries has been associated with a decline in trade union membership. Between 1980 and 2000 union density declined in 17 out of 20 OECD countries and rose in only three (Hamann and Kelly 2008). Furthermore, to expand on the example of trade unions, the relationship between trade unions and leftist parties has in many cases become more adversarial (Howell 2001), thus reducing the role of unions in mobilizing and channeling votes towards a specific party. In Spain, for instance, class could account for almost 20 percent of the variance in votes in 1982, but decreased to less than 6 percent in 1993. A mere 2 to 3 percent of the variance in votes for the leftist parties (the Socialist Party PSOE and the communist-leaning United Left, IU) was explained by trade union membership in the 1993 election, compared to 13 percent of the variance for a vote for a left or a right party in 1979 (Gunther *et al.* 2004: 270–5). The weakening ties between the trade unions and the Labour Party in Britain have also been well documented (Ludlam 2001; McIlroy 1998, 2009), and other countries show similar patterns (Burgess 2004). The bottom line of these changes is that in many countries, the traditional ties between parts of the electorate (e.g. working class) and corresponding political parties (e.g. labor or social democratic parties) have softened, and electoral volatility has heightened. All these developments including decreasing party membership and attachments, and rising support for new parties, are evidence of "a declining capacity on part of traditional parties to maintain solid linkages with voters, and to engage these voters and to win their commitment" (Bartolini and Mair 2001: 334), resulting in "parties' erosion of social anchorage" (Poguntke 2004: 1).

Overall, declining party loyalty means that "contemporary voters are less likely to enter elections with standing party predispositions" (Dalton *et al.* 2000: 49). Parties, therefore, see the need to reach out to voters that did not traditionally form their core support group, while at the same time attempting to maintain the support of their core clientele. How, then, can parties in government or in opposition reconcile different pressures for inflation control, fiscal restraint, and welfare state reform while acknowledging these electoral pressures?

Pacts as an electoral strategy

Parties and governments are in need of adding legitimacy to economic adjustment measures if they are also concerned with vote and office considerations in addition to meeting policy goals. Welfare state retrenchment and wage policies are not just economic problems, but are also part of the political agenda of parties that compete for votes. Given that "parties are responsive [to voters] and governments do attempt to carry out their policy pledges" (Keman 2005: 242) and that voters generally prefer a continuation of welfare state programs while governments profess the need to downsize, how do governments promote and sell their policies to the electorate? In order to minimize the electoral costs of implementing unpopular economic and welfare policies, parties can employ several strategies, such as obfuscation, division of potential opposition groups (those voter groups that would lose out as a consequence of the policies), and compensation of targeted victims of retrenchment (Pierson 1994). In addition, the type of program matters, and parties may be more successful when they implement cutbacks for programs affecting smaller, clearly delineated population groups (e.g. the unemployed) rather than programs with a more universal target population (Kitschelt 2001). Myles and Pierson (2001: 306) point out, for instance, that pension reform only "rarely" happens through unilateral government legislation; instead, negotiation with other constituencies is used as a blame avoidance strategy. The strategic framing of the issue – e.g. publicizing the need for budgetary discipline rather than emphasizing welfare cuts or targeting programs that have become delegitimized – also holds promise for governments' efforts to implement unpopular policies while minimizing electoral costs (Kitschelt 2001; Klitgaard 2007; Ross 2000b). To add more detail to this argument, Padgett (2005) reasons that parties' capacity to nurture public acceptance of cutbacks is highest when partisan cleavages on socio-economic issues are strong and mirrored in public opinion.

This reasoning, espoused in the existing literature, can be broadened along two dimensions: it can be extended to other potentially unpopular policies, such as wage restraint, which will affect a large proportion of the electorate; and second, the repertoire of blame avoidance strategies can be expanded. Social pacts are one way in which governments can attempt to diffuse responsibility for unpopular policies and, at the same time, enhance the legitimacy of those policies. We assume that governments have the option of either passing wage or other policies unilaterally through parliamentary procedure, or of negotiating social pacts with unions (and sometimes employers). In light of our observations about voters, parties, and governments, the pacts option might provide four advantages for governing parties: first, it could increase the legitimacy of unpopular policies by broadening the social coalition in support of the policies, thereby helping to construct a consensus around them (see Pizzorno 1978). Such a coalition might prove attractive to undecided voters, especially to those in favor of consensus politics. It might also help differentiate the pact party from rivals wishing to adopt a more unilateral rather than consensus-based approach to policymaking. The possible need for party leaders to differentiate their party from competitors is illustrated by the fact that on average, the ideological distance between the most extreme right and left parties and the degree of right-left polarization in the party systems of 15 West European countries decreased between the 1980s and the 1990s, thus reducing "the scope of policy offers for voters" (Volkens and Klingemann 2005: 156–7) despite the persistence of differences in patterns over time for individual countries.

Second, the process of negotiation involved in a social pact may help ensure that the costs of reform are distributed in ways that are acceptable to "economic voters." For instance, Green-Pedersen (2002: 34) contends that "voters might abstain from punishing the government if they can be persuaded that the retrenchment measures take away benefits from some undeserving group or improve the economic viability of the welfare state." Broadening the "retrenchment coalition" to include the social partners might signal just that, i.e. that the welfare cutbacks might be beneficial for a large share of the electorate.[10] Third, a social pact may help dissipate blame for the policies amongst other members of the coalition and thereby reduce the electoral costs falling on the government. Moreover, if pact negotiations fail, the unions can be blamed and the government can still claim credit for being decisive and willing to take responsibility for adjustment policies in the face of external economic pressures. Fourth, the implementation of policy reforms may prove easier and more efficient if government has enlisted the help of unions (Hassel and Ebbinghaus 2000). Insofar as voters seek to hold governments to account for their management of the economy, the successful implementation of labor market or welfare reforms may result in voters forming a favorable view of the government's economic competence. That in turn may help parties achieve their vote and office seeking goals.

Much of the reasoning in this chapter has revolved around governing parties' motivations to offer social pacts as a way to guard their electoral fortunes when embracing wage, welfare, or labor market reforms. Conversely, we can construct a parallel argument for why governments at other times prefer to act unilaterally and legislate reforms. For example, parties may actively repudiate pacts or attempt to undermine tripartism if party leaders believe that pacts are unlikely to produce the desired economic outcomes. The significance of this belief is underlined by the literature on economic voting that suggests a perceived deterioration in the economy could result in electoral losses for the governing party. Legislation may also prove attractive where a significant proportion of voters has become disillusioned with the consensus-based systems of policymaking that are the hallmark of social pacts and often associated with coalition government. In other words, where an electoral rationale indicates that legislation is more beneficial, we expect governing parties to do just that. The need to reform does not in and of itself steer the reform strategy of the government; instead, electoral factors contribute to governments' preference for pacts or legislation.

The role of institutions

The way electoral pressures and welfare reform affect policies are also mediated by the institutional framework as "Institutions allow representatives to escape attention and shift blame" (Anderson 2007: 281). The literature has identified several institutional factors that potentially matter for welfare reform, including the type of democracy (closely linked to electoral systems), and the geographical distribution of power (unitary vs. federal states).

The type of democracy – whether a majoritarian (or Westminster) system compared to a consensus system (often based on some form of proportional representation) – is one variable that may influence the offer of social pacts. For instance, Müller (2005: 250) summarizes existing findings stating "... whilst Westminster systems vest the incumbent parliamentary majority with the requisite opportunities to push their policies through, in systems with many institutional veto players, the position of the governing parties is much more constrained" (see also Swank 2001: 209). Furthermore, opposition to welfare reform can effectively use the veto points provided by additional layers of legislative process in the upper houses, thus making welfare reform more difficult to push through in federal systems (Hibbs 2006: 579; Pierson 2001: 414). Federalism does not only obscure responsibility, it also complicates the legislative process as new legislation has to be approved in two houses of parliament, which, according to some research, has slowed down the expansion of the welfare state (see Iversen 2006: 613). However, Obinger *et al.* (2005: 42–3) offer a more nuanced evaluation of the role of federalism. They conclude that not all upper houses are involved in legislative processes concerning welfare reform, and that federalism can in fact facilitate retrenchment as it reduces government accountability and makes it possible for the government to shift the blame to other levels of government (see also Swank 2001: 210–2). Again, the literature has identified the importance of federal institutions but has not yet produced a consensus on the effects of specific institutional arrangements for policymaking. We will develop the impact of the political institutions on governments' reform strategies in some detail in the comparative case studies that follow the quantitative analysis in the subsequent chapter.

Conclusion

We have reasoned so far that when parties and governments have considered the adoption of potentially unpopular economic reforms concerning wages, welfare, and labor markets they have also had to be concerned with the fact that these policies potentially undermine their vote and office seeking objectives, presenting them with acute dilemmas. Moreover parties and governments are confronted with growing electoral pressures emanating from an increasingly volatile and fluid electorate and the rise of new parties. And finally we have noted that voters hold the government responsible for the state of the economy and vote accordingly. These factors combine to shape the party or government choice to implement reforms through social pacts or through legislative procedure. We thus expect parties and governments engaged in economic reforms, especially incomes and welfare policies, but also labor markets, to consider the potential electoral response of the voters in addition to the implications for the economy when they make decisions on how best to pass these reform policies. Based on the literature on accountability and economic voting, changing voting behavior, the position of the party in the party system, and several institutional factors, we expect the specific mechanisms that prompt governments to prefer either pacts or legislation to vary by country and over time. We will explore some of this variation across countries in the next chapter. We then disentangle the relationships within countries and over time as well as some of the complex interactions between these factors in the comparative case study chapters.

4 Governments, voters, and social pacts in Western Europe

What accounts for the variation in the presence of social pacts or legislation to reform wages, welfare policies, and labor markets across countries and within countries over time in Western Europe? To obtain systematic evidence about the factors that privilege reform through pacts or legislation, this chapter presents a statistical analysis of variables that we expect to matter if our argument about electoral considerations and governments' reform strategies is valid. Chapter 2 summarized some of the prominent explanations the literature has proposed concerning the genesis of social pacts and pointed to the prominence of variables relating to economic institutions and labor relations. Chapter 3 laid out the reasoning for our focus on governments as political actors rather than just economic managers by linking governments to political parties and voters in an increasingly volatile and competitive electoral environment. We then explained how governments can use social pacts or legislation to minimize the potential electoral backlash to reforms. Here, we build on these literatures. In furthering the arguments presented in the previous two chapters, we hypothesize more specifically the conditions under which governments might be more likely to prefer pacts or legislation to embrace wage, welfare, or labor market reforms that are potentially unpopular with electoral constituencies.

Our hypotheses and variables follow from the arguments and findings on the crucial role of electoral politics in governments' decisions on reform strategy introduced in Chapters 2 and 3. Thus, we include spatial variables, such as party family and party locations on a left-right continuum; variables related to electoral dynamics and outcomes, such as party competition; types of governments; and legislative party fragmentation. We develop hypotheses about how they might affect the choice between pacts or legislation. Furthermore, we assume that the type of issue at hand (wages, welfare, or labor market) matters because reforms on some of these topics may, for example, meet with more resistance by large segments of the electorate than others. We also assume that some of these variables interact. Moreover, we include a series of economic, institutional, and industrial relations control variables, such as unemployment, welfare regime, and union density, since the existing literature (see Chapter 2) claims these variables are significant.

We set out to test how well electoral and government variables hold up when economic and industrial relations variables are included in our model. By analyzing data for 16 countries in Western Europe for over a quarter of a century (1980–2006), we identify patterns that hold across countries and over time. The comparative case studies in the subsequent chapters will provide more detail, untangle causal relationships, and account for some of the variation of our cases from the general patterns generated by the statistical analysis.

In this chapter, we introduce our variable definitions and measurements and formulate our hypotheses. Throughout, we expand on the literature discussed in the previous chapters to hypothesize how voting behavior and related variables might affect governments' choices of tripartism or legislation. We then discuss measurement issues and develop our models. Finally, we present and discuss our main findings concerning the variables that determine the probability of governments' preferences for reform through either pact offers or legislation.

Variables and hypotheses

Dependent variables

Our model specifies the ways in which pressures from the electorate and from other parties, mediated by additional factors, influence governmental decisions to favor pacts or legislation when pursuing reform policies. Therefore, our dependent variable is dichotomous: there is either a government offer of a social pact on the issues of wages, welfare and/or labor market reform or there is legislation proposed by governments on the same issues.[1] We coded separately any legislation proposed by governments in the wake of pact rejection by unions; as we are primarily interested in governments' initial preferences in pursuing reforms, we omit this category from our analysis. The measure of proposed legislation used in our models is therefore based on those cases where governments introduced legislation at the outset as an alternative to social pacts. Occasionally, some or all of the contents of social pacts were translated into legislative measures; however, we did not count these instances as separate cases of legislation because the initial motivation of the government was to include unions.

Independent variables

Party competition

In brief, our argument is that electoral pressures will affect the governing party's efforts, or that of the main party (defined as the party of the prime minister) in a coalition government, to minimize the electoral costs of unpopular reform through the offer of social pacts, rather than pursuing reform through legislation. The impact of electoral pressures may be enhanced (or reduced) by additional variables, in particular the governing parties' strength in the legislature and the type of government, whether single-party or coalition. Therefore, we chose variables to measure electoral pressures that also capture some salient consequences of electoral volatility. In other words we look at how changes in electoral outcomes, caused by changes in voting behavior, affect the capacity of leading parties to form governments and pass policies. We measure competition in two ways: parties' vote loss (or gain), and closeness of elections measured for the election preceding a pact or legislation. Change in vote shares for a particular party measures competition with respect to overall electoral support, and closeness of the election outcomes indicates the competitiveness of the election. A party may retain or gain votes but still experience electoral pressure because of the closeness of elections. Closeness of elections can be measured in the difference in votes (electoral competitiveness) between the two largest parties in an election (Gunther *et al.* 2004: 225; see also Bartolini 2002 for a discussion of the complexities of defining and measuring party competition).[2] The smaller the margin between the party with the highest vote share and the party with the second highest vote share, the more competitive is the election. Two hypotheses follow:

> *H1a*: Social pact offers will be more likely and legislation less likely when the previous election was more competitive.
> *H1b*: Social pact offers will be more likely and legislation less likely the more votes the governing party lost in the previous election.

Party family and party position

The literature discussed in Chapter 3 asserts that not all types of parties face the same dilemmas when they consider implementing welfare reforms.[3] Center-left or social democratic parties may be credited with more "welfare legitimacy" than conservative or center-right Christian Democratic rivals by their constituents and can therefore more easily pass unpopular welfare legislation without incurring severe electoral costs. Yet, as leftist parties tend to have closer ties to unions, they might be more inclined to include unions in bipartite or tripartite negotiations. Conservative parties, for their part, may be more likely to opt for pacts since they have a lower welfare state reputation and thus need to demonstrate their commitment to the principles of the welfare state. Christian Democratic parties might fall somewhere between parties to their left and right since Christian Democratic parties have traditionally been more supportive of welfare state development than conservative parties but less so than leftist parties (Green-Pedersen 2002: 35–7). Center parties, formerly agrarian parties, are prominent only in Scandinavia, where they have often acted in a way similar to the Christian Democratic parties elsewhere in Europe and played a key role in coalition formation, e.g. in Denmark and Finland (Damgaard 2003: 239; Gallagher *et al.* 2006: 250–1; Nousiainen 2003: 273). In sum, the literature has referred to different constraints faced by parties belonging to different party families, but it is not theoretically obvious how these differences affect parties' strategic choices of either pacts or legislation.

In addition to party family, party policy positions may also influence the choice of pacts or legislation. Unlike party family, party position – as measured by the popular Manifesto Research Group data (Budge *et al.* 2001; Klingemann *et al.* 2006) – fluctuates over time. Consequently, although social democratic parties tend to score below the midpoint of the scale and conservatives above the midpoint, the temporal fluctuations yield correlations between party family and party position that are quite modest (never more than 0.45) and suggest they are capturing different facets of political parties. Our second reason for exploring the Manifesto data is methodological: party locations are measured on an interval scale, which assists in the construction of interaction terms including party position. The use of four party family dummies in each of five interaction terms would have resulted in extremely unwieldy regression equations with an excessive number of variables.[4]

We also expect that different types of parties will react differently to changes in their vote share regarding their preference for policy reform strategies. For example, parties to the right that have traditionally been less willing to include unions in policy reforms may become more favorable to social pacts when they lose votes, and other things equal, the greater the vote loss, the greater the shift in their preferences. Conversely, leftist parties that have historically favored social pacts might be more likely to consider the legislative route to reform if they lose votes heavily compared to parties further to the right. Alternatively, leftist parties that incur a significant loss of votes might fear that voters are beginning to doubt their commitment to high wages and welfare state protection and thus continue to opt for pacts. The direction of the party family–vote change interaction is thus difficult to specify.

> *H2a:* The probability of governments' preference for social pacts rather than legislation is related to the type of party in government.
> *H2b:* The probability of governments' preference for social pacts rather than legislation is related to the main governing party's position in a one-dimensional policy space.
> *H2c:* Governments' choice of pacts or legislation will be influenced by the interaction between party position and vote distance to the second strongest party.
> *H2d:* Vote change is likely to affect parties differently depending on the position of the party in a one-dimensional policy space.
> *H2e:* The direction of the vote change is likely to affect parties differently depending on the position of the party in a one-dimensional policy space.

Type of government

According to the literature on government responsibility and accountability, voters endeavor to hold governments responsible for their economic policies, including labor market and welfare reforms (see Chapter 3). Moreover, the literature has also pointed to the connection between the capacity of voters to reward or punish governments and the properties of the government. The allocation of blame for unpopular policies is most easily established for single-party and majority governments compared to coalition and minority governments since the "clarity of responsibility" (Cheibub and Przeworski 1999: 230; Powell and Whitten 1993) is higher in these cases and voters can more easily identify who to reward or punish (see also Anderson 2007). The fact that single-party, majority governments are most susceptible to vote loss at subsequent elections (see Chapter 3) hints that such governments should be most likely to offer social pacts, compared to minority and coalition governments. At the same time, coalition governments face more uncertainty in the legislature than single-party majority governments because of the risk of coalition termination (Gallagher *et al.* 2006: 410) and should therefore be more willing to offer social pacts to forestall coalition collapse. Therefore, we test whether the type of government (single-party or coalition) is related to the probability of pact offers.

In addition, we can further distinguish between different types of coalitions and group them according to the location of their constituent parties in a one-dimensional policy space – in our case, a left-right continuum, reflecting the dominant cleavage in most West European societies (on the utility of the left-right continuum as an indicator of party position, see Müller and Strøm 2003: 8–9). Connected coalitions consist of parties located adjacent to each other on the continuum while in unconnected coalitions, not all parties are adjacent and instead one party (or several) is "skipped" to form a coalition. Examples of the former comprise a social democratic-socialist government or a conservative-liberal government in situations where these parties are located next to each other. An example of the latter would be a social democratic-conservative coalition that leaves out a center party located in-between these two parties. Theoretically we would expect connected coalitions to magnify the effects of the family of the dominant party, normally designated as the party of the prime minister (see Hypotheses 2a, b, and c). However, if policy positions display greater differences, as might be more likely in unconnected coalitions that do not have adjacent policy positions, it might be more difficult for the government to produce a coherent policy proposal that is acceptable to the partners in coalitions.

The type of government, in conjunction with party system attributes, also matters for the way policies are formulated and passed. Corporatism has proved more resilient when mixed, or unconnected, coalitions govern, and less so when two major party "blocks" dominate party competition. This is because interest organizations "whose allies control the government have strong reasons to bypass corporatist institutions in order to seek direct political influence" (Anthonsen and Lindvall 2009: 172). If, on the other hand, party competition patterns are different and result in unconnected coalitions, "interest organizations cannot expect their allies to remain in power for long without engaging in compromises with ideological opponents" and are therefore more likely to stick to compromise negotiations (Anthonsen and Lindvall 2009: 172). While we are concerned with social pacts rather than corporatism, the same logic can be applied to social pacts – different types of governing coalitions matter for the policy process. We thus assume that unconnected coalitions will experience more difficulty in reaching and implementing agreements because of their different policy positions, making it difficult to pass legislation. It might consequently be easier to secure reforms through social pacts rather than legislation as a way of "overriding" internal coalition opposition by shoring up support outside the legislative arena.[5]

Furthermore, the strength of the government is also of potential import although the literature points in contradictory directions. As already noted, the "clarity of responsibility" hypothesis suggests that minority governments are the least likely to be "punished" by the electorate, which might suggest they have only weak incentives to offer social pacts. On the other hand, minority governments might be *more* likely to offer social pacts than majority governments because they cannot necessarily rely on legislative support from other parties to pass reform legislation. Minority governments also tend to be of shorter duration than majority governments; minority coalitions are relatively short-lived, while single-party minority governments survive almost as long as majority coalitions. Single-party majority governments far surpass the other types of government in their ability to survive (Strøm 1990: 115–7). These findings support the claim that minority governments are in many ways weaker than their majoritarian counterparts and therefore more inclined to seek support for reform policies outside the legislative arena. Thus, minority governments – especially minority coalitions – might be more likely to offer social pacts as they are attempting to garner support for controversial measures they might not be able to pass in the legislature.

Moreover, we could hypothesize that the stability and longevity of the government might have an impact on the preference for pacts or legislation. Governments might be short-lived for a variety of reasons: because they are composed of either minority governments or majority coalitions (Strøm 1990: 116) or because the institutional and spatial factors in which parties operate allow them to end governments prematurely at relatively low cost to themselves (Mershon 2002). Either way, short-lived governments might have a more difficult time gathering parliamentary support for contentious reforms. By inference a long-lived government might be deemed less susceptible to electoral pressure and therefore perceive less need for social pacts. We will thus test whether the duration of a government is inversely related to governments' preference for pacts.

H3a: The strength of the government in the legislature will be inversely related to the choice of pact offers and directly related to the use of legislation.

H3b: The composition of government, whether single-party or coalition, will be related to the choice of pact offers or legislation.

H3c: Unconnected coalitions will be more likely than connected coalitions to offer social pacts when compared to single-party governments.

H3d: The duration of a cabinet will be inversely related to the incidence of social pact offers or legislation.

Effective number of parties

The composition, size, and stability of any coalition will depend in part on the party fragmentation in the legislature, measured as the effective number of legislative parties (Dalton *et al.* 2000: 41–2; Taagepera and Shugart 1989). The more fragmented the legislative party system, the less likely cross-party support for contentious legislation is to emerge, which is especially important for minority governments. Consequently we would expect social pacts to be more likely than legislation under such conditions. Furthermore, the fragmentation of the legislature is related to the ease with which voters can identify policy responsibility (see Cheibub and Przewoski 1999: 230), with a more fragmented legislature making this task more difficult than a less fragmented legislature.

H4: The higher the effective number of legislative parties, the higher the probability that the government will attempt policy reform through social pacts rather than legislation.

Type of issue

Based on propositions advanced in the existing literature, we assume that governments might vary their preferred reform path depending on the nature of the issue. We accordingly classify pact issues under three headings: wages, welfare, and labor market. "Wages" includes issues such as overtime pay and bonuses as well as hourly rates of pay while "welfare" refers to issues such as unemployment, sickness, maternity and disability benefits as well as pensions. "Labor market" reforms include employment protection laws, covering both dismissal and redundancy rights, collective bargaining structures, and issues such as work time.

Welfare reforms of any kind might potentially elicit more electoral backlash than policies of wage moderation, the subject of much of the pacts' literature to date. This could be because wage bargaining takes place on a biennial or triennial cycle in most EU countries; hence, a union policy of wage moderation in one round can be revised at the next bargaining round. Welfare reform, in contrast, tends to operate over a longer time span, is less likely to be reversed in future years, and is therefore likely to generate more resistance. With respect to the third category of government intervention – labor market reform – it could be argued that some forms of labor market flexibility, such as changes to temporary or part-time contracts, will affect only a minority of union members and will therefore prove less contentious than welfare reforms. However, the regulation of wages and collective bargaining structures (another aspect of labor market reform) is more central to union activities and objectives than welfare expenditure and is thus likely to prove more contentious. Consequently, social pacts may be less, not more, likely on welfare, compared to wages and labor market issues. Given these different lines of reasoning it is plausible to suggest some link between the type of issue and the incidence of social pacts but it is not possible to offer a hypothesis clearly stating which direction the relationship should take.

The literature also asserts that social democratic parties enjoy more legitimacy and have more credibility concerning their commitment to the welfare state compared to conservative parties, with Christian Democratic and Center parties in the middle. We thus also test for the interaction between party family and type of issue since theoretically, for example, parties to the right might seek out a pact on welfare reform to demonstrate their commitment to the welfare state but might legislate wage restraint, where they have less need to boost their legitimacy.

H5a: The incidence of social pact offers will vary across the three issues of welfare reform, labor market reform, and wages.
H5b: There will be an interaction between type of pact issues and party family.

Economic institutions

The varieties of capitalism literature could imply that the higher degree of coordination in the Coordinated Market Economies (CMEs) might provide the institutional infrastructure facilitating social pacts, while the lack of coordination in Liberal Market Economies (LMEs) may be less suited to lead to pacts. However, the simple distinction between CMEs and LMEs is problematic because these two categories display considerable variation in important aspects of their welfare systems that may be relevant in this study while at the same time providing little theoretical grounding for other cases in our sample, such as the Mediterranean mixed market economies. Molina and Rhodes (2007a) argue on the basis of the Italian and Spanish cases that these economies are a hybrid of the core LME and CME types that is linked to high levels of class conflict. That feature of the MMEs, in turn, may help explain the proclivity of governments in these countries to seek to incorporate trade union confederations into social pacts. Nonetheless, the VoC approach does not provide a solid explanation of the significant within-category variation in the European CMEs and LMEs (see also Crouch 2005). Thus, while assuming that the institutional configurations of national economies (including different types of welfare institutions) are important we combine the more nuanced distinction proposed by the literature on welfare regimes with the VoC approach, which adds a

Southern European variant, and distinguish four types of West European capitalism: the four Scandinavian economies, coordinated market economies with social democratic welfare states (Denmark, Finland, Norway, and Sweden); the five coordinated market economies with conservative welfare states (Austria, Belgium, Germany, Luxembourg and the Netherlands); the five Southern European economies (France, Greece, Italy, Portugal, and Spain); and the two liberal market economies (UK and Ireland).[6]

Furthermore, it makes sense to expect that governments react to the need for reform policies differently depending on the type of economy because striking variation appears between Northern, Central, and Southern Europe concerning the structures and levels of welfare spending and in levels of union density. For example, total social welfare expenditure as a percentage of GDP in 1990–93 amounted to 30.4 percent in Scandinavia but did not exceed 25.5 percent in Austria, Belgium and Germany and 24.7 percent in France and Italy (Swank 2002: 126, 165). Union density in 2004 averaged 75 percent in Scandinavia, 37 percent in central Europe, and 15 percent in Southern Europe (Hamann and Kelly 2008). Theoretically, we might expect more welfare pacts in Scandinavia in light of the proportion of GDP consumed by welfare and of the higher levels of union density. At the same time, the literature hints that pacts should be less common in the most coordinated economies because wage setting institutions are likely to be responsive to competitive pressures (Hassel 2006: 235–7), thus eliminating the need for pacts. But Hassel also notes that the responsiveness of the wage bargaining machinery is itself influenced by other factors, such as the degree of factionalism within unions. For Southern Europe, a similar variety of arguments could be advanced: On the one hand the high degree of bargaining coverage might mean wage bargaining institutions should be responsive to market signals without the aid of government intervention. On the other hand the high levels of class conflict and the lower degree of bargaining coordination might necessitate more, not less, state intervention in order to construct broad coalitions in favor of reform (Hamann and Kelly 2008; Molina and Rhodes 2007a: 245–7). Thus, we hypothesize a relationship between the incidence of pact offers (or legislation) and varieties of capitalism without being able to specify the expected patterns further.

> H6: The incidence of pact offers and legislation will vary across the different varieties of capitalism.

Control variables

Several control variables test for the effect of economic and industrial relations variables that might be associated with pact offers or legislation. Since the existing literature has identified these variables as significant in explaining the occurrence of social pacts, we include them to check whether our independent variables remain significant in the presence of these control variables.

The literature on European Monetary Union has referred quite explicitly to three variables identified in the Maastricht criteria, namely public debt, government deficit, and inflation (see Chapter 2). We include deficit and inflation but omit debt because the latter is highly correlated with deficit. Moreover, current account deficits have featured more heavily in discussions on EMU than debt. Further, since unemployment is a key macroeconomic indicator that influences governmental policy as well as voting behavior and can also affect union strength, we have included an unemployment measure. All economic variables were measured for the year preceding the pact offer or legislative proposal. In addition we created a dummy variable to explore the effect of EMU on differences in the incidence, properties, and correlates of pacts. We therefore distinguish pacts offered in the EMU period (1992–98) from pacts offered either before 1992 or after 1998.

The institutional political economy approach (see Chapter 2) proposes that three attributes of industrial relations systems influence government approaches to wage regulation: the degree of centralization of collective bargaining processes, the degree of coordination of bargaining outcomes, and the level of union density. The first two measures proxy the capacity of union confederations to implement tripartite agreements and should therefore be positively associated with the incidence of pact offers. Centralization and coordination appear to be highly correlated and the literature has often focused on the latter (e.g. Traxler *et al.* 2001). Accordingly, we use coordination and omit centralization. The density variable is meant to capture union power; however, it remains unclear whether pacts are more likely to be offered to strong union movements (because the gains to governments may be substantial) or to weak union movements (because the probability of union acceptance is high). Union bargaining power, however, is notoriously difficult to define and measure and the industrial relations literature disagrees on the subject (see Hamann 1993; Hyman 1994: 127–31; Kelly 1998: 9–13; Martin 1992). We are thus unable to control for an independent measure of union power apart from coordination and density.

Data, measurement, and model development

Appendix 2 lists our main dependent and independent variables and their measurement. We have already described our pacts and legislation dataset in Chapter 1. Our main dependent variables are all measured on a binary scale: in other words, governments either offer a social pact or they do not; and either they legislate or they do not. Given this property of the dependent variables, we employ logistic regression, which constructs the probabilities of binary outcomes in the light of a given set of independent variables.

The independent variables in relation to Hypotheses 1a and 1b on party competition include data on vote changes, measured in percentage point differences between the two elections prior to the pact offer or legislation. We coded the direction of change – gain or loss – separately from the magnitude of change in order to facilitate interpretation of the statistical results. We measure electoral competition as the vote distance between the first and second parties in the legislature in the election prior to the pact/legislation. One of our indicators of electoral pressures on parties is vote loss, which we measure as changes between the most recent pre-pact/legislation election and the one previous to that. However, a decline in vote shares sufficient to affect party policy may have occurred over a longer period of time, spanning several elections; we will return to this issue in our discussion of results. As already noted, our measurement of party location is twofold. First, party family is based on categories commonly used in the literature, namely Social Democratic, Center, Christian Democratic, Liberal and Conservative.[7] Although other parties, such as the Greens or far left, have occasionally participated in governments they have never constituted the main governing party (defined throughout as the party of the prime minister) in the 1980–2006 period. Second, we use the Manifesto Research Group data (Budge *et al.* 2001; Klingemann *et al.* 2006).

Our basic electoral politics Model (1) of pact offers includes the main variables contained in our argument:

$$
\begin{aligned}
\text{OFFER} &= \text{Constant} + \beta_1\text{VOTECH} + \beta_2\text{VOTEDIREC} + \beta_3\text{VOTEDIST} \\
&+ \beta_4\text{PTYPOS} + \beta_5\text{PTYFAM} + \beta_6\text{STRENGTH} + \beta_7\text{CONNECTED} \\
&+ \beta_8\text{UNCONNECTED} + \beta_9\text{DURATION} + \beta_{10}\text{EFFEC} + \beta_{11}(\text{VOTECH} \\
&\times \text{PTYPOS}) + \beta_{12}(\text{VOTEDIREC} \times \text{PTYPOS}) + \beta_{13}(\text{VOTEDIST} \\
&\times \text{PTYPOS}) + \beta_{14}(\text{WELFARE} \times \text{PTYPOS}) + \beta_{15}(\text{LABMKT} \times \text{PTYPOS})
\end{aligned}
$$

$$(4.1)$$

where OFFER is the probability of a social pact offer, VOTECH is the absolute change in vote for the main or single governing party, VOTEDIREC is the direction of vote change, VOTEDIST is the vote gap between the first and second largest parties in the legislature, PTYPOS is the left-right policy position of the main or single governing party, PTYFAM is the ideological family of the party of the prime minister, STRENGTH refers to the proportion of seats held by the government, CONNECTED indicates a connected coalition government, UNCONNECTED indicates an unconnected coalition government, DURATION refers to length of time the existing cabinet has held office and EFFEC refers to the effective number of parties in the legislature. The six final terms in the equation designate interactions between party position and four of the electoral variables as described in our hypotheses as well as interactions between party position and pact (or legislation) issue. In the case of coalition and single-party government we used the latter as our benchmark category so that the coefficients on the two coalition variables represent pact offer probabilities relative to a single-party government.

To assess the effect of other variables, drawn from the literature, and to test the robustness of our core variables when these other variables are included, we constructed a series of further models. Each of these comprised the variables in Model 1 with the following additions: Model 2 adds industrial relations and economic control variables based on the extant literature on social pacts; these variables are included in all subsequent models. Model 3 adds a variable capturing types of welfare regime in order to control for economic institutions:

> DENSITY refers to trade union density, COORDINATION refers to the degree of bargaining coordination exercised by peak union confederations, DEFICIT refers to government deficit as a proportion of GDP, INFLATION refers to the annual rate of change in the consumer price index and UNEMP refers to the annual percentage level of unemployment.

(4.2)

> DENSITY, COORDINATION, DEFICIT, INFLATION and UNEMP as well as NORTH, SOUTH and UKEIRE refer to the different categories of economic institutions within Western Europe with the CENTRAL European countries of Austria, Germany, and Benelux serving as the statistical benchmark.

(4.3)

Model 4 assesses whether the type of reform issue has an impact on the likelihood of governments offering social pacts rather than legislation:

> DENSITY, COORDINATION, DEFICIT, INFLATION and UNEMP as well as WELFARE and LABOR MARKET to refer to the content of social pacts and legislation with wages used as the benchmark category.

(4.4)

Model 5 adds the EMU time period as a control variable to the economic and industrial relations variables:

> DENSITY, COORDINATION, DEFICIT, INFLATION and UNEMP as well as TIME1 to refer to pact years between 1992 and 1998 and TIME2 to refer to pacts outside the EMU period, 1980–91 and 1999–2006.

(4.5)

Model 6 includes all of the above variables.

(4.6)

Results

Table 4.1 displays the results for our six regression models. Where our hypotheses are signed (1a and 1b on electoral competition and vote loss, 3a on government strength, 3c on type of coalition, 3d on cabinet duration, 4 on number of effective parties and 5a and 5b on type of issue) we have used

Table 4.1 Political, economic, and institutional correlates of pact offers (logistic regression)

	Model 1	Model 2	Model 3	Model 4	Model 5	Model 6
	Odds ratio (z)	Odds ratio (z)	Odds ratio (z)	Odds ratio (z)	Odds ratio (z)	Odds ratio (z)
Vote change	1.023 (0.61)	1.033 (0.78)	1.034 (0.80)	1.037 (0.86)	1.038 (0.87)	1.042 (0.93)
Direction vote change	2.384 (2.18)**	2.122 (1.79)**	1.986 (1.58)*	2.037 (1.65)**	2.222 (1.88)**	2.072 (1.63)*
Vote distance	0.991 (−0.30)	1.046 (1.25)	1.047 (1.23)	1.049 (1.30)*	1.043 (1.15)	1.047 (1.18)
Party position	0.939 (−3.17)***	0.939 (−2.69)***	0.943 (−2.41)**	0.938 (−2.70)***	0.939 (−2.66)***	0.942 (−2.40)**
Social Democrats	1.191 (0.36)	1.774 (1.07)	2.048 (1.25)	1.748 (1.02)	1.712 (0.99)	1.812 (1.01)
Center	5.004 (1.79)*	9.615 (2.40)**	15.462 (1.97)***	7.007 (2.04)**	10.17 (2.42)**	11.044 (1.71)*
Liberals	1.408 (0.30)	5.458 (1.16)	4.887 (1.10)	6.787 (1.30)	5.460 (1.16)	5.894 (1.21)
Christian Democrats	1.504 (0.78)	2.600 (1.57)	3.110 (1.70)*	2.150 (1.25)	2.928 (1.63)	2.763 (1.43)
Government strength	0.954 (−2.18)**	0.939 (−2.45)***	0.937 (−2.48)***	0.935 (−2.53)***	0.935 (−2.53)***	0.931 (−2.61)***
Connected coalition	0.502 (−1.31)	0.660 (−0.69)	0.744 (−0.47)	0.795 (−0.37)	0.697 (−0.60)	0.868 (−0.22)
Unconnected coalition	1.649 (0.55)	6.384 (1.58)*	7.416 (1.69)**	7.755 (1.72)**	6.860 (1.61)*	8.284 (1.73)**
Cabinet duration	0.999 (−0.28)	0.999 (−1.31)*	0.999 (−1.10)	0.999 (−1.42)*	0.999 (−1.02)	0.999 (−0.97)
Effective	1.988 (3.83)***	2.617 (4.31)***	2.493 (3.76)***	2.589 (4.16)***	2.532 (4.19)***	2.422 (3.55)***
Party position × vote change	1.005 (2.43)**	1.005 (2.13)**	1.005 (2.07)**	1.005 (2.21)**	1.004 (2.01)**	1.005 (2.01)**
Party position × direction vote change	0.947 (−2.26)**	0.958 (−1.60)	0.953 (−1.73)*	0.950 (−1.89)*	0.960 (−1.49)	0.949 (−1.81)*
Party position × vote distance	1.003 (2.06)**	1.004 (2.65)**	1.005 (2.66)**	1.005 (2.64)***	1.004 (2.58)**	1.004 (2.50)**
Party position × welfare	1.006 (0.26)	1.012 (0.45)	1.011 (0.40)	1.011 (0.41)	1.012 (0.47)	1.011 (0.41)
Party position × labor market	1.001 (0.03)	1.014 (0.55)	1.013 (0.51)	1.011 (0.43)	1.015 (0.58)	1.011 (0.43)

	(1)	(2)	(3)	(4)	(5)	(6)
Union density	0.951 (–3.61)***	0.951 (–3.61)***	0.954 (–1.72)*	0.948 (–3.69)***	0.952 (–3.46)***	0.950 (–1.80)*
Bargaining coordination	0.944 (–1.01)	0.944 (–1.01)	0.949 (–0.89)	0.956 (–0.77)	0.947 (–0.93)	0.962 (–0.62)
Deficit	1.067 (1.19)	1.067 (1.19)	1.071 (1.10)	1.058 (1.02)	1.076 (1.30)	1.066 (0.99)
Inflation	0.990 (–0.22)	0.990 (–0.22)	0.977 (–0.45)	0.964 (–0.76)	1.013 (0.23)	0.986 (–0.24)
Unemployment	0.985 (–0.28)	0.985 (–0.28)	0.968 (–0.53)	0.979 (–0.39)	0.987 (–0.22)	0.974 (–0.38)
Northern Europe			1.254 (0.17)			1.172 (0.11)
Southern Europe			1.851 (0.88)			1.331 (0.39)
LMEs			0.948 (–0.04)			0.804 (–0.17)
Welfare				0.319 (–2.22)***		0.307 (–2.24)***
Labor market				0.746 (–0.56)		0.705 (–0.66)
Time 1 (1992–98)					0.611 (–0.85)	0.533 (–1.04)
Time 2 (pre–92 and post–98)					0.692 (–0.64)	0.671 (–0.67)
Correctly classified	81.9%	83.6%	83.9%	83.2%	83.6%	81.5%
	N=292	N=286	N=286	N=286	N=286	N=286
	LR Chi²(19) =105.74	LR Chi²(24) =123.06	LR Chi²(27) =123.96	LR Chi²(26) =129.62	LR Chi²(26) =124.01	LR Chi²(31) =131.31
	Prob Chi²=0.000	Prob Chi²=0.000	Prob Chi²=0.000	Prob Chi²=0.000	Prob Chi²=0.000	Prob Chi²=0.000
	Log likelihood =–119.550	Log likelihood =–106.051	Log likelihood =–105.600	Log likelihood =–102.775	Log likelihood =–105.575	Log likelihood =–101.930
	Pseudo R²= 0.31	Pseudo R²= 0.37	Pseudo R²= 0.37	Pseudo R²= 0.39	Pseudo R²= 0.37	Pseudo R²= 0.39

Note: *** $p<0.01$, ** $p<0.05$, * $p<0.10$, two-tailed apart from the variables in bold, which are one-tailed.

Source: Hamann-Kelly dataset.

one-tailed tests; for all other hypotheses we report two-tailed results. We focus first on the electoral and government variables and then turn to the economic and institutional control variables.

Electoral competition – measured as the recent change in vote share for the main governing party – is strongly associated with the incidence of pact offers in Models 1–6. However, contrary to Hypotheses 1a and 1b the relationships are positive rather than negative.[8] Vote distance – the size of the vote gap between the first and second parties – and the magnitude of vote change appeared not to be significant. On the face of it, this might indicate that electoral pressures are not implicated in the genesis of social pacts. However, as noted in the measurement section of this chapter, we are acutely aware of the time-frame problem. Parties can suffer vote erosion over several elections before adjusting their policies, recovering their vote and securing election to office on the back of an increased vote share. Measurements confined to changes between the two most recent elections prior to a pact or legislation may still overlook the impact of electoral pressures over a long period of time and produce (potentially misleading) negative results. Thus, it is difficult to decide a priori what would constitute a reasonable time-frame for a range of political parties in 16 countries between 1980 and 2006, and we are aware that the results of our statistical estimation may not reflect these complex relationships. Furthermore, we also hinted at the fact that new governments likely experience a gain in votes (while incumbent parties that are reelected are more likely to experience vote losses, see Powell and Whitten 1993: 397–8), which further complicates the meaning of the statistical results. Lastly, the significant interaction terms between party position and size and direction of vote change as well as vote distance show that vote change and vote distance do matter, but in different ways for different parties, thus potentially canceling out their aggregate effect.

We can discern clear and strong party family and party position effects, in line with Hypotheses 2a and 2b. The Center parties were distinctive and were significantly more likely than the Conservatives to offer social pacts. In contrast, the coefficients for Social Democratic governments never reached significance. It is Center parties, not Social Democrats, that stand out from Conservative governments. The party position results also indicate that parties further to the right were the least likely to offer social pacts. The party position coefficients in Models 1–6 were all highly significant, mostly at the 1 percent or 5 percent levels. Thus, we cannot corroborate findings in the literature based on case studies that Conservative parties are more likely to offer pacts in an effort to boost their welfare legitimacy; nor can we extend the arguments of the corporatist literature that leftist parties are necessary to cooperate with unions on social pacts as our results indicate that Center parties are strongly involved in making pact offers.

We also found strong evidence of interaction effects between party position, electoral competition, and vote gain or loss, confirming Hypotheses 2c–e. The positively signed interaction terms in all six models mean that a large vote change (whether increase or decrease) and a large vote gap between the first and second parties were more important for parties of the right (higher scoring parties on the party position scale). Vote change and vote gap were less significant in explaining the behavior of left and center parties. The negatively signed interaction term for party position and *direction* of vote change in all six models means that vote *increases* were a stronger predictor of pact offers for parties of the left than for parties of the right.

In line with Hypothesis 3a we found a robust relationship between pact offers and the strength of the government in all six models. The smaller the seat share of the government, the more likely it was to make social pact offers. In other words, governments with only a minority of seats or a small majority are significantly more likely to offer pacts than their majority counterparts.[9] Evidence in relation to Hypotheses 3b and 3c shows that the relationship between the type of government, whether single-party or coalition, and pact offers was complex. Unconnected coalitions were more likely to offer social pacts, compared to single-party governments; yet, no statistically significant difference between connected coalitions and single-party administrations was discernible. The critical variable is the type of coalition rather than the type of government. The coefficients for the unconnected coalition variable were positively signed and highly significant in five of the six models. In contrast, the coefficients on the connected coalition governments were invariably insignificant. The odds ratios for the unconnected coalition variable were extremely high suggesting that unconnected coalitions were far more likely to offer social pacts than either connected coalitions or single-party administrations, confirming Hypothesis 3c.

We also hypothesized that short-lived governments should be more likely to make pact offers (Hypothesis 3d). Although the duration coefficients are negatively signed in all six models, they only reach significance in two of them. This leads us to conclude that while short-lived cabinets might tend to offer more social pacts than their longer-lived counterparts, this tendency is fairly weak once other variables, such as government strength and coalition type, are controlled for.

Hypothesis 4 proposed a positive relationship between the probability of pact offers and the fragmentation of the legislature. All our models confirm this hypothesis. In other words, the probability of pact offers rises significantly with an increase in the effective number of parties in the legislature. Legislative fragmentation appears to increase the probability of pact offers, perhaps because it is more difficult for governments to find sufficient support in the legislature to pass controversial reforms. On the subject of reform content, we hypothesized that the incidence of pact offers would vary between the issues of welfare, wages, and labor market reform (Hypothesis 5a). We found that pact offers were *less* likely on welfare compared to wages but there was no difference between labor market and wage issues (Models 4 and 6). When we examined the relationship between party family and pact/legislation issues (Hypothesis 5b) we found no relationship, contrary to some of the literature.

In other words, there was no evidence that Conservative parties were more likely to make pact offers on welfare reform compared to other parties or Social Democrats on wages.

Finally, we proposed the possibility of variation in the incidence of pact offers across the different welfare state categories without, however, being able to specify the direction of any such relationship (Hypothesis 6). The results for both Models 3 and 6 suggest the incidence of pact offers did not vary significantly across the different welfare state categories, a finding that could reflect the large degree of within-category variation. For example, in the Northern European group of countries, governments in Finland made 13 pact offers and legislated reforms only once whereas in Denmark the use of legislation was more common (six pact offers and eight cases of legislation). Within the two LMEs, Irish governments offered nine pacts to unions and employers while UK governments have offered none.

Adding the economic and institutional control variables in Models 2–6 further improves model performance somewhat (see Table 4.1). The pseudo R^2 value increases from 0.31 to between 0.37 and 0.39 and the number of significant party and electoral variables also increases, from eight to approximately nine or ten. All of the electoral and political variables that are significant in Model 1 remain significant in Models 2–6 and most of the odds ratios on individual coefficients are either unchanged or improved. The probability of pact offers is strongly associated with a low level of union density but is not related to bargaining coordination (contrary, e.g. to Hassel 2006). Maybe that is because governments expect organizationally weak unions to be more agreeable to negotiations. The former result possibly reflects the large number of pact offers in Spain where union density is relatively low by West European standards, as well as the relative dearth of pact offers in Sweden, Denmark, and Austria, where union density is relatively high. For the three economic variables we found no significant associations with pact offers in any of the five models in which they were included. Moreover, and as reported in Chapter 2, we found that when these three economic and two industrial relations variables were entered alone, none of them was significant and neither was the equation. This result is at odds with much of the literature that has argued that economic factors such as high levels of budget deficits and high unemployment have stimulated government interest in social pacts, although it is consistent with Avdagic's (2010) finding that economic pressures alone cannot explain the government decision to offer a social pact. The case studies in the subsequent chapters reveal that while economic problems are often implicated in government action to restrain wages and to reform welfare systems and labor markets, they do not have a clear and consistent effect on government behavior: Labor market reforms, for instance, have been initiated during periods of both high and low unemployment; all types of reforms have been tackled both through social pacts and through legislation. Instead, the non-significance of the economic coefficients likely reflects the facts that government behavior is influenced by electoral calculations, and that governments can choose between pacts and legislation. Furthermore, contrary to some of the literature, we did not find any effect of timing. There was no preponderance of pact offers in the 1990s during the run-up to EMU but rather, as the raw data suggest, pact offers have both predated and postdated the EMU period 1992–98. In light of the rather poor performance of many of the control variables, it is not surprising to see that Model 1, which consists only of political variables, still worked very well, with eight significant coefficients and a pseudo R^2 of 0.31.

In sum, pact offers to unions and employers were more likely when the main party recently experienced a big change in its vote total (an effect that was strongest for parties to the right). Pact offers were more likely where the government was dominated by left or centrist parties (Social Democrats or Center parties); where it comprised an unconnected coalition; and where a large number of parties populated the legislature. Pact offers were also more likely where union density was lower and less likely on welfare reforms compared to wages.

Our results also illuminate the factors associated with the use of legislation rather than pacts. Consequently, we found that reliance on legislation was associated with small vote changes over recent elections and with governments that were Conservative-led and comprised a connected coalition or a single-party administration in a legislature with a relatively small number of parties. Legislation was also more likely where union density was relatively high. In summary, all six models are highly significant (p<.0000), five of the six pseudo R^2 values fall in the range 0.37–0.39 and many of the odds ratios deviate significantly from 1.

Conclusion

The principal aims of this chapter were threefold: to construct hypotheses based on our electoral model, to operationalize the main variables required to test these hypotheses, and to explore through quantitative analysis their explanatory power in relation to social pact offers and legislation. We developed six groups of hypotheses relating to party competition, party family and position, type of government, type of coalition, fragmentation of the party system in the legislature, type of issue, and economic institutions. Once we had resolved a number of measurement and model specification issues, partly to minimize multicollinearity, we constructed an initial regression equation (Model 1) comprising 18 variables related to elections (13 single variables and five interaction terms). We then progressively added economic and industrial relations controls and a number of other variables into five successive regression models.

Overall the data support our main argument that the likelihood of governments choosing pacts or legislation is influenced by party competition, party family and position, and by attributes of the government and the legislature. While governments are obviously concerned with meeting economic targets, they are also concerned with the potential electoral costs of welfare reforms and wage policies that they might deem necessary to meet these economic targets. Our analysis of 16 West European countries between 1980 and 2006 allows us to draw some conclusions as to which governments are more likely to resort to pacts rather than legislation, and under which circumstances. We found that recent vote changes, the family and position of the main party and the type of coalition (where there was one) as well as the number of parties in the legislature are all significant factors in accounting for government choices. In addition, reflecting complex empirical realities, the party position of the main governing party mediated the impact of changes in electoral support. However, these variables did not all perform in the ways that we had hypothesized. In particular, pact offers seemed to be more likely where the main governing party had recently gained votes, not lost them, as often happens with new governments. It is possible that we have not identified the most suitable measures of electoral competition or that we have focused on an inappropriate timeframe in order to capture the effects of such competition. One of the important advantages of the accompanying case studies is that they allow us to explore the role of electoral competition in more depth than is possible in our quantitative analysis. Turning to our control variables, we found no support for the role of EMU and for the impact of inflation, deficits, unemployment, or bargaining coordination but some support for the role of union density. To complete our tests of arguments advanced in the literature, we could not confirm any robust effect of economic institutions (welfare state categories combined with varieties of capitalism) and we found that pacts were *less* likely to be offered on welfare reform compared to wages.

In sum, to explain government choices of reform strategies, it matters who governs, and how stable the government is, as well as what is at issue. These fundamentally political factors provide more powerful explanations than those relying on economic factors or economic institutions alone. Our data indicate that politics still matter, and that election results likewise still matter in deciding how reforms are implemented, and which political actors are involved in deciding on the details of reform. The subsequent comparative country case studies will disentangle some of these complex relationships and unveil the causal dynamics that have led governments to opt for legislation or pacts in specific situations.

5 The divergent trajectories of social pacts in the Liberal Market Economies

Ireland and the UK

Ireland and the UK are conventionally regarded as the only Liberal Market Economies (LMEs) in Western Europe. In both countries firms are said to rely heavily on markets to coordinate activities such as wage bargaining and training in highly decentralized bargaining systems (Hall and Soskice 2001b: 6–7, 19–20; Kitschelt *et al.* 1999: 435). Their "liberal" welfare states rely on means-testing to distribute comparatively modest levels of benefit (Esping-Andersen 1990: 52; Huber and Stephens 2001: 88–9); employment protection laws are weak by international standards (Hamann and Kelly 2008); their union movements have similar structures and density levels (Howell 2005: 122; Wallace *et al.* 2004: 146);[1] and both countries have a history of unsuccessful attempts at tripartite wage regulation in the 1970s. Amable (2003: 180–1) points out that the designation of Ireland as an LME is problematic because of the centralized bargaining and active labor market policies introduced since the late 1980s (see also Crouch 2005: 34–5). Nevertheless Ireland and the UK exhibit many institutional similarities sufficient to differentiate them from the CMEs of Western and Northern Europe.

Yet despite the similarities in institutions and structures, the most striking feature of these countries since the 1980s is the dramatic divergence in the forms of government intervention in wage determination and industrial relations. Irish policymaking in these fields has become synonymous with tripartite social pacts, supported to varying degrees by all five political parties that have participated in governments between 1987 and 2006 (Fianna Fáil, Fine Gael, Progressive Democrats, Labour, and Democratic Left) (Teague and Donaghey 2009). In stark contrast, successive UK governments have relied entirely on the legislative route to reform and neither Conservative nor Labour administrations have offered social pacts to the unions and employers.

Here, we illustrate how our model of electoral competition can make sense of these dramatic national differences. We show that the dominant party in Ireland – Fianna Fáil – came out in favor of social pacts in 1987 as a way of positioning itself between electoral rivals to its left and right and taking votes from both. Its electoral and parliamentary success over the ensuing years eventually compelled its rivals, originally opposed to social pacts, to change their positions on pacts in order to secure access to coalition governments. Governmental preference for pacts has been reinforced by the fragmentation of the legislature and the prevalence of minority administrations. In contrast, the repeated electoral and parliamentary success of the British Conservatives and the large seat majorities of successive single-party Conservative governments allowed them to repudiate tripartism and rely on the legislative route to reform. Labour's successive electoral defeats intensified the sharp factional debates inside the party as it tried to come to terms with the problems of reconciling full employment and low inflation. The weakening of the left wing of the party, especially after the 1983 electoral defeat, gradually enabled the center-right leadership to pull the party away from its commitment to tripartite regulation and towards an acceptance of conservative policy-making style.

Ireland

Industrial relations institutions and economic context

Irish trade union density levels peaked in the late 1970s at almost 55 percent before falling dramatically to just 35 percent in 2003. The single union confederation has no political party affiliation although some individual unions are affiliated to the Labour Party and support it financially. The level of industrial conflict was traditionally one of the highest in Western Europe but has declined significantly since the early 1980s. Employment protection legislation is relatively weak and in the early 1980s bargaining coordination was low (Hamann and Kelly 2008). The welfare system comprises low replacement ratios and widespread means testing, and is based on relatively low levels of taxation (Huber and Stephens 2001: 111).

Throughout the early 1980s, unemployment climbed rapidly as the Fine Gael–Labour administration pursued deflationary policies involving restraints on public spending, reduced tax rates and wage moderation (Roche 1997a: 194; see also Figure 5.1). Rising unemployment helped reduce price inflation from its 1980 level of around 20 percent to just 3–4 percent by the mid-late 1980s. Unemployment peaked in the mid-1980s then fell before briefly rising again in the recession of the early 1990s and then resuming its downward trajectory to approximately 4–5 percent. Inflation continued falling throughout the period and stabilized at between 3 percent and 5 percent. The government did face unusually high levels of public deficit and debt during the first half of the 1980s but both fell quickly from 1987 and government borrowing was eliminated after 1996. Finally, GDP growth rates were substantially above the EU average (see Figure 5.1).

The electoral and party system in Ireland

Elections to the Dáil, the national legislature, are conducted under the Single Transferable Vote form of proportional representation. Ireland has experienced a modest rise in the effective number of parties in the legislature, from 3.2 in

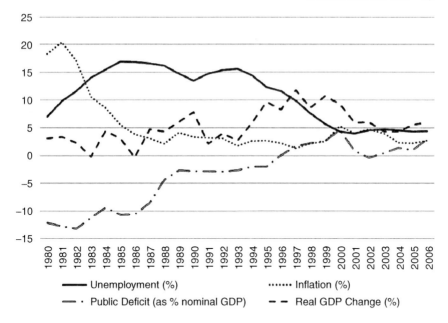

Figure 5.1 Main economic indicators, Ireland, 1980–2006.
Sources: OECD (June 2007; December 1999; December 1996).

the 1950s to 3.9 in 2002, and a more recent and dramatic decline in the vote share of the two major parties, Fianna Fáil and Fine Gael, from 84.4 percent (1982) to 64.0 percent (2002) (Webb 2004: 237). The Irish party system is peculiar in Western Europe because its two major parties are not rooted in the traditional cleavages of social class or religion but in the contending forces of the 1921–23 civil war (Murphy and Farrell 2002: 217–8). Ireland also possesses a recognizably liberal conservative party (Fine Gael) as well as a social demo-cratic party (the Labour Party) that is unusually weak by European standards (Laver 1992: 375). Furthermore, Fianna Fáil's manifesto positions approximate those of populist conservative parties such as the Gaullists in France or New Democracy in Greece (Gallagher *et al.* 2006: 245). Other authors, however, understand Fianna Fáil as a pragmatic, catch-all party with very few clear values or policy positions (Collins 2000: 332; Farrell 1999: 34; Gallagher 1985: 28). Since the 1980s these three main parties have been joined in the legislature by four additional parties, the liberal Progressive Democrats, the Greens, and two leftist organizations, the Workers' Party and Democratic Left.

In addition to the growing support for new parties, Ireland has displayed other trends similar to those found elsewhere in Europe: increased electoral volatility, declining turnout, and declining partisan identification (Dalton 2000: 25; Gallagher *et al.* 2006: 291–4). In 1978, 42 percent of voters felt "very or fairly close" to a particular party but by 1986 this figure had almost halved to just 22 percent (Mair and Marsh 2004: 240–1). Table 5.1 lists

Table 5.1 Election results, Ireland (Dáil), 1977–2006

	1977		1981		Feb. 1982		Nov. 1982		1987		1989		1992		1997		2002	
	% votes	# seats (%seats)	% votes	# seats (%seats)	% votes	# seats (%seats)	% votes	# seats (%seats)	% votes	# seats (%seats)	% votes	# seats (%seats)	% votes	# seats (%seats)	% votes	# seats (%seats)	% votes	# seats (%seats)
Fianna Fáil	50.6	84 (56.8)	45.3	78 (47.0)	47.3	81 (48.8)	45.2	75 (45.2)	44.2	81 (48.8)	44.2	77 (46.4)	39.1	68 (41.0)	39.3	77 (46.4)	41.5	81 (48.8)
Fine Gael	30.6	43 (29.1)	36.5	65 (39.2)	37.3	63 (38.0)	39.2	70 (42.2)	27.1	51 (30.7)	29.3	55 (33.1)	24.5	45 (27.1)	27.9	54 (32.5)	22.5	31 (18.7)
Labour	11.6	17 (11.5)	9.9	15 (9.0)	9.1	15 (9.0)	9.4	16 (9.6)	6.4	12 (7.2)	9.5	15 (9.0)	19.3	33 (19.9)	10.4	17 (10.2)	10.8	21 (12.7)
Progressive Democrats[a]									11.9	14 (8.4)	5.5	6 (3.6)	4.7	10 (6.0)	4.7	4 (2.4)	4.0	8 (4.8)
WP/DL[b]	1.7	0 (0.0)	1.7	1 (0.01)	2.2	3 (1.8)	3.1	2 (1.2)	3.8	4 (2.4)	5.0	7 (4.2)	3.5	7 (4.2)	2.9	4 (2.4)	0.2	0 (0.0)
Green Alliance[c]									0.4	0 (0.0)	1.5	1 (0.6)	1.4	1 (0.6)	2.8	2 (1.2)	3.8	6 (3.6)
Others	5.5	4 (2.7)	6.6	7 (4.2)	4.1	4 (2.4)	3.1	3 (1.8)	6.2	4 (2.4)	5.0	5 (3.0)	7.5	2 (1.2)	12.0	8 (4.8)	17.2	19 (11.5)
Total	100	148 (100)	100	166 (100)	100	166 (100)	100	166 (100)	100	166 (100)	100	166 (100)	100	166 (100)	100	166 (100)	100	166 (100)

Sources: See Appendix 1.

Notes:

[a] Formed December 1985.

[b] The WP (Workers' Party) formed 1970 as Official Sinn Fein; Democratic Left (DL) formed 1992 as a breakaway from WP before merging with Labour 1999. Voting figures record the combined WP and DL vote.

[c] Founded as the Ecology Party 1981; renamed Green Alliance 1984.

election results for Ireland since 1977 and demonstrates the dominance of Fianna Fáil, the dramatic fluctuations in the Fine Gael and Labour votes, and the growth of support for several new parties.

Electoral competition and the origins of the 1987 social pact in Ireland

The first contemporary Irish social pact, the Programme for National Recovery (PNR), was adopted in October 1987, nine months after the election that brought Fianna Fáil to power as a minority, single-party government. Since the 1987 pact successive governments and the union and employer organizations have signed six additional national agreements regulating wage rises, tax rates, employment and pensions, each one coming into force as its predecessor expired. This 20-year sequence means that Ireland has the longest unbroken coverage of social pacts of any country in Western Europe. It is generally accepted that the first pact emerged in response to the economic crisis of the mid-1980s (Hardiman 2002: 8; O'Donnell *et al.* 2007; Roche 2007: 396–7; Teague and Donaghey 2004: 16). Unemployment had climbed from 9 percent in 1980 to almost 17 percent in 1986 and the budget deficit in 1986 had remained stubbornly high at 10.6 percent of GDP, three times the OECD average (Figure 5.1). Following the collapse of centralized agreements at the end of the 1970s, the decentralized bargaining that prevailed between 1982 and 1987 was preferred by some employers in part because they were able to drive down the level of nominal wage settlements in line with price inflation (Roche 1997a: 199). An alternative interpretation is that other employers, as well as the 1982–87 Fine Gael–Labour government and many union leaders, took the view that Ireland was in the throes of a profound economic crisis that required radical policies for its solution. Thus, a "shared understanding" of the country's economic problem emerged that provided the foundation for the first social pact. Its perceived success in moderating wage growth and reducing unemployment encouraged the parties to repeat the policy of central agreements (O'Donnell and Thomas 2002: 185–6; see also House and McGrath 2004).

The economic crisis of the mid-1980s was clearly a powerful impetus for governmental action; however, political parties disagreed substantially about the most appropriate policies to solve the crisis. Our understanding is that the reemergence of social pacts was driven by the response of the main opposition party, Fianna Fáil (FF), to vote and seat losses and electoral defeat. Its 1987 proposal for a social pact was as much a political response to secure the party's reelection as an economic solution to high unemployment and public deficit. Fianna Fáil had ruled Ireland for most of the postwar period as a single-party government. After losing power following the 1973 election, however, Fianna Fáil's parliamentary performance continued to deteriorate and the other two main parties, Fine Gael (FG) and Labour, formed a coalition government for almost ten of the next 15 years (1973–77, 1981–82 and 1982–87). Fianna Fáil lost support in these years primarily to its main rival Fine Gael rather than

Table 5.2 Voting for Fianna Fáil and Fine Gael by social class, 1969, 1977, and November 1982 (in %)

		1969	1977	Nov 1982
Fiánna Fáil	Non-manual	32	20	25
	Skilled manual	13	23	22
	Unskilled manual	33	32	30
	Farmers	22	25	23
Fine Gael	Non-manual	34	31	35
	Skilled manual	12	14	18
	Unskilled manual	19	16	23
	Farmers	35	39	24

Source: Chubb (1987: 210).

to Labour, whose vote share also declined, from 11.6 percent in 1977 to just 6.4 percent in 1987 (Mair and Marsh 2004: 237; see also Table 5.1). Fianna Fáil lost out in the 1970s especially among middle class (non-manual) voters, as Table 5.2 shows, although it recovered some of these voters in 1982.

The origins of the 1987 pact go back to the November 1982 election, when Fianna Fáil was defeated and replaced by a Fine Gael–Labour coalition government. The party's influential and charismatic leader Charles Haughey initially sought to recover Fianna Fáil's vote share by reasserting its traditional nationalism on the issue of a united Ireland and its social conservatism on the issues of abortion and divorce (Mair 1987a: 215; 1987b: 33–6). However, these party positions antagonized some leading party members who favored fresh economic thinking to tackle the sharp rise in unemployment and in December 1985 broke away to form a new party, the Progressive Democrats (PDs). The PDs were a classic "conservative liberal" party in favor of income tax cuts, wage restraint, and reductions in welfare spending, but more progressive on social issues such as abortion and divorce law reform (Collins 2005; Gallagher *et al.* 2006: 249). Through the latter half of 1986 opinion polls granted the PDs around 15 percent of the popular vote, although its support came primarily from middle class supporters of Fine Gael rather than Fianna Fáil, the party from which it had broken away (Girvin 1987: 12; Laver *et al.* 1987: 104–8).

Fine Gael, much like Fianna Fáil, had also become a "catch-all" party with an electoral base spread across the social classes (see Table 5.2). It aimed at appealing both to conservative voters through its support for inward investment for example, and to manual and non-manual workers and small farmers through support for the welfare state (Mair 1987a: 213). From June 1981 to February 1982 Fine Gael formed a short-lived coalition with Labour and attempted to pursue cuts in public spending and income taxes and to restrain the growth of wages. Given this was a conservative-led government in a legislature with a relatively small number of parties it might have been expected to legislate wage restraint. On the other hand the government commanded only a minority of seats in the legislature and as an unconnected coalition it was vulnerable to policy disagreements: both of these factors pushed in the direction of social pacts. In fact, the government offered a social pact to the unions only to have it rejected.

The Fine Gael–Labour coalition reformed in November 1982, after two intervening governments lost confidence votes that year, but this time it had a majority in the legislature. The coalition predictably did not offer a pact to the unions throughout its four-year period in office and in April 1984 it legislated a limit on wage rises (Collins 1993: 107–10; Hastings *et al.* 2007: 14, 16, 28; Wallace *et al.* 2004: 382). As the end of its five-year term drew near, the Fine Gael leadership became increasingly concerned at the rise of the PD and worried by its own slump in the opinion polls. Throughout 1986 it was polling around 25 percent of the electorate, a 14-point drop from November 1982 surveys (Girvin 1987: 19, 27). The growing electoral threat posed by the neoliberal PD, as well as the mounting economic crisis, finally led the Fine Gael leadership to move sharply to the right. In its 1986 budget the government therefore promised cuts in income tax and public spending and higher interest rates (Mair 1987b: 37).

However, this new set of more conservative policies produced tremendous strains on the relationship with Fine Gael's leftist coalition partner. Labour's moderate leader Dick Spring had been elected to that post in November 1982 but had been subject to continual criticism from the party's well organized left-wing factions, as well as from some trade union leaders, for his support of Fine Gael conservative economic policies. In addition the party appeared to be paying an electoral price for its participation in office. In June 1984 Labour lost all of its Euro MPs; in June 1985 its local election vote share was halved to just 9 percent; and throughout 1986 its opinion poll rating hovered at a mere 4 percent (Collins 1993: 127–30; Marsh and Mitchell 1999: 48). In 1986, as the Fine Gael leadership moved to the right, the Labour Party leadership became increasingly fearful that the party would continue losing working class votes to the government's main critics from the left, Fianna Fáil and the Workers' Party. Faced with mounting electoral pressures and increased discontent from all levels of the party, Labour resigned from the coalition in January 1987 and precipitated a general election the following month. In order to distance itself from Fine Gael's neoliberal policies, Labour issued a radical Keynesian manifesto that called for increased government spending and borrowing to tackle unemployment, a wealth tax on big farmers, and protection of welfare expenditure (Girvin 1987: 23; Mair 1987b: 39–40). Although not quite as radical as its November 1982 manifesto, the document still placed Labour to the left of Fianna Fáil, despite the latter's strident criticisms of spending cuts (Budge *et al.* 2001: 28). Fine Gael, for its part, campaigned on a program of continued cuts in government spending, borrowing and taxation as well as privatization (Girvin 1987: 18).

Until early 1987 the Fianna Fáil leadership responded to the country's problems by campaigning on economic issues, openly attacking the government's spending cuts, and seeking to reposition the party as a catch-all organization of the political center. This move to the center was assisted by the November 1986 publication of a widely publicized report on economic strategy from the standing tripartite advisory body, the National Economic and Social Council. The report called for wage restraint, control of public spending, tax reform (not simply tax cuts), public sector reforms, and continued social protection for vulnerable groups (O'Donnell and Thomas 2002: 178–9). The Fianna Fáil leadership appropriated much of the report in its 1987 election manifesto Programme for National Recovery. It acknowledged the case for some restraint on public spending, notwithstanding its repeated attacks on Fine Gael spending cuts, to appease more conservative voters concerned about economic crisis and decline and win them back from the PD. However,

> In an attempt to attract a section of the trade union and working class support base the manifesto also committed Fianna Fáil to renew the process of tripartite consultation and social partnership which had been a feature of government policy during previous Fianna Fáil administrations.
>
> (Girvin 1987: 22)

As the 1987 election campaign got under way, "Fine Gael competed from the right; Labour had begun to rediscover a socialist heritage; and Fianna Fáil sought the centre ground through the revitalization of its socialist appeal" (Mair 1987b: 43).

The 1987 election afforded Fianna Fáil more votes but fewer seats than 1982, resulting in a single-party minority government. It duly offered and signed a social pact with the unions and the employers, the Programme for National Recovery (1987), designed to moderate wage growth and facilitate implementation of the Fine Gael spending cuts, which it had denounced only a few months previously (Girvin 1990: 5; Wallace *et al.* 2004: 386–7). Many national union leaders welcomed a return to tripartite policymaking, anxious to avoid the union exclusion then taking place in the UK under Margaret Thatcher (Baccaro and Lim 2007: 34–5; Wallace *et al.* 2004: 146, 223, 384).

Fianna Fáil's promotion of tripartite consultation can be traced back to its 1982 election defeat and to the electoral threats that emerged in subsequent years. The left-moving Labour Party and a resurgent Workers' Party potentially threatened its working-class base while the breakaway Progressive Democrats potentially threatened its more conservative base. In policy terms, Fianna Fáil was threatened from both left and right and its centrist manifesto therefore sought to appeal to a diverse range of voters in order to maximize its own vote and return to office. Once in power the pacts option was reinforced by the government's minority status and the increased fragmentation of the legislature, up from 2.56 to 2.90 (Mitchell 2003: 127). However, as the new Fine Gael opposition leader famously announced in autumn 1987 his party's support for the government's economic policies (the so-called "Tallaght strategy"), in theory Fianna Fáil could have legislated wage restraint with a substantial parliamentary majority (Roche 1997b: 50). The fact that Fianna Fáil chose not to legislate is consistent with our claim that the party had come to favor a social pact as a means of rebuilding its vote share.[2]

Electoral competition and the renewal of the 1987 pact

Fianna Fáil offered the 1987 social pact to the unions with little or no support from its four rivals: Fine Gael had turned against tripartism in the early 1980s; the Progressive Democrats were never in favor of pacts with unions; and both Labour and the Workers Party objected to the spending cuts and wage restraint at the heart of the pact (Hastings *et al.* 2007: 54–6). Yet between 1989 and 1997 all four of these parties held office in coalition governments and endorsed the wage pacts signed in January 1991, February 1994, and January 1997. Pacts became a regular feature of policymaking in Ireland in large measure because all of the potential governing parties came to support this approach, despite their initial skepticism or hostility. In this section, we set out to explain the radical shift in the positions of these four parties.

The 1989 snap election was called by Fianna Fáil to capitalize on its favorable poll ratings and secure a majority in the legislature (Marsh and Sinnott 1990: 101). Its election campaign highlighted two years of strong economic growth with low inflation and a modest fall in unemployment (see Figure 5.1). Yet the need for continued restraint on public spending meant that the party's "significant working class constituency ... would be seriously affected by cutbacks. Arrangements with the trade union could deflect some of the expected criticism" (Girvin 1990: 8). Fianna Fáil therefore pledged to renew the social pact when it expired in late 1990, controversially implying that the pact was responsible for the country's economic success (see Hastings *et al.* 2007).[3] Yet, although Fianna Fáil remained the largest party and its vote share was unchanged, it lost four seats while its nearest rival Fine Gael gained four. Leftist critics of the social pact also gained – Labour rose from 12 to 15 seats and the Workers' Party almost doubled its seats from four to seven – but the liberal PD lost heavily to the two big parties (Girvin 1990: 5–6, 13; see also Table 5.1). Fianna Fáil formed an unconnected coalition with the PDs despite their policy disagreements on relations with the trade unions and on social issues (Laver and Arkins 1990: 201–3; Marsh and Mitchell 1999: 56). With the economy continuing to improve during 1989 and 1990, the government proceeded to offer a new, three-year social pact, the Programme for Economic and Social Progress (PESP), which was finally agreed by the unions in January 1991. Although the new pact sought to limit wage growth, it was less restrictive on wages than its predecessor, the PNR (Wallace *et al.* 2004: 385).

In theory Fianna Fáil leaders could have responded to the 1989 election setback by abandoning social pacts and opting for legislation, a choice that its conservative coalition partner might well have supported. However, Fianna

Fáil had pledged in its election manifesto to renew the 1987 pact, thus effectively ruling out legislation as a strategic option. Although the PDs were critical of the 1991 pact, they were themselves under intense electoral pressure. The party's vote and seat totals had fallen sharply between the 1987 and 1989 elections and refusal to back the pact could have resulted in government defeat and another election with yet further seat losses (Collins 1992: 167, 200; Table 5.1). Consistent with our model, Fianna Fáil's continued support for social pacts after the 1989 election reflected its status as a center party that held only a minority of seats in a somewhat more fragmented legislature and was now part of an unconnected coalition. Moreover, as the expiry of the PNR pact approached in late 1990, Fianna Fáil suffered a serious defeat in the November 1990 presidential election, adding to the pressure to appease voters (Collins 1992: 199).

The continuation of social pacts 1994–2006

By January 1994 and the imminent expiry of the PESP social pact, Ireland had a new coalition government comprising Fianna Fáil and the Labour Party, formed after the November 1992 election. Fianna Fáil entered that election after two years of economic slowdown and rising unemployment and in the midst of a series of political scandals, one of which led to the resignation of the unpopular Prime Minister Haughey in January 1992 (Marsh and Sinnott 1993: 103). With its poll ratings slipping as it hemorrhaged support to a resurgent Labour Party, Fianna Fáil sought to protect its urban working-class base with a reassertion in the manifesto of its corporatist credentials: "Fianna Fáil will build on the consensus approach that we pioneered – bringing together employers, trade unions and farmers in an effective partnership to tackle unemployment" (Fianna Fáil cited in Girvin 1993: 13).

Although stressing the need for continued restraint on public spending and wage growth, in line with the Maastricht Treaty, the party placed far less emphasis on income tax cuts compared to Fine Gael and the PD (Budge *et al.* 2001: 28; Girvin 1993: 12–3; Kavanagh *et al.* 1998: 123). Although there was little popular support for tax or welfare cuts and a widespread belief that unemployment was the dominant issue in the election, the results were another disappointment for Fianna Fáil (Marsh and Sinnott 1993: 99). The party again lost seats and votes, falling to a total of 68 seats, its worst performance since 1954. However, as its nearest rival Fine Gael also lost seats the gap between the two parties actually increased fractionally. While the PDs picked up four more seats, the big winner was the Labour Party, whose vote share rose from 9.5 percent to 19.3 percent, affording it 33 seats in the legislature, its best performance ever. Following unusually prolonged coalition talks a majority Fianna Fáil–Labour administration was eventually formed in January 1993 (Mitchell 2003: 134). Just over one year later, in January 1994, the government again opened negotiations with the unions on a new round of wage restraint. The rate of increase in money earnings had slowed in 1993 as unemployment climbed for the third year in succession but the wage slowdown was modest: from 7.0 percent in 1992 to 6.4 percent in 1993 (European Commission 2003: 204). A new social pact, the Programme for Competitiveness and Work, was duly signed in February 1994.

In terms of our model the government's continued support for social pacts partly reflected its composition as a center-left administration. Moreover the fact that the government comprised a connected coalition would normally mean that the priorities of the larger partner – the centrist Fianna Fáil – would take precedence on issues it deemed highly salient. We can infer that the preference for pacts over legislation was salient for the Fianna Fáil leadership because its election manifesto contained an unequivocal commitment to renew the pact despite the fact that two previous social pacts had failed to stem its vote and seat losses. In 1992, as in 1989, the party therefore effectively eliminated its own strategic choice between pacts and legislation. For its part, the Labour Party had shifted significantly since the late 1980s, as leader Dick Spring responded to the dismal results of the 1987 election, when the party lost one-third of its votes and one-quarter of its seats after four years as junior partner in a coalition government with Fine Gael. Spring emulated the behavior of his British counterpart Neil Kinnock (see below), seeking to expel the "hard left" Militant faction of his party and simultaneously beginning to move Labour towards the center, toning down both its socialist rhetoric and its ambitious spending plans (Collins 1993: 163–4; Gallagher 1982; Girvin 1993: 4). Despite some differences with Fianna Fáil over public spending levels, the Labour leadership therefore agreed to endorse the 1994 pact, due to expire in early 1997 (Collins 1993: 206–7).

The Fianna Fáil–Labour coalition collapsed in 1994 following the resignation of Prime Minister Reynolds and was replaced by an unconnected coalition comprising Fine Gael, Labour, and Democratic Left. Until the early 1990s both Fine Gael and Democratic Left had been critical of the social pacts, albeit for very different reasons. Fine Gael, as a center-right party faced with competition from the PD, had not favored tripartism, fearing that to do so might result in vote losses to its right, while the Democratic Left had opposed the Maastricht convergence criteria on which the 1994 pact had been based (Girvin 1999: 4).

According to our model the new government could have opted for either pacts or legislation. Its majority status and the conservative character of the dominant coalition partner, Fine Gael, might have predisposed the government to pursue legislative reform. However three other factors pushed towards social pacts: the electoral performance of Fine Gael at the 1992 election, its relatively weak position in the 1994–97 coalition government, and the nature of the coalition and the fragmentation of the legislature. In the November 1992 election Fine Gael had slumped to its lowest vote share since 1948 and secured just 45 seats after campaigning on a neoliberal program of tax cuts, partly designed to compete with the PD on the right. However, as the PD vote share had fallen below 5 percent, Fine Gael leader John Bruton concluded that not only had the threat from the PD declined but so too had the electoral attractions of neoliberal promises of tax cuts. He therefore began to steer the party towards the political center and in doing so, according to Girvin (1999: 23), changed his negative view of tripartism "because of his experience in government [between 1994 and 1996] and his conviction that the Christian Democratic dimension of Fine Gael should be given prominence over the neo-liberal strain."

The second factor encouraging social pacts was the relative standing of the right and left parties within the coalition. Both of Fine Gael's coalition partners had performed exceptionally well in the 1992 election: Labour's 33 seats represented the highest seat total in its history while Democratic Left, formed only months before the election, obtained four seats. Consequently in the 15 member, three-party cabinet Fine Gael held a bare majority with eight ministries compared to seven for its left partners (Mitchell 2003: 146–7). Finally, as an unconnected conservative-left coalition that excluded the centrist Fianna Fáil, the 1994–97 government acted like many other similar governments in Western Europe and – as our model suggests – sought to include the social partners in the formation of potentially unpopular measures. These factors, in conjunction with the strength of the economy and the commitment of the Labour Party to a new social pact, led to successful negotiations with unions and employers between December 1996 and January 1997. In theory, Democratic Left, with four parliamentary deputies and one cabinet seat, could have voiced its opposition to wage restraint and voted against the pact. In practice its national leaders acted like office-seekers, demanding and obtaining enough concessions from Fine Gael and Labour (especially on anti-poverty measures) to enable it to vote in favor of the pact in cabinet and in the legislature.

Over the next decade, three more social pacts were offered by governments and accepted by unions and employers. In November 1999 the Fianna Fáil–PD government, formed after the 1997 election, offered a pact called Progress for Prosperity and Fairness, which was signed in March 2000. Fine Gael, as the main governing party 1994–97, had benefited from the country's rapid economic growth and its vote increased by 3.4 percentage points, yet it was unable to form a coalition and was replaced by Fianna Fáil, which had also recorded a significant increase in its vote (Table 5.1). The new Fianna Fáil–PD minority government was an unconnected coalition in a fragmented legislature. All of these factors inclined the government to a renewal of the social pact. In October 2002 and August 2005 fresh pacts were offered by a Fianna Fáil–PD coalition government reelected in 2002 following five years of strong economic growth and with increased seat and vote shares for both parties, a highly unusual outcome in Irish elections (see Table 5.1; Murphy 2003). In accordance with our model, the vote and seat increases for both parties and the unconnected character of the coalition (Fine Gael was excluded) both pointed in the direction of a renewed social pact offer. In addition, by the late 1990s all of the five main political parties had come to accept pacts as an integral component of government policy-making style. In effect the strategic choice of pacts versus legislation that lies at the heart of our model had been taken off the political agenda.

Summing up the Irish case

Pacts first emerged as a key and distinctive element in Fianna Fáil's drive for political power in 1987 and were criticized by all of the party's rivals. But under the pressures of electoral and parliamentary competition the next few years witnessed the emergence of

> a broad-ranging consensus ... most obviously within the social and economic domain, which ... reflects the reluctance of any of the major parties to isolate itself from its opponents, particularly now that it may need one or more of those opponents as coalition allies.
>
> (Mair and Marsh 2004: 248)

While economic problems constituted the agenda for government intervention in wage determination, each of the governing parties had to make choices about the advantages and disadvantages of pacts and legislation. We have reasoned that electoral and parliamentary competition helped steer Fianna Fáil, and then its competitors, down the road of social pacts. Within the space of ten years a cross-party consensus had emerged on the role of social pacts in forming and implementing government policy. Party leaders all became convinced there was no electoral gain, and potentially great electoral loss, if they departed from this orthodoxy. In Ireland's neighbor, the UK, a cross-party consensus about policymaking on economic and industrial relations issues had also emerged by the late 1990s. Its preference for union exclusion and legislation was radically different from Irish tripartism, yet the mechanisms of electoral competition that brought it about were almost identical.

The UK

Industrial relations institutions and economic context

British trade union density, like that in Ireland, peaked in 1979 at almost 55 percent before plummeting to below 30 percent by 2003. The union movement is dominated by a single confederation, the Trades Union Congress (TUC), which is not aligned to any political party, although some of its larger constituent unions are affiliated to the Labour Party. The level of industrial conflict, measured by days lost per 1,000 workers, has fallen substantially since the early 1980s. Employment protection legislation is relatively weak and bargaining coordination and centralization have both been low since the early 1980s (Hamann and Kelly 2008). The welfare system is based on low replacement ratios, widespread means testing and relatively low levels of taxation (Huber and Stephens 2001: 111). Throughout the 1980s and early 1990s successive governments were faced with historically high levels of unemployment, inflation, and public borrowing (see Figure 5.2). Unemployment climbed rapidly in the early 1980s as governments pursued deflationary policies but price inflation fell from around 20 percent to just 3–4 percent by the mid- to late 1980s (Howell 2005: 153–6). Unemployment decreased in the late 1980s, rose again in the early 1990s, and then commenced a long decline to approximately 4–5 percent in the early 2000s. Inflation declined throughout the period, stabilizing at 2–4 percent in the late 1990s. The high level of public deficit was lowered through the early 1980s but increased to an unprecedented 7.9 percent of GDP in 1993 only to fall again and disappear by the early 2000s.

The similarity in economic trends between the UK and Ireland is not surprising given the high degree of interdependence between the two economies. The UK was Ireland's main trading partner in the late 1970s and 1980s, accounting for 47 percent of exports in 1979 and 34 percent in 1986 (Kavanagh *et al.* 1998: 133). Substantial downturns in the larger UK economy are therefore quickly transmitted to its smaller neighbor, as evident from the synchronicity in the trends depicted in Figures 5.1 and 5.2. Consequently, we cannot explain radically different paths to policy reform – continuous social pacts in Ireland and their total absence from the UK – by reference to economic problems.

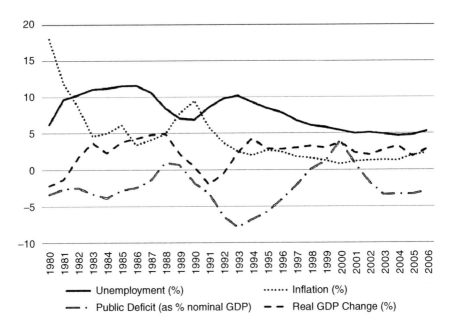

Figure 5.2 Main economic indicators, UK, 1980–2006.

Sources: OECD (June 2007; December 1999; December 1996).

The electoral and party system in the UK

Unlike Ireland, the UK employs the plurality, or "first-past-the-post," system for elections to the Westminster parliament. One consequence is that single-party, majority governments are typically formed by a party with only a plurality of votes. Moreover the disproportion between votes and seats means that governing parties can experience a significant vote decline without necessarily losing many seats or relinquishing office. Lijphart (1999) identifies this electoral system as a key component of "the Westminster model of democracy," characterized by a concentration of power in single-party, majority governments whose cabinets dominate the legislature. The party system is normally described as a "two-plus" system despite the rise in the number of effective parties in the legislature from just 2.13 in 1951 to 3.25 in 2001 and the associated erosion of the combined Labour and Conservative vote (Webb 2004: 22). The two main parties' share of the popular vote declined steadily from the 1951 peak of 97.2 percent; this erosion accelerated in the 1970s but even as recently as the 2005 election the Labour and Conservative parties still obtained 69.4 percent of the popular vote (Denver 2007: 10; see Table 5.3). Simultaneously, electoral turnout declined from 80.7 percent in the 1950s to an average of 60.3 percent for the 2001 and 2005 elections while electoral volatility more than doubled from an average of 4.3 percent in the 1950s to 9.3 percent in the 1990s (Denver 2007: 28; Gallagher *et al.* 2006: 291, 294). Finally, and again in common with other countries, the numbers of voters strongly identifying with a particular political party declined steeply between 1964 and 1997 (Dalton 2000: 25).

The conservative reliance on legislation

Prior to the 1980s both Conservative and Labour governments in the UK, like their counterparts in Ireland, were deeply involved in tripartite regulation of wages. Labour governments negotiated incomes policies with the unions between 1965 and 1969 and between 1974 and 1979, while the Conservatives negotiated three incomes policies with the trade unions between 1971 and 1973 (Davies 1983: 453–4). Yet by the 1990s the British Conservative and Labour parties had converged on the legislative route to reform and repudiated social pacts. Here, we discuss how Conservative policy emerged in response to the two electoral defeats of 1974 and was then reinforced by its success in the elections of 1979, 1983, 1987, and 1992. In a similar vein we show how Labour's abandonment of tripartite social pacts and its accommodation to legislative reform of industrial relations was a response to successive election defeats.

In office from 1979 until 1997, the Conservatives embarked on a far-reaching program of labor market reform through legislation. Often described as a policy of "labor exclusion" (e.g. Crouch 1986), its principal and ambitious aim was to undermine trade union power and thereby help eliminate the

Table 5.3 Election results, UK (House of Commons), 1979–2005

	1979		1983		1987		1992		1997		2001		2005	
	% votes	# seats (%seats)	% votes	# seats (%seats)	% votes	# seats (%seats)	% votes	# seats (%seats)	% votes	# seats (%seats)	% votes	# seats (%seats)	% votes	# seats (%seats)
Conservative	43.9	339 (53.4)	42.4	397 (61.1)	42.3	376 (57.9)	41.9	336 (51.6)	30.7	165 (25.0)	31.7	166 (25.2)	32.3	198 (30.7)
Labour	37.0	269 (42.4)	27.6	209 (32.2)	30.2	229 (35.2)	34.4	271 (41.6)	43.3	419 (63.6)	40.7	413 (62.7)	35.2	356 (55.1)
Liberal/ LibDem.	13.8	11 (1.7)	25.4	23 (3.5)	22.6	22 (3.4)	17.8	20 (3.1)	16.8	46 (7.0)	18.3	52 (7.9)	22.0	62 (9.6)
Others	5.3	16 (2.5)	4.6	21 (3.2)	4.9	23 (3.5)	5.9	24 (3.7)	9.2	29 (4.4)	9.3	28 (4.2)	10.5	30 (4.6)
Total	100	635 (100)	100	650 (100)	100	650 (100)	100	651 (100)	100	659 (100)	100	659 (100)	100	646 (100)

Source: See Appendix 1.

strikes, "restrictive practices," and "inflationary" wage demands, which Prime Minister Thatcher's government believed to be at the root of British economic decline (Lawson 1993: 431–6; Thatcher 1993: 93).[4] In 1980 the government introduced legislation to remove legal protection for solidarity action and abolish compulsory trade union membership. In 1982 it restricted the definition of a lawful industrial relations dispute thereby exposing union funds to third-party claims for damages. The same Act allowed employers selectively to dismiss strikers. In 1984 it introduced mandatory secret ballots of individual union members for the election of union executives, the endorsement of union political funds, and the decision to strike. The Acts of 1988, 1989, and 1990 extended the legal curbs on solidarity action and on the closed shop and expanded the grounds on which employers could dismiss workers engaged in union activity (Marsh 1992: 76–7). Concerning wage regulation, the government legislated in 1986 to restrict the jurisdiction of the Wages Councils, tripartite bodies created in the early 1900s to regulate wages and conditions in low-paying industries. On pensions, the government passed legislation the same year to reduce the replacement rate for state pensions, from its comparatively low level of 25 percent to 20 percent (Schulze and Moran 2007: 67–74). Following its fourth successive election victory (in 1992) the new Conservative government passed legislation that simply abolished the Wages Councils altogether.

These labor market and welfare reforms were components of a broader program of neoliberal policies designed to enhance the role of market forces in the regulation of economic life, in the private sector and especially in the public sector, to reduce inflation (if necessary, at the expense of employment), and to restore the authority of government (Gamble 1994: 34–5; Howell 2005: 155; Kavanagh 1997: 26; Thompson 2008). Union resistance and protests, most notably in the 1984–85 miners' strike, were overridden as the government pursued a policy of "management by confrontation," presiding over a steep decline in union membership and in strike activity (Ferner 1988; Waddington 2000: 585, 595). The flipside of the Conservatives' marked preference for legislation was a pronounced antipathy to social pacts and to other forms of tripartism, which according to Dorey (2001: 194) were "now deemed by most Conservatives as wrong in principle, and unworkable in practice." Thatcher asserted in 1979, while still in opposition, that all discussion of tripartite bodies "was at best irrelevant and at worst misguided" (Thatcher 1993: 94; see also Lawson 1993: 432). Similarly, when Chancellor Lamont abolished the tripartite discussion forum, the National Economic Development Council (NEDC) in 1992, he declared "The age of corporatism must be put firmly behind us" (Lamont quoted in Thomsen and Frølund 1996: 221; see also Tebbit 1989: 244).

However, Conservative policy towards relations with the trade unions was somewhat more complex than this picture suggests. First, while the government officially repudiated social pacts and tripartism, especially in the area of pay determination, and abolished a number of tripartite institutions (the training agency, the Manpower Services Commission in 1987 and the NEDC in 1992), other bodies were preserved: the Health and Safety Executive, the Advisory, Conciliation and Arbitration Service, and the Equal Opportunities Commission all survived beyond 1997 (Taylor 1993: 267–8). Second, many Conservative ministers and supporters of the prime minister kept open lines of communication to selected, "moderate" trade union leaders for occasional consultation on issues within their jurisdiction (Fowler 1991: 175–7; Lawson 1993: 147–9; Marsh and Savigny 2005: 170; Prior 1986: 157; Young, Lord 1990: 103–6; see also Taylor 2000: 247–54). These informal contacts suggest there may have been some concern among ministers to try and monitor, and possibly minimize, adverse reaction to the government's legislative approach and its abandonment of tripartism.

Electoral competition and the Conservative preference for legislation

The Conservative preference for legislation, in contrast to the Irish preference for pacts, cannot be explained by reference to the gravity of the economic problems in the UK throughout this period. Figures 5.1 and 5.2 illustrate that the Conservative governments of 1979–97 faced problems similar in nature if not in magnitude and timing to those in Ireland, particularly high unemployment and large public deficits, yet they chose to resolve them in fundamentally different ways. Nor do institutional arguments provide much insight into the differences in behavior between the two sets of governments. Both countries had experimented with tripartite pay regulation throughout the 1970s; both systems of collective bargaining were undergoing a rapid process of decentralization; union density was falling; both peak union confederations wielded only a limited degree of authority over their affiliated members; and the principal monetary authorities in both countries enjoyed a similar, and limited, independence from central government (Franzese and Hall 2000: 198; von Prondzynsi 1998; Waddington 2000).

We therefore turn our attention to the electoral dynamics that gave rise to the Conservatives' preference for legislation. Critical in their reappraisal of the strengths and weaknesses of social pacts and legislation were the major electoral defeats in February and October 1974, in which the Conservative vote shares dropped to their lowest levels since 1918. Between 1975 and 1977 competing interpretations emerged from the "corporatist" and "neoliberal" wings of the party as to why the Conservatives, electorally so successful in the 1950s with three victories in nine years, had lost four of the five elections between 1964 and 1974. There were equally stark differences of view as what they should do to recover votes and power. In 1977, two years after Thatcher became the Conservative leader, the party issued a major statement of its economic policy. Co-authored by Shadow Employment Secretary Prior, it criticized previous state incomes policies, especially those of the 1970–74 Conservative government, as well as the union power with which they were associated. Nonetheless it suggested a role for a loose form of tripartite consultation over pay and it ruled out drastic legislation against unions, except as a last resort (Dorey 2001: 175–8). In essence the "corporatist" wing of the party remained committed to the postwar Keynesian consensus on full employment and to the policy of working with the trade unions to control inflation via wage restraint. In contrast, a neoliberal program (*Stepping Stones*), published a few months later by some of Thatcher's close supporters, insisted on a "complete change in the role of the trades union movement" (Young, Hugo 1990: 107–15). While supporting tight monetary policy as a key instrument to control inflation, the program argued that this alone would be insufficient to restore economic growth unless trade union power was drastically curtailed (Taylor 2001: 126–7). According to Dorey (2009: 230–1), party leader Thatcher was privately sympathetic to the neoliberal case but cautious in public because of the potential electoral cost of confronting union power. It was the strike wave that ran from October 1978 into March 1979 (the "Winter of Discontent") that emboldened the neoliberal wing of the party because it turned public opinion against union power (Marsh 1992: 59). Opinion polls in the run-up to the election showed a marked voter preference for Conservative as compared to Labour policies on law and order, taxation, inflation, and unemployment, and strong support for their proposals to reform trade unions (Butler and Kavanagh 1980: 131, 328). The Conservatives swept into government with an eight-point rise in vote share, a seat gain of 62, and a 42-seat majority over all other parties combined (Table 5.3). According to Budge et al (2001: 25) the 1979 manifesto was the Conservatives' most "right wing" program since 1945. As a single-party conservative government that had gained votes and held a large majority in a legislature with only a small number of effective parties (2.87 in 1979 down from 3.16 in 1974), the party leadership could be confident of enacting its radical legislative reform program starting with the Employment Acts of 1980 and 1982.

Even these decisions were not quite as straightforward as they seemed because of the government's deteriorating popularity. Sharply rising unemployment (see Figure 5.2) eroded support for the government in the opinion polls throughout 1980 and 1981 and resulted in inner city riots in the summer of 1981. In addition the Social Democratic Party (SDP), formed in April 1981 as a breakaway from Labour, won spectacular by-election victories in 1981 and 1982 in traditional Conservative districts (Butler and Kavanagh 1984: 12–17; Jenkins 2007: 60–4). On the other hand, at one of her very rare meetings with TUC leaders (in June 1979) Thatcher reportedly found them so weak and ineffectual that she anticipated little effective resistance to her legislative program (Dorfman 1983: 120; Marsh 1992: 69).

The Conservatives fought the 1983 election in the midst of high and rising unemployment (Figure 5.2). At the same time, the opposition was deeply divided between Labour and an electoral alliance of the centrist SDP and the Liberal Party and the popularity of both opposition leaders lagged well behind that of Prime Minister Thatcher (Denver 2007: 119). Although its vote share fell slightly, the Conservatives secured 58 additional seats and an almost unassailable 144 seat majority over all other parties. Emboldened by this victory the government pressed ahead with a new round of legislative reforms, targeted now at the internal organization of trade unions. Some consultation with trade union leaders occurred over the issue of trade union political funds, many of which were used to finance the Labour Party. But the few meetings did not reflect government moves towards a possible social pact. The Conservative leadership was simply concerned that any perceived restriction of the union's financial support for Labour could lead in the future to similar restrictions on business funding for the Conservatives (Marsh 1992: 116–9). In 1986, two further pieces of legislation – the Wages Act and the Social Security Act – marked the first incursion by the Conservatives into the areas of pay determination and pensions respectively (see above). The latter issue was potentially difficult because opinion polls had shown growing voter support for higher spending on welfare and public services even at the expense of higher taxes. In 1979, just 37 percent of the electorate agreed with this proposition but by 1986, 72 percent did so (Wilensky 2002: 374).

The economy grew strongly between 1983 and 1987 and in 1986 unemployment began to fall, a trend that coincided with a renewed Conservative lead in opinion polls. That lead lasted until the June 1987 election, when the Conservatives won their third successive election victory (Butler and Kavanagh 1988: 10). While their vote share was practically unchanged at just over 42 percent and their majority somewhat reduced, they still led by 102 seats over all the opposition parties. Over the next three years, the single-party Conservative government introduced three further legislative measures to curb union power, in 1988, 1989, and 1990. In addition it enacted legislation in 1989 to abolish the legal protections afforded to dock workers and pave the way for privatization of the ports, a step that precipitated a short-lived and unsuccessful dockers' strike (Fowler 1991: 303–9; Turnbull *et al.* 1992). Finally, after becoming exasperated with union criticism of government training policy, it abolished the tripartite Manpower Services Commission in 1987 (Fowler 1991: 299–300). As Trade and Industry Secretary Lord Young wrote in 1988, "We have rejected the TUC; we have rejected the CBI ... we gave up the corporate state" (cited in Dorey 2001: 193). Nevertheless the Conservatives again found themselves badly trailing Labour in the opinion polls from mid-1989. With Thatcher's popularity as PM rapidly declining, she was replaced as party leader and prime minister in November 1990 by John Major (Butler and Kavanagh 1992: 14, 31), who secured another Conservative election victory in April 1992, with the party's vote share slipping just 0.4 percent although it lost 40 seats. This was a remarkable result because the economy was once more in recession, unemployment had risen again to almost 10 percent, and the Conservatives trailed Labour in the polls from mid-1991 (Butler and Kavanagh 1992: 14). However, early 1992 poll data suggested that only a small minority of voters blamed the new Major government for rising unemployment (Heffernan and Marqusee 1992: 305).

In terms of our model, the 1992 government found itself in a far less favorable position for legislation than all of its predecessors. Although it was a single-party, majority Conservative administration it had lost votes and a significant number of seats and seen its parliamentary majority dramatically reduced from 102 to just 21. Moreover the legislature was highly fragmented by the standards of the 1950s–70s. The balance of factors in favor of legislation rather than pacts had thus weakened considerably. Although the government did not offer social pacts, its legislative program was very limited both in scale and content. While each of the three Thatcher administrations (1979–83, 1983–87, and 1987–90) had enacted a number of far-reaching reforms of industrial relations, the Major administration passed only one industrial relations Act, in 1993. This minimal program did not reflect a lack of ideas – two consultative documents issued in the early and mid-1990s floated a range of radical proposals on topics such as strikes in essential services and the legal enforceability of collective agreements (Employment Department 1991; Department of Trade and Industry 1996).

The Conservative approach to industrial relations and labor market reform was repeatedly challenged by the Labour opposition in the 1980s. In the election campaigns of 1983 and 1987 Labour pledged to repeal the Conservative industrial relation legislation and return to social pacts with unions and employers. Yet when it came to power in 1997, the Labour Party had undergone a dramatic change in policy spurred by electoral competition.

Electoral competition and the Labour Party commitment to social pacts, 1979–87

Just as the Conservative election defeats of 1974 generated a period of sharp internal debate about policy direction, the years immediately after Labour's 1979 election defeat were marked by an equally bitter factional struggle (see Downs 1957: 300). Political debate in the party had intensified through the 1970s as party policy shifted leftwards towards more radical state intervention under the rubric of the Alternative Economic Strategy (AES) (Wickham-Jones 1996). Yet the senior party leadership remained in the hands of center and right social democrats opposed to key elements of the new party policy and adamant it would not be implemented by a Labour government (Panitch and Leys 2001). Their antagonism to the new policies resulted in 1973 in the formation of a left-led Campaign for Labour Party Democracy, which in turn led to the emergence of a center-right body, the Manifesto Group (Meredith 2008). Center-right leader and former Prime Minister Callaghan resigned in October 1980. His preferred successor, Denis Healey, was narrowly defeated by Michael Foot, who was backed by both the center-left and far-left of the party and the unions. Six months later one center-right group broke away to form a rival organization, the Social Democratic Party, which soon won a series of by-elections and was standing at 30–35 percent in voting intention polls, well ahead of Labour (Kavanagh 1997: 178–85). Left influence inside the Labour Party had been growing steadily since the 1970s and became evident in the contents of the 1983 Manifesto, one of the most left-wing British manifestos of the second half of the twentieth century (Budge *et al.* 2001: 25). It pledged a Labour government to nationalize key firms, introduce import and exchange controls, withdraw from the EU (then the EEC), and increase overall public spending while substantially cutting defense spending (Shaw 1996: 166–7). On industrial relations, the manifesto declared,

> At the heart of our programme is Labour's new partnership with the trade unions. Our policies have been worked out with them ... Our starting point in government will be to discuss and agree with the trade unions a *national economic assessment* ... This will set out the likely growth in the national output and how it could be shared.
>
> (Labour Party 1983: 9, emphasis in original)

Yet, mindful of the breakdown of Labour's incomes policy in 1978–79 under the pressure of union demands for "free collective bargaining," the manifesto stressed, "We will not, however, return to the old policies of government-imposed wage restraint" (ibid., 1983: 9).[5] Unions would therefore be heavily involved in government policymaking through this social pact and the "divisive" Conservative industrial relations legislation would be repealed (Dorey 2001: 201–10; Labour Party 1983: 9). Meanwhile party-union links continued to be very close with unions providing the bulk of Labour income and union leaders contributing heavily to policy formation (Minkin 1992: 420–40, 508–16).

According to our theoretical reasoning, vote loss in general is associated with a preference for legislation, but the interaction with party family hints that left parties that lose votes are likely to retain their commitment to pacts. In fact, the party's right wing did repudiate tripartism, as we would expect, but after successive policy defeats at the hands of the left, many of its supporters broke away to form the SDP (Crewe and King 1995).

In the 1983 election Labour obtained its lowest vote share (27.6 percent) since 1918 and its lowest seat total since 1935, only just beating the SDP–Liberal Alliance, which polled 25.4 percent of the vote (Thorpe 2001: 198). In the wake of this traumatic defeat and the Labour leader's immediate resignation, the party quickly elected a center-left leader, Neil Kinnock (and a center-right deputy leader). Kinnock believed that in order to win the next election Labour had to change its industrial relations policies, shifting the balance between tripartism – which he continued to support – and legislation (Heffernan 2000: 98; Kavanagh 1997: 186). He stated that on issues such as mandatory secret ballots the Conservative government's legislative approach to labor market reform was popular with most of the electorate and with most trade unionists and Labour should therefore accept the 1984 Act (Minkin 1992: 435–7, 470).[6] He also believed the party had to alter its image as a divided organization dominated by the trade unions and the far left. In 1985 he secured the expulsion of the far-left Militant faction from the party and also began the process of centralizing power in the hands of the national leadership (Feigl-Heins 2004; Seyd and Whiteley 2004: 54). Both Kinnock and the national Labour leadership remained firmly committed to the idea of a tripartite National Economic Assessment, in effect a social pact on wages, although there was no longer any reference – as in 1983 – to the pact being central to Labour's program and the 1987 manifesto provided very little detail about its content (Thompson 2006: 259). In addition, the manifesto promoted the idea of a new set of rights for individual employees under the heading "Democracy at the Workplace" and it also promised a statutory national minimum wage, despite the misgivings of some unions (Labour Party 1987; Minkin 1992: 428–31).

Electoral competition and Labour's abandonment of social pacts after 1992

Throughout 1986, opinion polls put Labour ahead of the Conservatives and following policy changes under Kinnock the 1987 manifesto was significantly to the right of its 1983 equivalent (Budge *et al.* 2001: 25; Butler and Kavanagh 1988: 10). The result of the 1987 election was therefore a serious blow to this electoral strategy. Although Labour's vote share rose 3 percentage points (equivalent to the fall in the SDP–Liberal vote) and it gained 20 seats, these small gains still left the Conservatives with a huge majority of 102. Moreover the Labour result only represented a "gain" when measured against the historically disastrous performance of 1983. Compared to Labour's performance over the whole century, its 30.8 percent share of the vote remained one of its worst ever election results. According to Heffernan (2000: 78) the impact of this result was to encourage the Labour leadership to embark on a "wholesale revision" of its 1983 and 1987 programs. In 1988, Kinnock therefore established a wide-ranging Policy Review with commissions to examine policy in seven areas, including employment and industrial relations. Although its ostensible remit was to examine the appropriateness of current policies in the light of changes in the economy and society, Shaw (1996: 181) concludes that "The driving force behind programmatic renewal in the Labour Party since 1987 has been the search for votes."

To that end Kinnock personally chose the conveners of each of the groups and then agreed the composition of each commission with its convener (Minkin 1992: 465–6). The Policy Review process, led by Kinnock, brought about a further shift in party policy on social pacts and legislation. While the 1987 manifesto had promoted the traditional case for a tripartite forum to implement a "light" form of pay regulation, the 1989 Policy Review report on "People at Work" abandoned this approach altogether:

> On pay generally, we reject a pay policy or any form of pay norm as being unhelpful and unworkable … money spent too generously on consumption today could prejudice jobs and services tomorrow.

> Our national strategy for industrial growth and skills training will help to remove the bottlenecks and overheating which at present push up inflation whenever we try to expand.
>
> (Labour Party 1989: 14)

This statement appears to represent a radical break with the party's traditional commitment to Keynesian demand management in favor of the type of labor market supply-side policies preferred by the Conservative government. Social pacts on pay and related issues were therefore replaced by the idea that market forces (on the product market side) and supply side measures (on the labor market side) would be sufficient to deal with inflationary pressures in the economy (Cronin 2004: 31). Less than a year later and as part of their ongoing attempts to portray Labour as a party that was friendly to business, Labour leaders came out in support of a fixed sterling exchange rate through membership of the Exchange Rate Mechanism (ERM). In theory the monetary discipline of the ERM would mean that high wage settlements would quickly translate into higher and uncompetitive prices and then into higher unemployment as jobs were lost. Alarmed at the prospect of rising unemployment, the Labour leadership soon revived the idea of a National Economic Assessment and included it in the 1992 election manifesto (Wickham-Jones (2000: 21; 2009):

> Every autumn, we will make a *State of the Nation* report on the British economy. Our national economic assessment will then allow employers, trade unions and other social partners to consider Britain's competitiveness and the competing claims on national output. These considerations will be an important influence on collective bargaining.
>
> (Labour Party 1992: 5)

Meantime, on the issue of Conservative legislation, the Policy Review moved Labour still closer to an acceptance of both the process and substance of the 1980s legal reforms of trade unions and industrial relations. In the early stages of the Policy Review it emerged that the "People at Work" group was proposing to reassert the 1987 policy of rejecting the Conservative approach to labor market reform and repealing most of its industrial relations legislation despite a December 1987 warning from Kinnock's economic policy adviser John Eatwell that a restoration of union power would be "an electoral liability" (Eatwell cited in Wickham-Jones 1995: 471). Kinnock worked with union leaders late spring 1989 to secure their support for a more accommodating stance that would combine some form of tripartism with support for legislated reforms. For example, instead of rejecting the restrictions on solidarity action introduced in 1980 and 1982, Labour now proposed simply to "review the boundaries of lawful industrial action," a process that might well include a negotiated agreement with the trade unions (Hughes and Wintour 1990: 150–2; Labour Party 1989: 25). Another sign of his determination to adopt a more favorable stance towards legislative reform occurred when the Conservatives initiated a Bill in 1990 that would finally render the closed shop unlawful. Supported by his new Employment spokesperson, Tony Blair, Kinnock abandoned Labor's long standing support for the closed shop and his antagonism to legislated labor market reform and declared that the party leadership would not oppose the Conservative proposals nor even insist on consultation with the unions (Fowler 1991: 325). Although the Policy Review had declared that specific pieces of recent industrial relations legislation would be repealed and others reviewed, the 1992 manifesto, with input from Tony Blair, came close to accepting that Conservative industrial relations laws would be accepted almost in their entirety, boldly declaring "there will be no return to the trade union legislation of the 1970s ... There will be no mass or flying pickets" (Labour Party 1992: 11).

At the time of the 1992 election Labour had been ahead in the polls for over a year and remained narrowly in the lead until polling day (Butler and Kavanagh 1992: 14). Once again, however, the Conservatives won the election although Labour increased its vote share by 4.2 percentage points and gained 42 additional seats. Because the opinion polls had raised Labour expectations of victory the final result was "an even more crushing disappointment" (Shaw 1996: 192). When Tony Blair was elected party leader in 1994, he argued that although the party's acceptance of labor market legislation had improved its electoral performance, the party had still not distanced itself sufficiently from its association with trade unions (Fielding 2003: 1; Hay 1999: 140; McIlroy 1998; Mandelson and Liddle 1996: 42–3). In July 1994 he declared that "Trade unions will have no special and privileged place. They will have the same access as the other side of industry" (cited in Dorey 2001: 218). In a 1996 public lecture Blair confirmed that, like Thatcher, he too had now repudiated "corporatism" when he declared that "I reject ... as out of date and impractical, the recreation or importation of a model of the corporate state popular a generation ago" (Blair cited in Dorey 2001: 218). The idea of a National Economic Assessment, a tripartite forum to discuss wages and related issues, was finally buried.

Labour fought the 1997 General Election on its most rightist manifesto in at least 60 years and secured a historic victory, gaining almost 9 percentage points in vote share and an additional 148 seats to grant it a parliamentary majority of 187 (Budge *et al.* 2001: 25; Cronin 2004: 37–8; see also Table 5.3). Although according to our model, new governing parties that gain votes are more likely to offer social pacts than legislate, the government's large majority in the legislature strongly reinforced its manifesto repudiation of social pacts, although it did create a tripartite commission to recommend the level of the new statutory minimum wage and to monitor its effects. In the Foreword to *Fairness at Work*, Labour's 1998 legislative proposals on the national minimum wage and on union recognition, newly elected Prime Minister Blair confirmed that Labour had finally come to accept the Conservative program of industrial relations legislation and now shared its preference for legal reforms enacted without union consultation and in the face of union opposition, as evident from the following statement: "The days of strikes without ballots, mass picketing, closed shops and secondary action are over. Even after the changes we propose, Britain will have the most lightly regulated labour market of any leading economy in the world" (Board of Trade 1998: 2). Although the number of meetings between union leaders and ministers increased in comparison to the years of the Major administration, it did not return to the frequency of contact even in the Thatcher years, let alone that of the 1970s (Marsh 2002: 148; Marsh and Savigny 2005: 171).

In the 2001 election Labour retained almost all of its seats (413 out of 419) although its vote share dropped 2.6 points. An electorally successful social-democratic party with a substantial vote and seat gap over its nearest rival might well have opted to pursue social pacts particularly as it began to consider issues such as reforms to state pensions, welfare benefits, and public services that could, in theory, have been discussed and agreed with trade unions. Moreover opinion polls conducted during the election campaign showed that health care and education were rated as the two most important issues by voters as a whole (Butler and Kavanagh 2002: 237). On the other hand as a single-party administration with a large majority it could just as readily secure its objectives through legislation. In fact public service reform became a highly contentious issue under the second Blair government and significantly soured its relations with the union movement, leading two small unions, the Railworkers and the Firefighters, to disaffiliate from the party (Kelly 2005: 78; Ludlam 2004: 76). In 2003 and 2004 Labour lost two by-elections in seats it had previously held, the first time the Blair government had suffered such losses. These defeats, coupled with worries about a decline in union electoral finance, led party leaders (not the government) to negotiate a series of general policy commitments late 2004 with the leaders of affiliated unions, the so-called "Warwick Agreement" (Bewley 2006). Although Labour's vote share fell by 5.5 points and it lost 57 seats in the 2005 election, it still commanded a parliamentary majority of 53 and therefore continued as a single-party, majority administration functioning without social pacts.

Summing up the British case

Despite the existence of similar industrial relations institutions and economic problems to those found in Ireland, a succession of British governments, both Conservative and Labour, converged on a fundamentally different approach to policymaking. Both parties have implemented welfare and labor market reforms through legislation and neither offered social pacts to the unions. We have argued that it was electoral competition that first impelled the Conservatives to abandon tripartism and opt for a tough program of legislated labor market reform. Successive majority governments were able to legislate reforms through the 1980s and did so at virtually no electoral cost until 1992. The repeated electoral failure of the Labour Party, coupled with the absence of any competition on its left, gradually led the latter to abandon tripartism and emulate the policies of its Conservative rival.

Conclusion

Ireland and the UK are conventionally regarded as the only liberal market economies in Western Europe, with similar economic and industrial relations institutions and patterns of government intervention until the late 1970s. Thereafter the forms of government intervention in industrial relations radically diverged as successive Irish governments came to rely on social pacts while their British counterparts, Conservative and Labour alike, both repudiated pacts in favor of legislation. We have shown that the economic and institutional similarities between the two countries, reinforced by high levels of mutual trade, limit the usefulness of economic and institutional accounts of this divergence. In contrast we have demonstrated that electoral competition, party family, government and coalition types, and the number of effective parties in the legislature have played highly significant roles in both countries.

In Ireland, electoral competition led Fianna Fáil to promote the idea of a social pact as part of its strategy to move into the political center and take votes from its socialist and neoliberal rivals. Initially the four competitor parties to Fianna Fáil were hostile to social pacts but by 1994 all of them had switched to a pro-pact position as they were forced to respond to the pro-pact position of the pivotal party, Fianna Fáil. Of the two conservative parties, the PD had lost votes and seats in the 1989 election and votes (but not seats) in the 1992 election. Although vote losses for such a party might have pushed it towards legislation, its weakness in the legislature and its status as a junior partner in an unconnected center-led coalition had modified its antagonism to pacts. Fine Gael had suffered a dramatic loss of votes and seats in 1992 and also began to abandon its neoliberal antagonism to pacts once it entered an unconnected coalition with two left parties (Labour and Democratic Left), both of which had now reversed their stance and favored pacts.

In Britain, the Conservatives responded to electoral defeats in 1974 by eventually repudiating tripartism and social pacts as an approach to policy-making and the associated concessions to union power they believed respon-sible for their electoral problems. The legislative assault on the trade unions that followed their 1979 election victory was reinforced by two subsequent victories in 1983 and 1987, all of which led to single-party, conservative majorities facing a deeply divided opposition. Throughout the 1980s, there-fore, the Conservative preference for legislation and its antipathy to social pacts was reinforced by electoral success. The evolution of Labour policy was also fueled by election defeats, starting in 1979 and only ending with the Labour victory in 1997. After first polarizing to the left, the Labour Party from 1984 onwards moved steadily to the right, each election defeat both encouraging and helping successive leaderships progressively dismantle Labour's commitment to social pacts as it converged on the legislative reform policies of its successful rival. By 1997 electoral competition had eliminated all traces of social pacts from the Labour manifesto, weakened the influence of the unions over the party, and brought Labour to an acceptance of most of the Conservative labor relations legislation. Labour was able to pursue this approach both because of the absence of an effective party on its left and also because the centralization of power inside the party insulated its leaders against periodic rank and file revolts (Kitschelt 1999: 344).

Although Irish and British governments displayed radical differences in their approaches to policymaking, the former favoring pacts and the latter legislation, these differences were generated by the same set of mechanisms, that of electoral and parliamentary competition.

6 Social democracy between pacts and legislation in Scandinavia

Sweden and Finland

The Scandinavian economies present a puzzle: On the one hand they are often discussed as a group because they display many similarities in their industrial relations systems and welfare regimes. On the other hand governments in Denmark, Finland, Norway, and Sweden have adopted very different approaches to wage regulation, labor market intervention, and welfare reform, as Table 6.1 exemplifies. While the dominant reform strategy in Finland and Norway has privileged social pact offers rather than legislation, Denmark and Sweden have displayed the opposite pattern, with a preponderance of legislation and relatively few pact offers. Between 1988 and 2006 successive Finnish governments have offered 13 pacts to the social partners despite the fact that the country has been ruled by majority governments throughout the entire period, a feature that would have facilitated a purely legislative process of reform (Nousiainen 2003: 266–7). In contrast, both conservative and Social Democratic governments in Sweden, normally minority administrations, have sought to bypass union negotiation and legislate on labor-related issues on five occasions since the beginning of 1990. Moreover, in the wake of pact rejections they have resorted to legislation on three further occasions.[1] It is these substantial national differences in the approach to reform that constitute the focus of this chapter.

We examine the contrasting experiences of Sweden and Finland and relate electoral competition and the properties of parties and governments to the differing preferences for pacts and legislation despite the countries' institutional and economic similarities. The Swedish and Finnish economies both performed relatively well during the 1980s with average or above-average GDP growth (compared to the rest of the OECD) and public account surpluses. Both then experienced severe economic contraction, high unemployment and large current account deficits in the early 1990s. Yet governments in the two countries responded in very different ways to these ostensibly similar problems.

In brief, our argument is that from the early 1970s the highly successful Social Democrats in both countries faced growing electoral challenges from center and conservative parties. The differences in their choices of pacts and legislation are due to critical differences in the patterns of electoral competition.

Table 6.1 Pact offers and legislation in the Scandinavian economies, 1980–2006

Country	Pact offers (Issues)	Legislation (Issues)
Denmark	6 (7)	8 (9)
Sweden	6 (8)	6 (6)
Finland	13 (16)	1 (1)
Norway	10 (12)	0 (0)

Source: Hamann-Kelly database.

The Swedish conservatives became the most successful of the non-left parties after 1976, supplanting the Center Party, and their neoliberal program posed an acute and growing electoral threat to the Social Democrats (SAP). The SAP's response was to move to the right, weakening its ties to the unions and showing an increased willingness to enact reform through legislation rather than tripartite negotiation. In Finland, in contrast, the electoral threat to the Social Democrats had for most of the postwar period been evenly divided between the Center and the conservatives. Since 1991, however, it was the Center Party that became, and still remains, the largest of the non-left parties. The powerful position of the Center Party, as well as the continued strength of the far-left, resulted in the main Finnish parties' convergence on a policy-making style favoring social pacts.

Sweden

Industrial relations institutions and economic context

Swedish industrial relations are characterized by high union density (78 percent in 2003), which is partly based on the Ghent system of union involvement in unemployment benefits (Western 1997: 58–9), although the union monopoly over benefit administration was removed in the early- to mid-1990s (Böckerman and Uusitalo 2006). The manual confederation (LO) is the largest of the three existing strong union confederations. LO still has organizational links to the Social Democratic Party (SAP) though these have weakened in recent years (Allern et al. 2007). The collective bargaining system is highly coordinated and supported by encompassing employer organizations although the structure of collective bargaining became far more decentralized since the 1980s (Kjellberg 1998: 74–7; Lilja 1998: 173–4). State intervention in collective bargaining has been rather limited and levels of industrial conflict (days lost per 1,000 employees) since 1980 have been low by Western European standards (Hale 2008: 35; Sweeney and Davies 1996: 155). Employment protection legislation was relatively strict in the early 1980s and has changed very little since then (Hamann and Kelly 2008). The welfare system comprises a high proportion of universal benefits, high replacement ratios, relatively little means testing, and is based on high levels of taxation (Huber and Stephens 2001: 111). Expenditure on social protection as a percentage of 2001 GDP was relatively high at 28.9 percent compared to the EU-15 average of 24.0 percent (Pestieau 2006: 22).[2]

From 1980 to 1990 the unemployment rate was below the OECD average; the high inflation rate of the early 1980s fell by the end of the decade, and public finances were in surplus most years. In the early 1990s, however, the economy experienced an acute economic crisis and unemployment rose from 1.7 percent in 1990 to 9.4 percent in 1994 (Figure 6.1). In 1995 Sweden joined the EU, but chose to remain outside the EMU (Benner and Vad 2000: 420–1).

Given the high levels of labor and employer organization, the long tradition of industrial relations cooperation, and the history of centralized bargaining, one might have expected successive governments to have sought negotiated wage and welfare reforms through social pacts. The strength of the union movement and the links between the manual unions and the SAP arguably militated against the use of legislation to secure contentious reforms. Yet these predictions are not borne out. Before explaining the governmental predilection for legislation we first describe the electoral and party system.

The electoral and party system in Sweden

Sweden has a proportional electoral system with a 4 percent national vote threshold for representation in the 349 seat, unicameral legislature, the Riksdag.

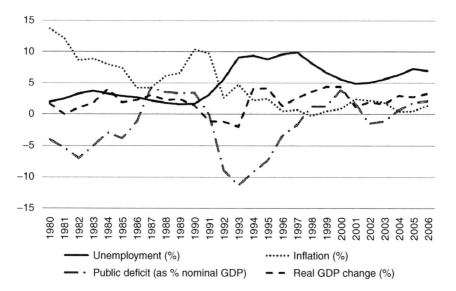

Figure 6.1 Main economic indicators, Sweden, 1980–2006.

Sources: OECD (June 2007; December 1999; December 1996).

Until the early 1980s, five main parties competed in elections, the Left Party, the Social Democrats (SAP), the Centre Party (formerly the Agrarian Party), the Liberals, and the conservatives (officially known as the Moderate Party). The SAP was easily the most successful of these parties, heading the Swedish executive continuously between 1932 and 1976 either in a majority coalition with the Centre Party or more commonly as a single-party minority administration (Arter 1999a: 57). In common with many other European countries, Sweden has recently experienced increased electoral volatility, reflected in the rise of new parties and declining success for the Social Democrats, out of power between 1976 and 1982, between 1991 and 1994, and again since 2006 (Aylott and Bolin 2007; Table 6.2). In 1988 the Greens secured representation for the first time and in 1991 the Christian Democrats surpassed the 4-percent threshold, as did a conservative protest party, New Democracy (Bergman 2003). Between 1932 and 1994 the SAP's vote share averaged almost 45 percent and only once fell below 40 percent, in the electoral defeat of 1991. However, in the 1998, 2002, and 2006 elections its vote share averaged just 37 percent (Arter 2006: 69; see also Table 6.2). Class voting has weakened over the postwar period: whereas the proportion of manual workers voting SAP was 72 percent in 1956 and 65 percent in 1988, it fell to 50 percent in 1991 (Arter 1994: 76; Widfeldt 2001: 74). Partisan identification and electoral participation have similarly declined: 50 percent of the electorate identified with a particular party in 1976, but just 41 percent did so in 1988 (Arter 1994: 76). Electoral turnout declined by 10 points between the early 1990s and 2006 (Gallagher *et al.* 2006: 291). In short, the electoral arena has become far more uncertain since the 1980s.

Legislation and pacts in Sweden in the 1990s

The recent phase of legislation and social pacts emerged only with the economic problems of the late 1980s and the severe economic contraction of 1991–94 (see Figure 6.1). In February 1990, halfway through its three-year term, the minority, single-party Social Democratic government tried to legislate a wage freeze and strike ban. The measures were reluctantly accepted by the LO leadership but rank and file protests and parliamentary opposition forced the government to withdraw these controversial measures (Pontusson 1994: 37). The government lost the 1991 election, and the new conservative-led government enjoyed more success with its legislation to reform welfare benefits and pensions, thanks to Social Democratic support. The replacement rates for unemployment and sickness benefit were both reduced and the indexation of pensions to prices was adjusted downwards (Huber and Stephens 2001: 248–9; Schludi 2005: 92–5). The conservative–Centre coalition lost the 1994 election and the new Social Democratic minority government offered a wage and employment pact to the unions in 1996. When this was rejected, the government proceeded with legislation and the following year legislated again, only this time without any attempt at negotiating a pact.

Table 6.2 Election results, Sweden (Riksdag), 1979–2006

	1979		1982		1985		1988		1991		1994		1998		2002		2006	
	% vote	# seats (%seats)	% vote	# seats (%seats)	% vote	# seats (%seats)	% vote	# seats (%seats)	% vote	# seats (%seats)	% vote	# seats (%seats)	% vote	# seats (%seats)	% vote	# seats (%seats)	% vote	# seats (%seats)
Left Party	5.6	20 (5.7)	5.6	20 (5.7)	5.4	19 (5.4)	5.8	21 (6.0)	4.5	16 (4.6)	6.2	22 (6.3)	12.1	43 (12.3)	8.4	30 (8.6)	5.9	22 (6.7)
SAP	43.2	154 (44.2)	45.6	166 (47.6)	44.7	159 (45.6)	43.2	156 (44.7)	37.6	138 (39.5)	45.3	161 (46.1)	36.4	131 (37.5)	39.9	144 (41.3)	35.9	130 (39.5)
Greens							5.5	20 (5.7)	3.4	0 (0.0)	5.0	18 (5.6)	4.5	16 (4.6)	4.6	17 (4.9)	5.2	19 (5.8)
C	18.1	64 (18.3)	15.5	56 (16.1)	10.1	44 (12.6)	11.3	42 (12.0)	8.5	31 (8.9)	7.7	27 (7.7)	5.1	18 (5.2)	6.2	22 (6.3)	7.9	29 (8.8)
CD	1.4	0 (0.0)	1.9	0 (0.0)	2.3	0 (0.0)	2.9	0 (0.0)	7.1	26 (7.5)	4.1	15 (4.3)	11.8	42 (12.0)	9.1	33 (9.5)	6.6	24 (7.3)
FP	10.6	38 (10.9)	5.9	21 (6.0)	14.2	51 (14.6)	12.2	44 (12.6)	9.1	33 (9.5)	7.2	26 (7.5)	4.7	17 (4.9)	13.4	48 (13.8)	7.5	28 (8.5)
MP	20.3	73 (20.9)	23.6	86 (24.6)	21.3	76 (21.8)	18.3	66 (18.9)	21.9	80 (22.9)	22.4	80 (22.9)	22.9	82 (23.5)	15.3	55 (15.8)	26.2	77 (23.4)
Others	0.8	0 (0.0)	0.2	0 (0.0)	0.5	0 (0.0)	0.7	0 (0.0)	7.9	25 (7.2)	2.2	0 (0.0)	2.6	0 (0.0)	3.1	0 (0.0)	5.7	0 (0.0)
Total	100	349 (100)	100	349 (100)	100	349 (100)	100	349 (100)	100	349 (100)	100	349 (100)	100	349 (100)	100	349 (100)	100	329 (100)

Source: See Appendix 1.

Notes: V = Vänsterparteit (Left Party); SAP = Socialdemokratiska Arbetareparteit (Swedish Social Democratic Party); MP, Miliöparteit de Gröna (Green Party); C = Centernparteit (Center Party); CD = Kristdemokratiska Samhällsparteit (Christian Democratic Society Party); FP = Folkpartiet Liberalerna (Liberal People's Party); MP = Moderata Samlingsparteit (Moderate Unity Party).

Despite losing seats and votes in the 1998 election, the government was able to remain in office. It offered two further pacts (December 1998 and November 2001), but proceeded with legislation in response to the unions' rejection of both offers. The newly elected 2006 conservative government swiftly legislated cuts in unemployment benefits in an attempt to drive down the level of unemployment, which was still high at 7.0 percent.

How can we account for the preponderance of legislation over pact offers and for the apparent cross-party consensus on the virtues of legislating reform? Perhaps by the 1990s the institutions facilitating social pacts had seriously eroded. The centralized bargaining structures that operated for much of the postwar period had been effectively dismantled by the employers in 1983 following a bitter industrial dispute in 1980 (Mahon 1999: 127). Moreover the antagonism between employer and union organizations in the 1980s was compounded by interconfederal relations that were sometimes strained and difficult partly owing to tensions between public and private sector unions (Kjellberg 1998: 98). Yet these features of industrial relations were also found in other countries, including Finland and Italy, where social pacts, rather than legislation, came to dominate government intervention into labor markets and welfare regimes. To explain the emerging cross-party willingness to resort to legislation in Sweden we need to examine the evolution of party competition and its effects on the leading party, the SAP.

Political polarization during the 1970s and 1980s

After peaking in 1968 at 50.1 percent, the SAP vote slipped over the next three elections to 42.7 percent by 1976, before recovering slightly in 1979 to 43.2 percent (Benner and Vad 2000: 413–9; see also Figure 6.2). In the 1973 election the combined Social Democrat and Left Party seat total failed to exceed that of the center-right for the first time since 1945; three years later the Social Democrats suffered a traumatic electoral defeat, forcing the party into opposition for the first time since 1932. From 1976 until 1982 the country was ruled by four different governments drawn from the Center, conservative, and Liberal parties. Although the Center Party lost 22 seats in the 1979 election, the main beneficiary was not the SAP, which gained only two seats, but the resurgent conservatives, who gained 18 seats and almost 5 percentage points in vote share. The conservative party had moved towards the right through the 1970s, advocating neoliberal policies of privatization, cutbacks in public spending, and cuts in income tax (Fulcher 2002: 289; Pontusson 1994: 30; Ruin 1983: 168). Its vote share rose significantly, from 15.6 percent in 1976 to 23.6 percent in 1982, elevating it to the dominant non-socialist party and the main electoral threat to the SAP by the early 1980s (Boreus 1997: 283; Callaghan 2000: 68–70; Volkens and Klingemann 2002; Table 6.3).

In response to the 1979 election defeat – the second in three years – the SAP began to rethink the problems and limitations of some of its traditional employment, fiscal, and welfare policies (Nygård 2006: 374–5; Pontusson 1994: 34). This process was difficult because the party was divided between a traditional left wing, anxious to retain close relations with the LO and cooperate with the Left Party, and an increasingly influential conservative wing led by Kjell-Olof Feldt, SAP Finance Minister (1982–90). Feldt was keen to promote competitiveness through deregulation and was hostile to the more radical policies of the 1970s, such as the Meidner Plan for Wage Earner Funds that had antagonized the employers and helped boost the electoral fortunes of the conservatives (Immergut and Jochem 2006: 120; Pontusson 1994: 34–5; Sassoon 1996: 742).[3] Once reelected in 1982 following the collapse of the center-right coalition, the SAP sought to encourage economic growth through an eclectic mix of policies, often described as a "Third Way" between Keynesianism and neoliberalism (Jochem 2000: 123). This extended to currency devaluation, deregulation of the financial sector (including exchange controls), privatization, and wage restraint, but it also included a very limited form of wage earner funds and protection of public services and welfare spending (Benner and Vad 2000: 422–3; Kitschelt 1994b: 15; Pontusson 1994: 29, 35–6). Although the SAP did not formally pursue social pacts with the unions in the 1980s, Prime Minister Palme met union and employer leaders informally in 1984 and again in 1986 to encourage moderation in wage settlements, offering tax cuts as a quid pro quo (Kjellberg 1998: 89).

These policies, including the dilution of the wage earner funds, had now seriously alienated the LO leadership. Its conference therefore voted in 1986 to abandon the collective affiliation of local unions to the party, maintaining the affiliation only of those individuals who wished to join the party. In 1987 the SAP congress endorsed this historic measure, its leadership perhaps conscious of the fact that union power had become increasingly unpopular in opinion polls and that the party now received only 20 percent of its income from the unions, down from 40 percent in 1970 (Allern *et al.* 2007: 624–5; Aylott 2004: 72–7; Pontusson 1994: 38–9). In addition, the SAP faced a political threat because its traditional ally, the Left Party, was threatening to withdraw support from the SAP government and leave it to rule as a minority administration (Aylott 2003: 372). The growing separation between the leaderships of the LO and the SAP arguably weakened the likelihood of pacts offered by an SAP government and of any such offers being accepted by the LO.

Social democratic legislation in 1990

Although the SAP remained the largest party after both the 1985 and 1988 elections, its vote was diminished by 2.4 points and it lost 10 seats over the two elections, a surprising result given that unemployment declined every year between 1983 and 1988 (Lindström 1986; Micheletti 1989; van der Brug *et al.* 2007: 99). Moreover, the legislatures became increasingly fragmented with a rise in the effective number of parties from 3.09 in 1982 to 3.66 in 1988 (Bergman 2003: 196). The minority Social Democratic administration, reelected in 1988, was almost immediately faced with a sharp deterioration in the economy. Inflation began to rise, reaching double figures by 1990, while slow growth and rising unemployment after 1990 strained public finances (Benner and Vad 2000: 425–6; see also Figure 6.1). A program of income tax cuts and consumption tax rises, agreed with the Liberals and heavily criticized by the LO leadership, made little impression on the economy. It did, however, erode SAP support in opinion polls, pushing it below 30 percent, and boosted that of the neoliberal conservatives and the Christian Democrats through 1989 and early 1990 (Arter 1994: 77; Widfeldt 1992: 73). In early 1990 inflation was close to the level that would have triggered a clause in the 1989–90 collective agreements permitting renegotiation of wage rises (Kjellberg 1998: 89). Anxious to avoid a fresh round of inflationary pay settlements and still trailing the conservatives in the opinion polls, the SAP cabinet therefore proposed the legislation described earlier, including a pay freeze and compulsory reference of industrial relations disputes to arbitration, in effect, a strike ban (Fulcher 2002: 291; Iversen 1999: 145; Kitschelt 1994b: 27).

Our model suggests that a Social Democratic minority government that had lost votes and seats just 18 months previously in a fragmented legislature would have been likely to reach out to unions and employers in a social pact. A tripartite pact might have aided government efforts of "blame avoidance" although it was unclear whether such an agreement was possible and how long it would have taken to secure given the growing policy disagreements between union and government leaders in the preceding years. However, what proved critical in the Swedish case was not just the magnitude of electoral threats to the SAP but the source of those threats. Opinion polls suggested the SAP was losing support most heavily among pro-market, unionized blue collar voters who were switching to the conservatives (Kunkel and Pontusson 1998: 18; Widfeldt 2001: 74). Decisive, *legislative* action to deal with inflation might therefore undercut voter drift to the right and restore the SAP's electoral support. Although reliance on legislation might alienate some left-wing voters, it was not clear how many would defect to the Left Party because of its divisions and disarray following the 1989 events in Eastern Europe (Dunphy 2004: 148). These workers would be even less likely to switch to other non-socialist parties, because they were also proposing to legislate austerity policies similar to those of the SAP (Kunkel and Pontusson 1998: 20). Finally, evidence indicates that relations between the non-socialist parties were improving and that the anti-SAP opposition was becoming more united, thereby increasing the chances of the non-socialist bloc displacing the SAP and forming the next government (Kitschelt 1994a: 172). In fact, this development came to fruition later in the year when the conservatives and the Liberals issued a neoliberal manifesto, "A New Start for Sweden," proposing a legislative program of cuts in sick pay and income tax and abolition of

the wage earner funds (Widfeldt 1992: 74). The SAP government's calculation was that although the use of legislation was controversial, it would be
passed in the Riksdag and thereby demonstrate that the SAP could be just as
tough and effective as the conservatives in its anti-inflation policy (Fulcher
2002: 291; Moses 1998a: 214–5; Volkens and Klingemann 2002).

Despite the passage of an amended, watered-down bill and the resignation
of the controversial SAP Finance Minister, the Social Democrats lost the 1991
election to the conservatives, who campaigned on a strongly neoliberal manifesto (Pontusson 1994: 37). This was the SAP's third defeat in 15 years and
its lowest vote share since 1928 (Widfeldt 1992: 75). Since the Left Party
also lost votes it appeared that former SAP voters had predominantly moved
to parties on its right (Sainsbury 1991: 37; Sainsbury 1992: 160; see also
Table 6.2).

Conservative legislation, 1991–94

The new government was a four-party, minority, connected coalition led by
the conservatives and also included the Centre Party, the Liberals, and the
Christian Democrats. Our model and the evidence in Chapter 4 suggests that
other things equal a minority administration in an increasingly fragmented
legislature is more likely to pursue pacts rather than legislation for contentious
reforms (Bergman 2003: 196). In this case, however, more factors pushed in
the direction of legislation. The government was led by the Conservatives,
who moreover had gained votes to record their second-highest ever vote share.
Within the connected governing coalition it was the policies of the main
party, the conservatives, that held sway and their policy was to take measures
on the economy without union involvement or consultation. The quantitative
analysis in Chapter 4 showed that the more rightist the party position, the
more likely it was to opt for legislation rather than social pacts. In line with
this approach, and just months after the election, the employers' confederation SAF organized a public seminar under the title "Farewell to Corporatism"
and simultaneously withdrew several hundred of its representatives from a range
of tripartite bodies including the National Labor Market Board (Immergut
and Jochem 2006: 123; Lindvall and Sebring 2005: 1061). The government
then claimed it would be unfair to allow such bodies to have "one-sided
representation" from the unions but not the employers and proceeded to
replace union representatives with its own "independent" candidates (Pesthoff
2002: 298–301).

The SAP, now the main opposition party, initially continued its electoral
strategy of pursuing conservative fiscal policies despite its election defeat,
supporting much, though not all, of the government's legislation on welfare
retrenchment (Nygård 2006: 367). It therefore voted in support of the
government's proposed cuts in sickness benefits and the pension indexation
formula, increased consumption taxes, entry into the EU and the radical
pension reform finally enacted in 1994 despite the exclusion of the unions

from the discussions (Anderson and Immergut 2007: 371, 377–8, 388; Widfeldt 1995: 207). At the same time it opposed measures such as increased provision for temporary contracts and reductions in wealth taxes (Mahon 1999: 138; Pontusson 1994: 48–9). When the economy continued to experience severe difficulties in early 1993, the SAP changed course and began to oppose the government in the legislature, a move that significantly increased its opinion poll ratings (Widfeldt 1995: 207). In the 1994 election campaign, all four main parties (SAP, conservatives, Liberals, and Center Party) argued for austerity policies and "tough decisions" and all of their programs were positioned well to the right of those issued at the previous election (Budge *et al.* 2001: 38–9; Widfeldt 1995: 209). Indeed the SAP manifesto was the most conservative document in the party's history and was somewhat to the right of public opinion, which remained strongly opposed to growing income inequality and to public sector retrenchment (Holmberg 2000: 164–5; Immergut and Jochem 2006: 125). Although it lost some votes to the Left and the Greens, both of whom made modest gains, its own vote recovered dramatically to 45.3 percent and it was able to form a single-party minority administration (Madeley 1995: 426). Remarkably, the Conservative vote also increased a little, despite the parlous state of the economy under its management (Table 6.2).

The Social Democrats 1994–2006: between pacts and legislation

As a single-party minority administration that had gained votes but held only 46 percent of seats in the Riksdag, we would predict the Social Democratic government to prefer pacts over legislation. In June 1996 the government did offer a pact to the social partners but following union rejection it proceeded to introduce two pieces of legislation in late 1996 and early 1997. How can we account for the government's actions? In its first two years in office it introduced restrictive budgets and presided over strong economic growth. However, unemployment remained at around 9 percent and eroded support for the government. In the 1995 European Parliament elections the combined vote of the Left Party and the Greens (29 percent) exceeded that of the SAP by one percentage point (Kunkel and Pontusson 1998: 6). The same year also witnessed the highest level of strike activity since 1980, with major stoppages among public sector workers on the issue of wages (Mares 2006: 124). In June 1996 therefore the government decided to tackle unemployment by introducing a fixed time limit on the duration of unemployment benefits (Björklund 2000: 156). Rather than repeat the legislative approach of 1990, which had alienated the unions and arguably contributed to its 1991 election defeat, the minority government opened talks with the unions to try and secure their agreement, as our model would predict. However, when talks broke down in October 1996 amidst union protests and demonstrations, the government proceeded with legislation that allowed employers to circumvent legal regulations on redundancy by negotiating local agreements

(Ahlberg 1997; Timonen 2003: 97). The government was able to switch tactics because its close working relationship with the Center Party provided the SAP government with 54 percent of votes in the Riksdag, enough to pass legislation and ignore Left Party opposition (Dunphy 2004: 150–2; Madeley 1999: 189; Mares 2006: 117–8).

Although the economy improved in 1998 with strong growth and a fall in unemployment, both the governing SAP and its informal ally, the Center Party, suffered heavily in the election that year (Figure 6.1 and Table 6.2). The SAP recorded an even worse result than in 1991, this time losing votes to the Left Party, whose all time high vote of 12.1 percent may have reflected support from former Social Democrat voters angry about cuts in welfare spending (Arter 1999b: 298; Timonen 2003: 71). However as the non-socialist parties lacked a majority of seats and the Left and the Greens were prepared to lend tacit support to the SAP, the Social Democrats were able to continue in office as a single-party government. Technically this was a minority government with just 34 percent of seats but the addition of its two parliamentary allies brought the seat total to 54 percent. One obvious advantage of including these two parties informally in government was that left-wing voters, critical of government policy, would have no obvious place to defect. One inference from the 1998 election is that austerity policies, failed pacts, and a reliance on the legislative route to reform alienated leftist SAP supporters and voters and led them to switch to the Left and the Greens. On the other hand, the SAP's severe vote loss did not translate into loss of office, as it had done in 1991, because the legislature was highly fragmented, with divisions between the conservative and Center opposition parties, and because the Left and the Greens were prepared to support the government despite their exclusion from the cabinet (Bergman 2003: 218–9).

According to our model, a left government that is technically a minority administration coming to office in a more fragmented legislature after a major vote and seat loss, should have a strong incentive to negotiate unpopular reforms with the social partners rather than enact them through legislation (Bergman 2003: 196). In fact, in "its policy statement, the new government declared its ambition to give cooperation between the social partners increased significance, in the belief that voluntary agreements provide long-term and stable solutions" (Berg 1999; see also Nygård 2006: 372).

Within days of the election, the employers' organization and the main union confederations began talks on a "Pact for Growth" centered on wage bargaining structures and outcomes and dispute resolution. By December, however, the talks had broken down and the following year the government used its informal parliamentary majority to introduce legislation creating a Mediation Authority to help resolve industrial disputes (Berg 1999). In November 2001 the government again approached the social partners for discussion on reforms to sickness benefits and talks continued well into the following year. In the September 2002 election the SAP recorded a rise in its vote share to 39.9 percent and an increase of 13 seats, the first time an incumbent Social Democratic administration had seen its vote share climb since 1968 (Widfeldt 2003). Despite the Left Party's loss of 13 seats, the three-party "Red–Green" informal coalition (SAP, Left Party, and Greens) increased its seat total by one and the two minor parties (the Left and the Greens) were granted "observer seats" in several cabinet committees (Bergman 2003: 218). Talks on sickness benefits quickly resumed but faced with union opposition and a walkout by the employers, the government finally abandoned the process in December 2002. In line with our model, the government was emboldened by its electoral success and its relatively secure position in the Riksdag and proceeded to legislate in 2003.

By the time of the next election the government had presided over four years of steady economic growth even though unemployment stood at 7.0 percent, two points higher than when the government had assumed office in 2002. Poll data indicate that employment was the most important issue among voters, in contrast to 2002, when it ranked in sixth place, and the priority given to employment damaged rather than helped the Social Democrats (Aylott and Bolin 2007: 629). The non-socialist bloc achieved an unprecedented level of pre-election policy agreement – the "Alliance for Sweden" – thanks partly to the conservative's move towards the center following its disastrous performance in the 2002 election. The result was a four-party conservative-led majority connected coalition. Armed with a majority in the Riksdag, the new government proceeded as we would predict and immediately legislated cuts in unemployment benefits (Lundberg 2007).

Summing up the Swedish case

The most common accounts of the Swedish labor and welfare reforms of the 1990s locate them as the result of a growing mismatch between existing institutions and the requirements of a more open, globalizing economy. Radical reforms, it is claimed, had to be undertaken by whatever government was in office, either with or without trade union cooperation and involvement. The economic crisis may well have been the trigger for policy reforms but the ambivalent attitude of the SAP towards social pacts and its proclivity for legislation cannot be explained by the economic crisis alone. What was critical in the Swedish case was the conjuncture of an economic crisis with a political crisis in which Social Democratic political hegemony came under increasing threat from the right. The Swedish conservatives performed sufficiently well to defeat the Social Democrats three times in just 15 years (1976, 1979, and 1991) and the SAP responded to the erosion of its vote and to the volatility of the electorate by moving to the right in order to recover voters switching to its main rival. This move entailed both substantive shifts in several policy domains as well as an increased willingness to legislate reforms in the face of union hostility. Central to the SAP's strategy was the calculation that legislating unpopular reforms would gain more votes from the right than would be lost to the left. The official minority status of all SAP governments since 1982 did not obstruct the legislative route, as we might have expected, because of informal cooperation between the SAP and one or more of its parliamentary opponents. Only when the party suffered severe electoral losses to the left in 1998 and was obliged to govern with the support of the Left and the Greens in a highly fragmented legislature did it show a serious willingness to secure union cooperation through social pacts.

Finland

Industrial relations in Finland are based on high union density (74 percent in 2003) in part (similar to Sweden) because of the Ghent system of union involvement in unemployment benefits (Western 1997: 58–9). Although the union role in benefit administration was reduced in the 1990s, density has remained high (Böckerman and Uusitalo 2006). Members are organized in three union confederations, of which the manual confederation (LO) is the largest and the most heavily involved in party politics through its organizational links to the Social Democratic Party (SDP) (Allern et al. 2007). The collective bargaining system displays a high level of coordination and is supported by encompassing employer organizations (Lilja 1998: 173–4). State intervention in wage bargaining has been prevalent in Finland especially since the first major incomes policy agreement in the postwar period, signed in 1968 and followed by a succession of two-year agreements throughout the 1970s and early 1980s (Elvander 2002: 131; Kauppinen and Waddington 2000: 196). Levels of industrial conflict (days lost per 1,000 employees), however, are among the highest in Western Europe (Hale 2008: 35; Sweeney and Davies 1996: 155). The level of employment protection was relatively high but has been reduced since the 1980s (Hamann and Kelly 2008). The welfare system, like that in Sweden, is based on a high level of taxation and relatively generous universal benefits (Huber and Stephens 2001: 111). Social protection expenditure as a percentage of GDP was 24.8 percent in 2001, somewhat lower than in Sweden, but still above the EU15 average of 24.0 percent (Pestieau 2006: 22).

The country's economic trajectory since the early 1980s has been very similar to that of Sweden. From 1980 to 1990 the unemployment rate was below the OECD average; the inflation rate fell during the 1980s; and the public finances were in surplus for every year of that decade. In the early 1990s, however, there was a sudden and dramatic rise in unemployment, from 3.2 percent in 1990 to 16.8 percent in 1994 (Figure 6.2). In 1995 Finland joined the EU and in 1999 it also joined the EMU (Benner and Vad 2000: 420–1).

The electoral and party system in Finland

Finland has a proportional electoral system without any vote threshold for representation in the 200-seat, unicameral legislature, the Eduskunta.

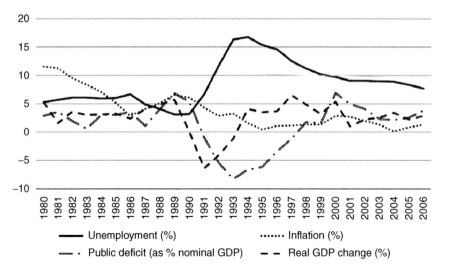

Figure 6.2 Main economic indicators, Finland, 1980–2006.
Sources: OECD (June 2007; December 1999; December 1996).

Until the 1980s five parties were normally represented in the legislature, the Left Wing Alliance (formerly the Communist Party), the Social Democrats (SDP), the Centre Party (formerly the Agrarian Party), the Liberals, and the conservatives. The Greens entered the legislature in 1987 (see Table 6.3). In contrast to Sweden the Center Party was for many years the strongest of the non-left parties, ahead of the conservatives while the Liberals trailed in third place (Arter 1999a: 76). The Social Democratic vote has averaged 25 percent since the late 1940s, significantly lower than that of the Swedish SAP but also more stable. At the same time the Left Party has performed much better than its Swedish counterpart, averaging 20 percent of the vote until the mid-1970s and on two occasions (1946 and 1958) actually exceeding the Social Democratic vote total (Arter 1999a: 71–2; Nousiainen 2003: 264). Electoral volatility has increased steadily in Finland since the 1960s, reflected especially in the rise of new parties, seven of which have entered the legislature since 1970, including the Christian Democrats in 1970 and the Greens in 1983 (Arter 1999a: 102). Changes in government have been equally far-reaching, as two of the main governing parties in the postwar period – the Center Party and the Social Democrats – were forced into opposition in the late 1980s and early 1990s respectively. In contrast to Sweden's record of minority single-party governments, Finland has been governed for much of the post-1945 period by broad, surplus coalitions (Nousiainen 2003: 266–7). Electoral turnout has been falling steadily since the 1960s and declined by ten points between the early 1990s and 2006 (Gallagher *et al.* 2006: 291). In Finland, as in Sweden, the political parties operate in an increasingly uncertain environment.

Table 6.3 Election results, Finland (Eduskunta), 1979–2006

	1979		1983		1987		1991		1995		1999		2003	
	% vote	# seats (%seats)	% vote	# seats (%seats)	% vote	# seats (%seats)	% vote	# seats (%seats)	% vote	# seats (%seats)	% vote	# seats (%seats)	% vote	# seats (%seats)
VAS	17.9	35 (17.5)	13.5	27 (13.5)	13.6	20 (10.0)	10.1	19 (9.5)	11.2	22 (11.0)	10.9	20 (10.0)	9.9	19 (9.5)
SDP	23.9	52 (26.0)	26.7	57 (28.5)	24.1	56 (28.0)	22.1	48 (24.0)	28.3	63 (31.5)	22.9	51 (25.5)	24.5	53 (26.5)
VIHR*					4.0	4 (2.0)	6.8	10 (5.0)	6.5	9 (4.5)	7.3	11 (5.5)	8.0	14 (7.0)
KESK	17.3	36 (18.0)	17.6	38 (19.0)	17.6	40 (20.0)	24.8	55 (27.5)	19.8	44 (22.0)	22.4	48 (24.0)	24.7	55 (27.5)
SKL	4.8	9 (4.5)	3.0	3 (1.5)	2.6	5 (2.5)	3.1	8 (4.0)	3.0	7 (3.5)	4.2	10 (5.0)	5.3	7 (3.5)
KOK	21.7	47 (23.5)	22.1	44 (22.0)	23.1	53 (26.5)	19.3	40 (20.0)	17.9	39 (19.5)	21.0	46 (23.0)	18.6	40 (20.0)
Others	14.4	21 (10.5)	17.1	31 (15.5)	15.0	22 (11.0)	13.8	20 (10.0)	13.3	16 (8.0)	11.3	14 (7.0)	9.0	12 (6.0)
Totals	100	200 (100)	100	200 (100)	100	200 (100)	100	200 (100)	100	200 (100)	100	200 (100)	100	200 (100)

Source: See Appendix 1.

Notes: *Founded in 1987

VAS = Vasemmistoliito (Left Alliance); SDP = Suomen Sosialidemokraattinen Puolue (Social Democratic Party of Finland); VIHR = Vihreä Liitto (Green League); KESK = Suomen Keskuta (Center Party); SKL= Suomen Kristillinen Liitto (Christian League of Finland); LKP = Liberaalinen Kansanpuolue (Liberal People's Party); KOK = Kansallinen Kokoomus (National Coalition Party; Conservatives).

Social pacts in Finland

Whereas Sweden's recent history has privileged legislation over pacts, Finland shows almost the opposite tendency: pacts were prevalent in the 1980s and 1990s while policy reform through legislation was relatively rare. Governments intervened frequently in wage bargaining in the late 1960s and 1970s following the abolition of wage indexation in 1968 but less so in the early 1980s (Elvander 2002: 131). In 1988 social pacts were resumed, with a tripartite agreement on wages promoted by a conservative–Social Democratic coalition government, followed by another wage pact in 1990. As the economic crisis of the early 1990s intensified, the newly elected Center–conservative coalition government secured union support for a pact on wages, taxation and pensions. Subsequent wage pacts were signed in October 1992 and May 1993. However, relations between the Center–conservative government and the trade unions were at times also highly conflictual. In late 1992 and early 1993 government proposals for radical reforms of welfare and labor markets met with union threats of general strikes (Kauppinen 2000: 166–7). The new government that came to power in 1995 – the so-called Rainbow Coalition of Social Democrats, Far Left, Greens, and conservatives – largely abandoned the policy of legislative reforms and union exclusion and secured union support for a series of pacts over the next eight years, on wages, welfare benefits and pensions. Even when unions rejected the government proposals and talks broke down in September 1999, the government resisted the temptation to legislate and renewed the offer of a social pact the following year. When the government was defeated in 2003, the new Center-led coalition nonetheless continued the policy of union inclusion through social pacts.

At first glance the predominance of pacts in Finland compared to legislation in Sweden is surprising given the institutional and economic similarities between the countries. At the same time, Finland features a stronger tradition of state intervention in industrial relations, which, coupled with the high degree of centralization of the actors and coordination of collective bargaining, might suggest an institutional bias in favor of pacts in Finland. However, we argue instead that the bias towards pacts in Finland reflects the structure of the party system and the composition of governments. Whereas Swedish party politics has long been dominated by the Social Democratic Party in competition with the conservatives, party politics in Finland has been characterized for almost half a century by competition between three big parties, the Social Democrats, the conservatives, and the Center Party. Relatively speaking, the Center party is much stronger in Finland compared to Sweden and has exerted a profound influence on industrial relations policy despite the increased electoral support for the conservatives in recent years.

The rise of the conservatives and the promotion of union inclusion

In Finland, as in Sweden, the conservative party enjoyed increased electoral success through the 1970s and 1980s. For most of the postwar period its vote share was approximately two-thirds of that going to the Center Party but in 1970 it overtook the latter, polling 18 percent, slightly more than the Center Party's 17.1 percent. Over the next 17 years the conservative vote increased steadily until it peaked in 1987 at 23.1 percent, just one point behind the Social Democrats (Table 6.3). The 1987 election was historic: the conservatives secured their highest ever vote share and entered government for the first time since 1963, the total left vote was the lowest since 1944, the Liberal performance was one of their worst in 40 years, and electoral turnout was the lowest in 30 years (Arter 1987: 170). Government formation in the wake of the election was equally historic because although the Center vote share had remained stable throughout this period at approximately 17–18 percent, the party was excluded from government for the first time in postwar history. Whereas the electoral success of the Swedish conservatives was based on a significant policy shift to the right, the Finnish conservatives had shifted policy on public spending and welfare reform only to a very limited extent because of public concern about the need to create jobs, revealed in pre-election polls (Arter 1987: 172, 175; Budge *et al.* 2001: 40–1; Holmberg 2000: 168; Nygård 2006: 370). They constructed a broad, surplus coalition including the Social Democrats and two minor parties from the center and right.

During its four-year period in office the government offered and success-fully negotiated two wage pacts with the unions, in 1988 and 1990. Its intervention was driven by economic concerns, in particular rising inflation and public borrowing despite strong economic growth (Figure 6.2). Several components of our model would suggest the new government might have been inclined to legislate either on wages or on welfare expenditure in order to rein in the public deficit. It was led by a conservative Prime Minister whose party had increased its vote and seat share significantly at the recent election; his four-party coalition controlled 66 percent of seats in the legisla-ture; and the legislature itself had become less fragmented because of the concentration of seats held by the three main parties (Nousiainen 2003: 266). Yet, several properties of the government and the legislature rendered legisla-tion difficult and created stronger incentives to offer pacts. First, although the conservatives held the post of Prime Minister, they occupied only a minority of seats in the cabinet; as the Social Democrats were the largest party in the legislature they secured the plurality of seats in the new govern-ment. Second, the exclusion of the Center Party meant that Prime Minister Holkeri headed an unconnected, four-party coalition and a successful legisla-tive program would therefore have required significant compromise with his coalition partners. This was true despite the fact that the Social Democrats had become more sympathetic to elements of the neoliberal consensus spread-ing throughout Western Europe from the 1980s, particularly on the issue of welfare reform (Budge *et al.* 2001: 41; Kiander 2005: 93). Finally, the moder-ation of the Finnish conservatives was reinforced by a particular political institution, the rule requiring legislation to have the support of two-thirds of the legislature – 134 votes out of 200 – rather than a simple majority. Although the rule was abolished in 1992, this unusually high vote threshold provided an incentive for surplus coalitions, which sometimes had to secure support for their legislative program from opposition parties (Isaakson 1994: 93). With 131 seats the 1987 government was just three votes short of the two-thirds threshold.

The Center–conservative government and the limits to union exclusion, 1991–95

The economic recession that spread across Western Europe in the early 1990s was particularly acute in Finland because it coincided with the collapse of the Soviet Union, the country's main trading partner, and also exposed the country's over-dependence on forestry exports (Berglund 1995: 461; Moses 1998b: 87). Within the space of just three years (1990–93) unemployment leapt from 3 percent to over 16 percent, the economy shrank by almost 12 percent and the public finances plunged into deficit after a decade of healthy surplus (Figure 6.2). This economic disintegration had a profound impact on the governing parties, dramatically reducing their standing in the opinion polls in the 18 months leading up to the March 1991 election (Berglund 1991: 257). While the ruling conservatives and Social Democrats both lost votes and seats in the election, the opposition Center Party was arguably rewarded for its unrelenting criticism of the old government, scoring its highest ever vote share of 24.8 percent and emerging as the largest party in the legislature for the first time since 1962. The Social Democrats obtained their worst result since 1962 and chose not to enter the government for the first time in 25 years (Arter 1991: 178). The Center Party leader therefore built a coalition with the conservatives and two smaller center-right parties but was still 12 votes short of the two-thirds majority needed for legislation.

The quantitative analysis in Chapter 4 indicates that Center parties comprise the party family most likely to offer pacts. As the dominant partner in a center-right coalition that had gained votes in the recent election and faced a highly fragmented legislature, we would therefore expect the pro-pact inclination of the Center party to be highly influential in government decision making. Although technically a majority administration, in its first year the Aho government was subject to the two-thirds rule in the legislature; thus, legislation would have required support from at least one of the opposition parties (Nousiainen 2003: 267). In the face of the economic recession the new government therefore opened talks with the unions and employers in September 1991 on wage moderation. Two months later all three groups signed the Tripartite Stability Pact and the government announced a devaluation of the currency (Moses 1998b: 85). By autumn 1992 unemployment had climbed to 12 percent and was still rising while the economy was continuing to contract. In response, the government proposed a new social pact to the unions and employers, combining wage moderation and reductions in unemployment benefits. When the unions rejected the proposed benefit cuts, Prime Minister Aho hinted at a potentially radical departure from the established consensus on tripartism and suggested the government might exclude the unions and legislate. The background to this threat was the recent abolition of the two-thirds rule for the passage of legislation. With 58 percent of seats in parliament the coalition government now held a working majority, a factor our model suggests would lower the probability of pacts and increase the probability of legislation.

Faced with an unacceptable erosion of benefits as well as the possibility of exclusion from policymaking, the union confederations began to mobilize for a general strike in November 1992. In the face of this threat the government quickly withdrew the proposed benefit cuts and the social partners simply agreed on a new round of wage moderation (Dunphy 2007: 39; Kiander 2005: 100). In spring 1993 the government turned its attention to youth unemployment and proposed to reduce starting wage rates for young workers in order to encourage their recruitment. Once again, however, the unions rejected the policy and threatened a general strike and once again the government withdrew its plans and settled for a new, two-year agreement on wage restraint (Kauppinen 2000: 166–7). Nonetheless, it succeeded in creating a new and lower level of unemployment benefit for those workers without earnings-related benefits (Timonen 2003: 92–3).

One factor that lay behind the government's acquiescence to union demands was its fear of an electoral backlash and growing support for the Social Democrats if it tried to curb the highly popular universal benefits (Timonen 2003: 61). The SDP had performed well in the October 1992 local elections with 27.1 percent of the vote compared to 22.1 percent in the 1991 general election and clearly posed a threat to the Center Party (Arter 1995: 197). As a result, the degree of welfare retrenchment between 1991 and 1995 was very limited (Kiander 2005: 101).

The return of the Social Democrats and of union inclusion

In the run-up to the 1995 election the main governing parties, the conservatives and the Center Party, were trailing badly in the polls (Berglund 1995: 462). Although the economy had returned to growth in 1994 and early 1995 and inflation had been reduced to less than 2 percent, unemployment remained at a historically high level of around 16 percent (Figure 6.2). The election resulted in vote and seat losses for the ruling Center and the conservative parties but substantial gains for the Social Democrats, who recorded their highest ever vote share at 28.3 percent (63 seats) as well as a small gain for the Left Alliance. Although the Social Democrats had been critical of the outgoing Center-led government, their own policies were actually very similar. Indeed most parties agreed on the need for public spending cuts (the Left Alliance was the exception), although they disagreed on the precise programs to be targeted and on the way in which cuts should be implemented (Arter 1995: 195; Berglund 1995: 464). The SDP had been losing votes and seats throughout the 1980s to the Center and the conservatives and in response had shifted rightwards, arguing the case for welfare retrenchment, tight control of the money supply, and limited privatization (Berglund 1991: 259; Kiander 2005: 93). Although rightward moves were checked prior to the 1991 election they were resumed following the election defeat of that year, especially after Paavo Lipponen was elected party Chairman in 1993 (Arter 2003: 155). In a *Financial Times* interview November 1994, for instance, he declared that "We need a real paradigm change ... We have to get more flexibility and reduce labour costs and social security costs" (quoted in Sassoon 1996: 742).

After the election the Social Democrats quickly constructed a five-party surplus, unconnected coalition comprising the Left Alliance, the Greens, the conservatives, and the right-wing Swedish People's Party (the "Rainbow Coalition"). The Left Alliance and the Greens were invited to join the government for the same reason the Social Democrats were anxious to secure union cooperation, namely to enhance the legitimacy of potentially unpopular policies (Jungar 2002: 67, 77). The vote gains for the SDP, the majority status of the government, and the reduced fragmentation of the legislature would have facilitated reliance on legislation, other things being equal. However the government was an unconnected coalition embracing parties from the far-left to the conservatives, and the problems in negotiating such a complex coalition raise the probability of union inclusion in policymaking. In addition, the two governing parties most likely to be critical of pacts, the conservatives and the Swedish Peoples' Party, both lost votes in the 1995 election and their anti-pact views arguably carried less weight as a consequence. The new government therefore offered two social pacts to the unions, on pensions (in May 1995) and on wages and welfare cuts (in June 1995). Although negotiations lasted several months, agreements were finally reached in August and September respectively. Two years later the tripartite incomes policy was renewed for another two years. One major problem faced by the government early in its term was union opposition to proposed changes in unemployment insurance. When the unions threatened a general strike for April 1996, the third such threat in five years, the government rescinded its proposals, fearful of the electoral consequences of alienating the trade unions (Timonen 2003: 61). The government then reopened talks with the unions just 18 months later on a new wage pact and quickly reached agreement.

Over the term of the "Rainbow Coalition" the economy improved considerably: GDP growth averaged an impressive 5.6 percent 1995–98 and unemployment fell from 15.4 percent in 1995 to a little over 10 percent by the end of 1998. Inflation remained very low at less than 2 percent and the public finances were back into surplus in 1998, one year before the election (Figure 6.2). The reforms to national pensions and welfare benefits were supported by large majorities in the legislature and were backed by the trade unions and the employers (Nurmi and Nurmi 2001: 148). In part this was because the government shied away from reforming the income-related benefits of most concern to trade union members and concentrated instead on universal benefits (Timonen 2003: 187). Nonetheless the Social Democratic party was punished in the election, losing 12 seats, while the conservative party, which had held the Finance Ministry in the outgoing government, actually gained votes and seats, as did the Center Party (Nurmi and Nurmi 2001: 149; Table 6.3). As the SDP remained the largest party in the legislature it was able to initiate the process of government formation and chose to reconstitute the old five-party surplus coalition, once again excluding the Center Party (Arter 2000: 180).

The pro-pact inclination of the old "Rainbow Coalition" was reinforced by the significant vote and seat losses incurred by its dominant partner, the SDP, and the new government therefore continued the policy of union inclusion that had arguably helped secure its reelection. However, talks on a new wage norm broke down in September 1999 as several industrial unions were keen to pursue more aggressive wage demands now that unemployment was falling and the economy growing strongly (Kauppinen 2000: 171–3). The resulting sectoral wage bargaining round was marked by an unusually high level of strikes (Hietanen 2000). As in 1996, the government was undeterred by this experience and again proposed a wage pact in September 2000 succeeding in securing union agreement. This set the pattern for the next three years with another wage pact and a pensions pact, both in 2002 (Kangas 2007: 284–6). The 2003 election followed four more years of steady economic growth, low inflation, and a modest fall in unemployment (Figure 6.2). The Social Democrat vote rose a little at the expense of its conservative coalition partner but the main winner was the Center Party, which became the largest party in the new legislature and initiated the formation of a new center-left coalition government, excluding the conservatives.

In the election campaign the parties differed in their emphasis on economic policy, with the conservatives more favorable to tax cuts while the Social Democrats and the Center Party pledged to maintain public services (Nurmi and Nurmi 2004: 559). However, in light of the steady succession of social pacts signed since the early 1990s, the conservatives were anxious not to appear as an anti-union party and in the course of the campaign repeatedly pledged their support for the tripartite approach to policymaking (Arter 2003: 155). The new Center–Social Democrat government did legislate public sector pension reform in 2004 but stated this was modeled on the tripartite agreement for the private sector in 2002 and did not therefore require fresh negotiations with the unions (Kangas 2007: 287). Nevertheless, the government continued the tradition of negotiating a wage pact with the unions, finally securing their agreement to a two-year deal in November 2004.

Summing up the Finnish case

Government regulation of wages and reform of pensions in Finland since 1980 has occurred almost entirely through social pacts. These have been offered by unconnected coalitions containing at least three parties and some-times as many as five parties. Such broad coalitions are far more likely to offer pacts than pursue legislation and the only government that did attempt legis-lative reform was a connected coalition of the center-right. Party family effects have also proved critical in the Finnish case because the combined electoral strength of the far left, Social Democrats, and Center has signifi-cantly constrained the degree to which the conservatives were able to move to the right. The government option for pacts was reinforced before 1992 by the de facto minority status of successive governments that lacked the two-thirds of seats required for legislation. After 1992 and the presence of majority coalitions, the pacts option was reinforced by the continuing fragmentation of the legislature and through party family effects, as succes-sive unconnected coalition governments were dominated first by the left (Social Democrats, far-left, and Greens) and later by the Center and the Social Democrats.

Conclusion

A succession of governments in Sweden and Finland sought to moderate wage growth, restrain welfare spending and reform pensions. But whereas Swedish governments showed a far greater willingness to legislate reform rather than pursue social pacts, Finnish governments, led variously by conservatives, Center, and Social Democratic parties, opted almost invariably for union inclusion in policymaking through social pacts. It is true that Finland has a longer history than Sweden of state involvement in wage determination through tripartite pay agreements; yet, as evident from the contrasting cases of Britain and Ireland (Chapter 5), a history of tripartism in the 1970s is no guarantee of its continuation in the 1980s and 1990s. It has also been argued that unions in Finland have been more willing to compromise with govern-ments on issues such as wage restraint, compared to their Swedish counter-parts. While the level of real wage increases has been lower in Finland than Sweden throughout the 1990s and 2000s, Finnish unions have also displayed higher levels of strike activity including strikes against government policy (European Commission 2003: 205–6). In other words it cannot be said that Finnish unions have proved to be more "moderate."

We propose that a major part of the Swedish–Finnish difference in the incidence of pacts and legislation derives from differences in the patterns of electoral competition and in the governments of the two countries. In Sweden elections in the 1980s and 1990s became polarized between a rising conservative party and a declining though still powerful Social Democratic party with an increasingly unstable voter base. With the Center and far left vote in decline, the electorally successful conservatives pulled the Social Democrats to the right. Our model predicts that successive vote losses by minority Social Democratic governments in an increasingly fragmented legislature would have increased the likelihood of pacts as a way of dealing with electoral competition. Yet the evidence shows the SAP became so committed to austerity policies that it was willing to legislate reforms even at the price of union exclusion from policymaking. While union exclusion might lose some votes to the Left (and to the Greens) the electoral threat from the neoliberal conservatives was deemed far more significant. Moreover, the sharp differences among the non-SAP parliamentary opposition, divided between far left, Green, Center, and conservative parties, made it difficult for the opposition to exploit the minority status of successive SAP governments. Second, these same divisions allowed the SAP periodically to reach informal voting arrangements with one or two opposition parties and overcome its minority status. Legislation in Sweden was also pursued, as we would predict from party family, by right-center coalitions, in 1991–94 and from 2006. Once again the minority status of the 1991–94 administration was obviated by divisions among the opposition parties.

In Finland, in contrast, the far-left and the Center parties were much stronger than in Sweden while the Social Democrats were considerably weaker with around 25 percent of the vote. The Finnish Social Democrats certainly moved to the right during the 1980s and became increasingly willing to retrench the welfare state. But the electoral presence and threats from the far left and the Center meant that union exclusion never came to hold the attraction for the Finnish Social Democrats that it did for its Swedish counterpart. The position of the conservatives also differed significantly between the two countries. The Finnish conservatives faced much greater and more successful competition from the left and center, and their electoral losses – in 1991 and 1995 – only reinforced their support for social pacts when they participated in the Social Democrat-led coalition governments of 1995–2003. The dominance of pacts in the Finnish system was reinforced by the effective minority status of pre-1992 governments; by the broad, unconnected character of the coalition governments typically found in Finland; and by the high degree of fragmentation of the legislature. In short, electoral and parliamentary competition in Sweden led to a cross-party consensus more favorable to legislation, but in Finland resulted in a party consensus around social pacts.

7 Cycles of social pacts in the Mediterranean economies
Spain and Italy

Spanish and Italian governments have offered more social pacts to unions and employers between 1980 and 2006 (25 and 17 respectively) than most other governments in Western Europe; in contrast, their willingness to pursue reforms through legislation has been close to the cross-national average. This proclivity for social pacts is somewhat surprising considering the countries' economic and industrial relations institutions. Both Spain and Italy are generally considered to be part of the "Mediterranean" variety of capitalism, alternatively referred to as "statist" or "mixed" (e.g. Hall and Soskice 2001b).[1] Although the literature has not developed a coherent theoretical framework that establishes the characteristics that tie Mediterranean economies (MEs) together, MEs lack the "institutional complementarity" typical of both CMEs and LMEs and might thus be prone to "underperform" economically (see Hancké *et al.* 2007b: 13–14; Molina and Rhodes 2007a: 223). According to Molina and Rhodes (2007a: 225), MEs feature production systems that are relatively fragmented, a prominent role of the state in the economy, fragmented and unevenly developed welfare systems, and high rates of strike activity (see Hamann and Kelly 2008; Hale 2008). Bargaining centralization and coordination scores place Italy and Spain around mid-table for Western Europe even taking into account the declines since 1980. Thus, "the institutional preconditions for national pacts are particularly weak, and the potential for conflict – over both labor market and social policy reform – especially high" (Rhodes 2001: 168). Nevertheless, the high incidence of social pacts in both countries has generated some discussion about the institutional and other factors driving this mode of policymaking (e.g. Baccaro and Lim 2007; Molina 2005; Molina and Rhodes 2007a; Pérez 2000a; Royo 2007). The other striking feature of both countries is that pact offers have fluctuated considerably over time and in ways that do not appear to be closely synchronized with economic trends. In the late 1980s, for instance, the number of pact offers declined sharply in both countries before rising again from the mid-1990s and tailing off again in the early 2000s (more so in Italy than Spain). Neither the stability of the economic institutions nor economic trends can account for these temporal fluctuations. Instead, we seek an explanation for these patterns in the varying electoral fortunes of the main political parties and probe electoral variables to illuminate shifts over time in government preferences for pacts and legislation.

Spain

Industrial relations institutions and economic context

Spanish industrial relations are dominated by two major union confederations in addition to several smaller sector-specific and regional unions. The UGT was historically tied to the Socialist Party (PSOE) but their close relationship first became more distant and then ruptured in the late 1980s when the UGT officially "divorced" from the PSOE (see Gillespie 1990) and refused to endorse the PSOE in the 1989 election for the first time ever. The Workers' Commissions, CC.OO., were born in resistance to the Franco dictatorship, developing close ties to the Communist Party (PCE) and positioned to the left of the UGT. While the relationship between the two union confederations was competitive until the late 1980s, they have since moved towards cooperation in what has become known as "unity of action" (Hamann and Martínez Lucio 2003). Union affiliation has been low in comparison with other West European countries since the early 1980s and recovered from a low of 13 percent in 1980 to over 20 percent in the early 1990s, stabilizing at approximately 16 percent since the mid-1990s (Jordana 1996: 215; Visser 2006: 45). Yet, due to extension clauses, bargaining coverage is high (about 80 percent) while bargaining coordination remains somewhat fragmented. Spanish unions have displayed a high capacity to mobilize workers in strikes, both as part of regular bargaining as well as in general strikes (Rigby and Marco Aledo 2001), which were organized in 1985, 1988, 1992, 1994, and 2002. Union strength is generally established through workplace elections to works committees, the outcome of which entitles unions to bargaining rights at the workplace level but also at higher levels, including in national-level bargaining.

Turning to the economy, Spain has recorded steady GDP growth along with a relatively modest public deficit since the late 1980s (see Figure 7.1) although the level of unemployment ranks among the highest in Western Europe. The Spanish welfare state is relatively small in comparison to other countries in Western Europe (including Italy); whereas high unemployment has generated periodic pressure for reforms of unemployment benefits, its pension system has experienced less retrenchment than its Italian counterpart.

The electoral and party systems

The Spanish party system is dominated by two main parties operating at the national (state-wide) level. At the outset of democracy in 1977, these two parties were the UCD (Union of the Democratic Center), a center-right alliance of about a dozen smaller parties ranging from the center-left to the right, and the Socialist Party (PSOE) to the left. When the UCD imploded after its

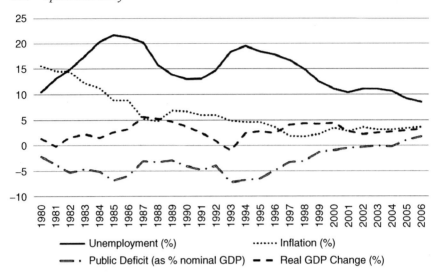

Figure 7.1 Main economic indicators, Spain, 1980–2006.
Sources: OECD (June 2007; December 1999; December 1996).

disastrous performance in the 1982 general election, the PSOE became the dominant party, while the conservative Popular Party PP (operating as Popular Alliance, AP, prior to 1989) established itself as the second major party. By the mid-1990s it had become the main opposition party and had closed the gap to the PSOE from almost 15 percentage points of the vote and 68 seats in 1989 to just 4 points of the vote and 18 seats in the 1993 election (Table 7.1). In addition, a smaller leftist third party operates at the national level, the United Left (Izquierda Unida, IU), which formed after the 1986 election and includes the Communist Party (PCE). These three parties are joined in several of Spain's 17 autonomous communities, or regions, by a range of regionalist (also referred to as nationalist, or non-statewide) parties, some of which are also represented in the Congress of Deputies, notably the Catalan parties CiU (Convergence and Union) and ERC (Republican), the Basque PNV (National Basque Party), and the Coalición Canaria (CC). All of these parties have exerted considerable political power as they have on occasion supported minority governments of both the left and the right.

The party system owes its shape in part to the electoral laws, which combines a proportional representation system with small district magnitude, a threshold of 3 percent at the district level, and the usage of the d'Hondt system of seat allocation. This lends the system a majoritarian twist, rendering it one of the least proportional PR systems in Western Europe and thus strongly favoring the development of a two-party dominant system (Field and Hamann 2008; Hopkin 2005a). Since the first democratic elections in 1977, three parties have formed the executive either as single-party majority or minority governments: the center-right UCD (1977–82), the

Table 7.1 Election results, Spain (Congreso de los Diputados), 1979–2006

	1979 % votes	1979 # seats (%seats)	1982 % votes	1982 # seats (%seats)	1986 % votes	1986 # seats (%seats)	1989 % votes	1989 # seats (%seats)	1993 % votes	1993 # seats (%seats)	1996 % votes	1996 # seats (%seats)	2000 % votes	2000 # seats (%seats)	2004 % votes	2004 # seats (%seats)
UCD	34.8	168 (48.0)	6.8	11 (3.1)												
CDS			2.9	2 (0.6)	9.2	19 (5.4)	7.9	14 (4.0)								
PSOE	30.4	121 (34.6)	48.1	202 (57.7)	44.1	184 (52.6)	39.6	175 (50.0)	38.8	159 (45.4)	37.6	141 (40.3)	34.2	125 (35.7)	42.6	164 (46.9)
AP/PP	6.1	10 (2.9)	26.4	107 (30.6)	26.0	105 (30.0)	25.8	107 (30.6)	34.8	141 (40.3)	38.8	156 (44.6)	44.5	183 (52.3)	37.7	148 (42.3)
PCE/IU	10.8	23 (6.6)	4.0	4 (1.1)	4.6	7 (2.0)	9.1	17 (4.9)	9.6	18 (5.1)	10.5	21 (6.0)	5.5	8 (2.3)	5.0	5 (1.4)
CiU	2.7	8 (2.3)	3.7	12 (3.4)	5.0	18 (5.1)	5.0	18 (5.1)	4.9	17 (4.9)	4.6	16 (4.6)	4.2	15 (4.3)	3.2	10 (2.9)
PNV	1.7	7 (2.0)	1.9	8 (2.3)	1.5	6 (1.7)	1.2	5 (1.4)	1.2	5 (1.4)	1.3	5 (1.4)	1.5	7 (2.0)	1.6	7 (2.0)
ERC									0.8	1 (0.3)	0.7	1 (0.3)	0.8	1 (0.3)	2.5	8 (2.3)
CC									0.9	4 (1.1)	0.9	4 (1.1)	1.1	4 (1.1)	0.9	3 (0.9)
Others	13.5	13 (3.7)	6.2	4 (1.1)	9.6	11 (3.1)	11.4	14 (4.0)	9.0	5 (1.4)	5.6	6 (1.7)	8.2	7 (2.0)	6.5	5 (1.4)
Total	100	350 (100)	100	350 (100)	100	350 (100)	100	350 (100)	100	350 (100)	100	350 (100)	100	350 (100)	100	350 (100)

Source: See Appendix 1.

Note: UCD = Unión del Centro Democrático (Union of the Democratic Center), CDS = Centro Democrático y Social (Democratic and Social Center), PSOE = Partido Socialista Obrero Español (Spanish Socialist Workers' Party), AP/PP = Alianza Popular/Partido Popular (Popular Alliance/Popular Party), PCE/IU = Partido Comunista de España/Izquierda Unida (Communist Party of Spain/United Left), PDC/CIU = Pacte Democràtic per Catalunya/Convergència i Unió (Democratic Pact for Catalonia/Convergence and Union), PNV = Partido Nacionalista Vasco (Basque Nationalist Party); ERC = Esquerra Republicana de Catalunya (Republican Left of Catalonia); CC = Coalición Canaria (Canarian Coalition). Percentages are rounded.

leftist PSOE (1982–96 and again since 2004), and the conservative PP (1996–2004). Furthermore, significant shifts in voters' preferences – and by implication in the party system – have been facilitated by low party membership and a very low party member/voter ratio, among the lowest in Europe (Katz 2005: 101–2),[2] which means that voter attachments to parties are relatively weak and can transfer easily.

Pacts and legislation in Spain

Several factors in Spanish politics privilege decision making by the executive through unilateral legislative acts but also through reforms negotiated with the social partners, especially regarding welfare issues. The prevalence of single-party governments, the concentration of power in the executive (Chari and Heywood 2008), and the small effective number of legislative parties[3] seemingly facilitate the legislative route to reform. Yet, executive power is mitigated when the governing party has just a small lead over its nearest competitor, especially when the prime minister heads a minority government that depends on the support of other parties to pass legislation in parliament. At the same time, the Spanish welfare state is relatively small in comparison to other countries in Western Europe (see Rueda 2007: 180) so that governments face considerable challenges if they want to "justify welfare cost-containment measures ... given that it can hardly be argued that the social protection system is oversized" (Chuliá 2007: 500).[4] Thus, it is perhaps not surprising that instances of welfare retrenchment legislation have been relatively infrequent in Spain, particularly in light of the fact that the Spanish welfare state experienced some degree of universalization as well as some expansion (especially in the areas of health and old-age pensions) despite aspects of rationalization (Guillén *et al.* 2003). In fact, the percentage of GDP spent on social protection increased from 18.1 percent in 1980 to 22.5 percent in 1991/92, before being reduced to 18.9 percent in 2001 (Gunther *et al.* 2004: 360).

This context sets the stage for the pattern of emergence, decline, and reappearance of social pact offers in Spain. Bi- or tripartite national agreements (sometimes comprising only the social partners but not the government) were offered and signed at the onset of Spanish democracy in the late 1970s and lasted until the mid-1980s; pact offers decreased slightly and were met with more frequent union rejection while reform through legislation occurred more frequently from the mid-1980s to the mid-1990s, after which pact offers became more prominent again. Pact offers were somewhat less visible again after the 2000 election, but resurfaced more prominently after 2004. Pacts in Spain have varied greatly in their contents, ranging from encompassing pacts including wage setting in the 1980s to the regulation of specific issues such as part-time work and pension reforms in the 1990s. They have also varied with respect to the signatories: governments both of the left and the right, one or both major union confederations, and for the most part – but not always – the main employers' organizations. Moreover, pact offers or legislative actions do not neatly mirror the ups and downs of the Spanish economy, and neither do they correspond easily to the EMU period. Pacts were offered more frequently during the early 1980s, while GDP growth was slow, but also during the latter part of the 1990s, when the economy grew relatively fast and the public deficit was declining. At the same time, during the early 1990s when pact offers occurred with less frequency and reform through legislation was more prominent, public debt grew and GDP growth slowed down. After 2000, pact offers became less frequent and legislation was more common even though GDP growth slowed from over 4 percent in 2000 to just over 2 percent in 2002 and inflation rose from 2.2 percent in 1999 to 3.6 percent in 2002 (the deficit, however, remained low at under 1 percent) (see Figure 7.1). The government's preference for pacts or legislation thus does not seem to correspond closely to economic patterns.

To explain the oscillating pattern of pact offers in Spain we thus steer away from the economic and institution-focused approach adopted by much of the recent literature and instead assume an actor-centered model that understands governments' pact offers as politically contingent and influenced by electoral dynamics (see also Hamann 2001). Pact offers in Spain appear to be affected by the strength of the government and by the direction of vote change: pact offers have been particularly noticeable when a new party assumed government responsibilities, an outcome generally linked to relative gains in votes. However, vote gains by incumbent parties did not result in more frequent pact offers, a finding that resonates with our theoretical reasoning on electoral pressures. Other variables identified as significant in our cross-national analysis (e.g. type of coalition) are of less relevance for the Spanish case, which has always featured single-party governments (majority or minority). Given Spain's relatively shorter history of electoral democracy, we also discuss factors relating to the context of democratization. While economic pressures – and various aspects of European economic and monetary integration in particular – may well have provided crucial motivations for adjustment policies, we propose that political and electoral factors correspond better to the choice of pact offers or legislation pursued by the government at particular times.

Social pacts, legislation, and the PSOE governments

The pacts of the late 1970s until the mid-1980s have often been interpreted not as some form of neo-corporatism, but rather as attempts to construct a broad social support coalition outside parliament in order to stabilize the economy at the height of a recession and protect the new democratic regime during a period of instability (see e.g. Fishman 1990; Hamann 2001). In fact, the democratic transition in Spain itself is commonly referred to as a "pacted" transition, comprising a series of pacts between political elites that resulted in, or at least facilitated, the restoration of democracy (e.g. Gunther 1992; Karl and Schmitter 1991; Maravall 1993; Preston 1986; Share 1986). In many ways, the pacts of the 1980s appeared to be an extension of this type of elite settlement or "consensus" involving new actors. Parliamentary negotiations of issues such as the constitution and broad economic targets, as in the Moncloa Pacts of 1977,[5] were now extended to issues such as employment creation and industrial relations and included organized labor and employers while excluding opposition parties. Several of the early pacts were bipartite agreements between employers and unions with the government being a bystander, notably the Basic Interconfederal Agreement (ABI, 1979) on labor market regulations and the Interconfederal Framework Agreement (AMI, 1980–81) focusing on wage policy.[6] The first tripartite pact was the 1982 National Employment Agreement (ANE), popularly – and tellingly – known as the *Pacto de Miedo* (Pact of Fear), signed with the UCD government after the 1981 military coup attempt during which military officers took the entire parliament hostage as a new government was about to take office. This time period was characterized by heightened political instability and party system fluctuation.

The UCD, the governing party after the 1977 and 1979 elections, virtually disappeared from the electoral landscape in 1982 when its vote share plummeted from 35 percent in 1979 to 6.8 percent in 1982 (see Table 7.1). Electoral volatility between these two elections was 42.3 percent, the "highest among more than three hundred elections held in thirteen European countries since 1885" (Gunther *et al.* 2004: 216–7).[7] Thus, when the PSOE was elected in 1982 with a majority of seats in the lower house of parliament (202 out of 350), not only had the nascent democracy recently survived a coup attempt, but its party system had also undergone a profound reconfiguration, and it could not be taken for granted that the vote distribution would stabilize immediately. Perhaps predictably, Prime Minister Felipe González sought to build and express support for democracy and his PSOE government through pacts even though he was heading a single-party majority government that would have allowed him to legislate reforms. The Economic and Social Agreement (AES), proposed in September 1984, was signed by the government, the employers, and one of the major union confederations, the UGT, and aimed to restrain wage growth for 1985–86. The government also engaged in an unsuccessful attempt to reach agreements on social security and pension reforms in 1985, which resulted in a general strike called by just one of the two union confederations (CC.OO.) and was eventually adopted as legislation (see Rueda 2007: 183).

At the same time, the new democracy became more consolidated after the 1982 election and the uncertainties of the transition began to give way to routine democratic policymaking when the legitimacy of the Socialist victory remained unchallenged by the military. Furthermore, the party system stabilized with the PSOE's return to office in 1986, again with a majority of the seats despite a small loss of votes and seats, and electoral volatility declined to 11.9 percent after the 1986 election (Gunther *et al.* 2004: 217). Once the PSOE had been reelected and Spain had joined the European Community in

1986, just two pact offers were extended during González' second term: a 1986 agreement on pension reform and the unsuccessful attempt to negotiate wages in 1987. Instead, the government opted in 1988 for legislation to curb youth unemployment, which then stood at 36.1 percent for young men and over 50 percent for young women, more than double the EU 12 average of 16.5 percent for males and 22.5 percent for females (Bertram 1994: 275). The unions heavily criticized the measures as both insufficient and inappropriate for dealing with unemployment of young people since they would at best create an even larger share of temporary contracts (already at approximately 30 percent of total employment). Both confederations called for a general strike in December 1988 in protest. About 80–85 percent of workers nationwide followed the strike call (Aguilar and Roca 1991: 17; Delaney 1988), considerably above Spain's union membership.[8] At the same time, leaders from both major union confederations also attacked the government for not having complied with the terms of previous agreements (Estivill and de la Hoz 1991; Recio and Roca 1998: 149; author interviews with union leaders, Madrid, fall 1991).

In many ways, this development paralleled moves from a consensus-building policy-making process towards more majoritarian decision making by the government. This trend was facilitated by the majoritarian aspects of the Spanish political institutions (see Chari and Heywood 2008; Field 2008; Field and Hamann 2008; Hopkin 2005b; Gunther *et al.* 2004) and became increasingly prominent after the government was reelected with an absolute majority in 1986. Having a large and secure majority and leading the second strongest party, the conservative AP, by 79 seats in the Congress of Deputies, the PSOE government was in a position to pass many of its economic, labor market, and welfare reforms unilaterally. Between 1982 and 1986, about 89 percent of all government bills were passed, and slightly less (86 percent) for the subsequent legislature (Field 2005: 1084, note 6).[9] The majority of the bills that failed to pass were not rejected by parliament, but instead either expired due to parliamentary elections, or were withdrawn (Field 2005: 1084).[10] González' government thus needed neither parliamentary support from other parties during this period, nor broader social support from the unions to pass controversial policies, and the pressures of European economic integration and the adjustment policies necessary to modernize Spain provided the justification for the policies. As a former PSOE Minister of Labor expressed with reference to the late 1980s, the Socialist government "preferred to make policies with the support of the unions, but we can do it just as well without them" (author interview, Madrid, fall 1991). Unions, for their part, expressed little interest in signing encompassing new pacts including wage components despite several government offers (see Astudillo Ruiz 2001; Gunther *et al.* 2004: 384; Maravall 1993: 119).

In the subsequent general election of 1989, the PSOE again incurred vote and seat losses and was allocated exactly 50 percent of the seats in Congress (Table 7.1). The PSOE's vote share had been diminished by over 4 percent while the IU, to the left of the PSOE, had gained an equivalent vote share.

Yet, the PSOE still had a margin of almost 70 seats over the second largest party, the PP, and was able to rule without forming legislative coalitions since the four deputies of the Basque party HB refused to take their seats, thus granting Prime Minister González an effective, though slim, parliamentary majority.

The early 1990s witnessed both pact offers and cases of reform through legislation, reflecting the political realities rather than economic trends alone. For example, in 1991 the PSOE government proposed negotiations for a Social Pact for Progress (*Pacto Social para el Progreso*), designed to strengthen Spain's position in the Single European Market. The negotiations failed due to union opposition to the proposed wage restraint (EIRR 1992, 224: 26). The following year the government adopted cuts in unemployment benefits in its unilateral Maastricht Convergence Plan. Just a few months later, in the face of rising unemployment, the government proposed tripartite negotiations on incomes policy but the unions rejected such a policy (Pérez 2000b: 349).

Why, though, did the government not impose wage policies unilaterally as its first course of action, as it had done on occasion in the past, and instead made a new pact a pivotal point in its campaign leading up to the 1993 election? Pérez (2000b: 349) cites electoral pressures on the PSOE as one factor given the "PSOE's slipping support in the elections ... Fearing an outright defeat, the PSOE had proposed a new Social Pact ... as a key element in its electoral campaign." Negotiations were started, but eventually broke down over disagreements between the unions, employers, and the government on the labor market reform. Unions, for their part, were unwilling to accept global social pacts as they feared these would legitimize the government's economic policies, while they were more willing to negotiate more limited agreements, which did not include wage policies (Maravall 1993: 119).[11]

The government's introduction of a strike law, mandated by the constitution, also met with vehement union opposition, resulting in negotiations of the Bill with the unions. Even though an agreement on the law was reached, the Bill was never passed as it failed to make it through the legislative process prior to the election in 1993, which was called early, and was not reintroduced under the new government. The government's parliamentary position weakened even more after the 1993 election, when the PSOE's seat share fell to 159 seats out of 350, forcing González to form a minority cabinet (Table 7.1). To bolster its legislative strength, the PSOE relied heavily on the Catalan nationalist party Convergencia i Unio (CiU) to pass bills. CiU therefore had significant influence in determining the government's economic austerity policies and promoting the liberalization of the labor market (Gunther *et al.* 2004: 385). While in principle open to pacts, the CiU opposed the pacted labor market reform (Pérez 2000b: 349–50). After negotiations with the unions broke down in November 1993, the government passed the 1994 labor market reform unilaterally, prompting the unions to call a general strike (Aguar *et al.* 1999: 60; Rhodes 1997).

Despite the failed attempts at agreements, the PSOE thus began to offer pacts more frequently, as could be expected in light of the government's lack of a legislative majority and the small seat margin over its competitor, the conservative PP, and on some occasions agreements were reached. The most notable of these agreements was perhaps the Toledo Pact on pension reform in 1995, based on one year of consultations between a parliamentary commission and non-parliamentary groups including unions and employers but also academics and public administration representatives. The resulting recommendations were subsequently passed unanimously in Congress (Chuliá 2007: 535).

The reemergence of pacts under the PP government

The trend towards pact offers rather than legislation, reemerging during the last Socialist term in office, was accentuated once José María Aznar's conservative Popular Party (PP) won the 1996 election and formed a minority government. Social pacts on welfare reforms were offered and signed with increased regularity and frequency without, however, containing wage clauses. The first big pact on pensions was the October 1996 Agreement on the Consolidation and Rationalization of the Social Security System (ASEC) between the Aznar government and the unions, based on the 1995 Toledo Pacts (Chuliá 2007: 538). Over the next few years, national-level agreements between the government and the unions (and sometimes employers) were reached on a variety of labor market issues, such as rural employment, employment stability, and part-time work.

The economy cannot provide an exhaustive explanation for the resurgence of pacts: inflation and unemployment rates were both falling in the late 1990s, the public deficit was shrinking rapidly, and the GDP growth rate climbed steadily to reach 5.0 percent in 2000 (Figure 7.1). If the economy had provided the main impetus for social pacts, we should have witnessed wage pacts as a way of addressing inflationary wage pressures. Pacts on incomes policy, however, were noticeably absent; instead, unions engaged in voluntary coordination of wage restraint, such as the 2001 bipartite Interconfederal Agreement on Collective Bargaining (ANC 2002). In fact, Gunther *et al.* (2004: 386) conclude that the PP government "took advantage of good economic conditions and established a new climate of dialogue with the trade unions." Thus, the argument that the economic pressures alone prompted the government to return to social pacts to achieve wage moderation lacks plausibility – pacts were neither clearly linked to the economy, nor were they necessitated by institutional factors, such as the need to negotiate incomes policies.

Instead, political and electoral factors constitute an integral part of the explanation for the reemergence of pacts. In particular, the importance of party family as well as the strength of the government becomes evident for the first Aznar government. For one, Aznar's election in 1996 marked the first time since the transition to democracy that a conservative party ruled the country. Until the late 1980s, the PP had suffered from the connections of its leadership to the Franco dictatorship and lacked democratic legitimacy. Aznar represented a new, younger generation of leaders, concerned with raising the democratic legitimacy of the party. Broadening the policy-making process from the parliamentary setting to include unions and employers was one such strategy of raising legitimacy (see Gunther *et al.* 2004: 389). Similarly, the PP faced the problem that "in the eyes of many voters its conservative-liberal ideology placed it under suspicion of wanting to cut back welfare benefits" (Chuliá 2007: 538). Agreements with the unions better legitimized welfare reforms and demonstrated more commitment to the welfare state than if the government had opted for unilateral legislation. The PP's shift towards the center was apparent in its 2000 electoral program, which praised the virtues of dialogue with the social partners (Partido Popular 2000) and was ratified during the nineteenth party congress in 2002, when the PP defined itself as a party of the "reformist center, servicing the general interests of Spain" (Partido Popular n.d.).

Second, Aznar's PP lacked a majority in parliament and thus had to form a minority government, supported by smaller regional parties. The PP commanded just 15 seats more than the largest opposition party, the PSOE. Again, broadening the support coalitions for controversial policies strengthened the government's position. Furthermore, polls and election results indicated that Spanish voters did not desert the PSOE in 1996 because of an ideological turn to the right or because of their criticisms of the government's economic policies, but rather because of growing resentment towards the increasing number of political corruption scandals involving the PSOE (Heywood 1995: 726; Pérez-Diaz 1999). Similarly, the relatively small margin of victory – the PP won just 1.2 percent more votes than the PSOE – also indicated that the electorate had not undergone a massive shift to the right. Despite voting for the PP, Spanish voters continued to support "collective goods" and the provision of welfare measures by the state (Gunther *et al.* 2004: 389). Thus, Aznar's inclusion of the unions appealed to some of the large number of centrist or center-left voters, "central to the electoral fortunes" of the PSOE.[12] Martínez Lucio (2002: 270) concludes that the PP tried to attract groups of voters that were willing to change their party preference. Thus, Aznar embraced an "ambiguous, neoliberal centrism" and an electoral catch-all strategy to reach out to the median voter (Gunther *et al.* 2004: 389).

These electoral strategies make sense considering that electoral volatility had more than doubled from 4.4 percent for the 1993–96 period to 10.1 percent between the 1996 and 2000 elections (Gunther *et al.* 2004: 217), indicating that voters were in general less tied to "their" party and that their vote could not be taken for granted. This was true both for the losing PSOE, but also for the winning PP, especially given the narrow vote distance between them. A similar picture emerges with respect to electoral and parliamentary competitiveness. The periods of highest electoral and parliamentary competitiveness, defined as the difference in the share of votes or seats respectively between the two largest parties, spiked at 4.0 (1993) and 1.3 (1996) for electoral competitiveness and 5.1 and 4.3 for parliamentary competitiveness in the same elections (Gunther *et al.* 2004: 226). After the 2004 elections, electoral competitiveness was 4.9 percent and parliamentary competitiveness reached 4.6 percent (authors' calculation based on Table 7.1). These periods of heightened competitiveness coincided with periods during which governments offered pacts with increased frequency (after the 1993, 1996, and 2004 elections) while the surge in pact offers in the early 1980s occurred subsequent to the extreme electoral volatility in 1982. Thus, Aznar's move to reach out to the median voter and negotiate reforms is consistent with electoral pressures and party competition.

The 2000 election returned Aznar and the PP to office with an absolute majority of seats in Congress – the governing party held 183 seats, 58 more than the PSOE, and the PP had gained almost 6 points more of the vote and 27 seats compared to the previous election while the PSOE had lost almost 3.4 percentage points of the vote and 16 seats. The PSOE suffered from leadership struggles after the resignation of long-serving Prime Minister and party leader Felipe González in June 1997, and the party ventured a new electoral strategy by forming a pre-electoral alliance with the leftist IU. These personnel and strategic changes were not rewarded by the voters, as the election outcome attests.

With a stronger position in the legislature, the relationship between the PP government and the unions became less cooperative. While some pacts were offered and signed (e.g. a 2001 update of the 1996 pension agreement and a pact on Health and Safety in 2002), the government also pursued reform through legislation, such as a labor market reform in 2000–01. Conflict and disagreement became perhaps most visible in the June 2002 general strike against the government's proposed reforms of the unemployment benefits system. Following the strike and a series of additional mobilizations, the government withdrew almost all of these restrictive reforms. Moreover, anti-inflationary measures were now pushed through unilaterally by the government using decree laws (Gunther *et al.* 2004: 392).

Social pacts under Zapatero's PSOE government, 2004–06

The reelection of the PSOE under the leadership of José Luis Rodríguez Zapatero in 2004 ushered in a new period of government cooperation with the unions. The election of the PSOE was unexpected after polls had consistently predicted a renewed victory of the PP. Many observers link the unpredicted election outcome not so much to voters' criticisms of the economy, which was doing quite well with economic growth, low inflation, and relatively low levels of unemployment, as to the consequences of the government's reaction to, and interpretation of, terrorist attacks on commuter trains in

Madrid just days before the election (see, for example, Chari 2004; Torcal and Rico 2004). This "perceived manipulation of the situation by the government" (Chari 2004: 962) was particularly important as Aznar's government had joined the coalition forces in Iraq against the preferences of the majority of Spaniards, many of whom participated in a general strike against the war in April 2003. As a result, electoral volatility was high during this election, especially among those voters that might otherwise have supported the leftist IU, many of whom voted for the PSOE to maximize its chances of winning. In addition, nearly half a million PP voters switched to the PSOE (Chari 2004: 960).

Prime Minister Zapatero had won the election, but not by enough votes or seats to enable him to form a majority government. He was, however, able to find parliamentary support from the leftist IU as well as the Catalan leftist party ERC (see Table 7.1). The minority government, backed by other leftist parties, immediately announced its intention to build a cooperative and inclusive relationship with the unions. Consequently agreements on a labor market reform and a new Workers' Statute for the Self-Employed were signed in 2006 shortly after the new government took office (Martín Artiles 2007). Pact offers were also made concerning training and a pension reform, all of which were signed by unions and employers.[13]

Summing up the Spanish case

In conclusion, the Spanish case illustrates that economic factors are not sufficient to explain fully the existence, absence, or the type of pacts. Existing explanations that focus on factors other than the economy center on political exchange (e.g. Molina 2006); on institutional factors, such as the fact that unions compensate for "organisational weakness at the lower levels of the bargaining system" with "peak interconfederal coordinated articulation" (e.g. Molina 2006: 655); or on the unions' interests and strategies (e.g. Astudillo Ruiz 2001; Royo 2006). Certainly, political exchange and actors' interests are important to understand why social pacts occur. Yet, governments' strategies are at least in part driven by their interest in electoral performance, which suggests an interaction of political parties not just with unions and employers but also with other parties. Neither economic nor institutional factors translate easily into the absence or presence of pact offers in Spain. The varied patterns of social pact offers within an institutional framework that has by and large been relatively stable (e.g. fragmented bargaining institutions) are more easily accommodated by considering the electoral dynamics and the position of the parties in the party system and in the legislature. Certainly, the political context of Spain as a democratizing country was crucial, especially during the early years of the democracy, but elections and their outcomes have proven pivotal in explaining the patterns of social pacts in Spain.

Italy

Industrial relations institutions and economic context

The Italian trade union movement is divided on political lines, although links between unions and parties began to weaken considerably in the 1970s. The CGIL was traditionally allied to the Communist Party (PCI); the CISL emerged from the tradition of Christian Democracy while the UIL is a secular and socialist confederation. Relations between the confederations have varied over recent years although all three confederations compete for votes in "works council" elections. Union density in Italy was much higher than in Spain, peaking at around 50 percent in the late 1970s before declining to under 35 percent in the 2000s.[14] Bargaining coverage is high, at approximately 80 percent, and the degree of bargaining coordination is moderate, as in Spain. Italian industrial relations are highly adversarial with a high strike rate. The labor market, however, is less regulated than in Spain with far fewer restrictions on dismissal and redundancy and a far lower proportion of temporary workers.

The Italian economy performed poorly by EU standards since the early 1990s: the GDP growth rate was significantly below the EU15 average while its public deficit was somewhat above the EU average (see Figure 7.2). Levels and trends in unemployment resembled Western European averages.

The electoral and party systems

Until its reform in 1993, Italy's proportional representation system resulted in the legislative representation of many parties, as well as the dominance of

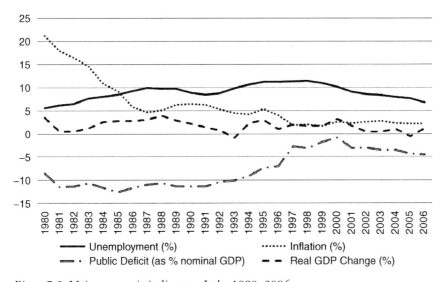

Figure 7.2 Main economic indicators, Italy, 1980–2006.

Sources: OECD (June 2007; December 1999; December 1996).

a single party, the Christian Democrats (DC). Consistently the largest party during the post-1945 period, the DC was present in every government until 1994, either as a single-party or coalition government. Conversely, the main opposition party, the Communists (PCI), were always excluded from government (Verzichelli and Cotta 2003: 435, 442). Under the 1993 electoral reforms, 75 percent of deputies in both houses are elected in local districts under a "first past the post" plurality system while the remaining deputies are elected through PR in large constituencies with a 4-percent threshold. The new rules were designed to reduce the number of parties in the legislature and to encourage pre-election agreements among parties. Since 1994 every general election has been fought between two blocs of parties (on the center-left and the right) as well as a number of smaller parties.

Electoral support for the DC and PCI began to decline after 1976 while the Socialist Party (PSI) vote began to erode in the early 1960s (Bardi 2004: 113; see also Table 7.2). Turnout was traditionally above 90 percent but fell steadily from 93.4 percent in 1976 to 87.3 percent in 1992 (Bardi 2004: 118). Voters' party identification declined while their willingness to switch parties increased. In 1978 almost half the electorate (46 percent) described themselves as "strongly" identifying with a political party but by 1992 just 30 percent did so (Bardi 2004: 118). Electoral volatility therefore increased throughout the 1980s, climbing from 8.3 percent in 1983 to 14.4 percent in the 1992 election (Mair 2006). Furthermore, new parties entered electoral contests starting in the mid-1970s (Verzichelli and Cotta 2003: 437).

However, between 1992 and 1994 the party system was almost completely overturned as the investigations of Milanese magistrates gradually unearthed a vast network of bribery and corruption that stretched across the established political parties (Bufacchi and Burgess 2001: 62–74; Rhodes 2001: 186–9). Many DC and PSI leaders were indicted on corruption charges in 1992–94, resulting in the fragmentation of the DC into a number of small parties and the dissolution of the PSI in 1994 (Leonardi and Alberti 2004: 121). Two years earlier the PCI had transformed itself into the Democratic Party of the Left, provoking a left-wing breakaway, the Communist Refoundation. The corruption scandal and the new electoral law certainly posed new and serious challenges for Italy's political parties. These proximate causes of political problems emerged in a context where the major parties were already facing serious difficulties because of the longer-run electoral threats and pressures just described (Newell and Bull 1997: 81–3).

Social pacts and legislation in Italy

Governments in Italy have signed numerous social pacts since 1980. Most famous are the agreements signed by all three social partners in July 1992 and July 1993 in the throes of the political crisis precipitated by the corruption scandals and in the midst of mounting economic crisis. They have also sometimes enacted reforms through legislation, notably in the late 1980s,

Table 7.2 Election results, Italy (Camera dei Deputati), 1979–2006

	1979		1983		1987		1992		1994		1996		2001		2006	
	% vote	# seats (%seats)	% vote	# seats (%seats)	% vote	# seats (%seats)	% vote	# seats (%seats)	% vote	# seats (%seats)	% vote	# seats (%seats)	% vote	# seats (%seats)	% vote	# seats (%seats)
RC							5.6	35 (5.6)	6.0	39 (6.2)	8.6	39 (6.2)	5.0	35 (5.6)	5.7	41 (6.5)
PCI/PDS	30.4	201 (31.9)	29.8	198 (31.4)	26.6	177 (28.1)	16.1	107 (17.0)	20.4	164 (26.0)	21.1	164 (26.0)	16.6	167 (20.5)	30.4	220 (34.9)
PSI	9.8	62 (9.8)	11.4	73 (11.6)	14.3	94 (14.9)	13.6	92 (14.6)	2.2	0 (0.0)	0.4	0 (0.0)	1.0	6 (1.0)		
PSDI	3.8	20 (3.2)	4.1	23 (3.7)	2.9	17 (2.7)	2.7	16 (2.5)								
PRI	1.9	9 (1.4)	2.9	16 (2.5)	2.1	11 (1.8)	2.9	17 (2.7)								
DC	38.3	262 (41.6)	32.9	225 (35.7)	34.3	234 (37.1)	29.7	206 (32.7)	15.7	33 (5.2)	6.8	33 (5.2)	14.5	80 (12.7)	6.6	39 (6.2)
FI									21.0	113 (17.9)	20.6	113 (17.9)	29.4	123 (19.5)	23.1	137 (21.8)
PLI	1.9	9 (1.4)	2.9	16 (2.5)	2.1	11 (1.8)	2.9	17 (2.7)								
MSI/AN	5.3	30 (4.8)	6.8	42 (6.7)	5.9	35 (5.6)	5.4	34 (5.4)	13.5	109 (17.3)	15.7	109 (17.3)	12.0	93 (14.8)	12.0	71 (11.3)
LN			0.3	1 (0.1)	1.3	1 (0.1)	8.6	55 (8.7)	8.4	117 (18.6)	10.1	117 (18.6)	3.9	59 (9.4)	4.5	26 (4.1)
Others	8.6	37 (5.9)	8.8	36 (5.7)	10.5	50 (7.9)	12.5	51 (8.1)	12.8	55 (8.7)	16.7	55 (8.7)	17.6	73 (11.6)	17.7	96 (15.2)
Total	100	630 (100)	100	630 (100)	100	630 (100)	100	630 (100)	100	630 (100)	100	630 (100)	100	630 (100)	100	630 (100)

Source: See Appendix 1.

Note: RC = Rifondazione Comunista (Communist Refoundation); PCI = Partito Communista Italiano (Italian Communist Party); PDS = Partito Democratico della Sinistra (Democratic Party of the Left); PSI = Partito Socialista Italiano (Italian Socialist Party); PSDI = Partito Socialista Democratico Italiano (Italian Social Democratic Party); PRI = Partito Repubblicano Italiano (Italian Republican Party); DC = Democrazia Christiana (Christian Democracy); FI = Forza Italia; PLI = Partito Liberale Italiano (Italian Liberal Party); MSI = Movimento Sociale Italiano (Italian Social Movement); AN = Alleanza Nazionale (National Alliance); LN = Lega Nord (Northern League).

mid-1990s, and early 2000s (Compston 1995; Regini and Regalia 1997). Yet the shifting *pattern* of social pacts and legislation over time does not correspond to trends in the main economic indicators. Social pacts were largely abandoned between 1984 and 1992 despite the continuing rise in public deficits and in unemployment and they were abandoned again after 2002 despite sluggish growth and a rising deficit. In contrast, they were resumed between 1995 and 1998 even though public borrowing was falling (Ferrera and Gualmini 2004: 59–63, 81). To understand the cyclical pattern of pacts and legislation we examine the electoral pressures faced by the main political parties.

Social pacts in the early 1980s

In July 1982 the five-party government headed by Republican Prime Minister Spadolini proposed a wage pact to the three union confederations (CGIL, CISL, and UIL) and the employers' organization Confindustria. The agreement, signed in January 1983 by the new DC Prime Minister Fanfani, restrained wage growth through a downward revision of the wage indexation formula of the *scala mobile* in exchange for tax and benefit concessions (Regini and Regalia 1997: 210–1). The pact was offered against a background of major economic problems: unemployment had risen to 6.5 percent by 1982 and was climbing rapidly; the public deficit had reached 11.4 percent of GDP in the same year; and inflation exceeded 16 percent, one of the highest rates in the EU (Negrelli and Santi 1990: 158–60; see also Table 7.2). The large government majority in both houses and the stability of its total vote between the elections of 1976 and 1979 suggest that it might have preferred to rely on legislation, particularly in light of the union rejection of its previous pact offer in December 1981. However, our model implies that as a connected coalition dominated by center and leftist parties it would be more inclined to offer pacts.

While governments continued to consult unions informally throughout the remainder of the decade and to enact a number of labor market reforms, the 1983 agreement is generally considered as the culmination of a cycle of agreements that began in the aftermath of the "hot autumn" strike wave of 1969 (Compston 1995: 314–6; Lodovici 2000: 276).[15] Yet the demise of social pacts after 1983 cannot be explained by any moderation or diminution of the country's economic problems. Unemployment had increased since 1975, peaking in 1987, while the public deficit averaged 11 percent of the GDP (three times the EU average) throughout the 1980s and into the mid-1990s (Ferrera and Gualmini 2000: 366–7; see also Table 7.1). Critical to the virtual disappearance of social pacts was the electoral strategy of the PSI in response to vote and seat losses in the previous decades.

The demise of social pacts after 1983

Between 1963 and 1976 the PSI had acted as a junior partner in DC-led coalition governments for nine years. Yet over that period, the PSI vote continued to fall from its postwar peak of 14.2 percent (1958) to a new postwar low of 9.6 percent in 1976, just when its closest rival, the PCI, reached a record high vote of 34.4 percent. Not only had the PSI strategy of power-sharing with the DC afforded the party very little influence over government policy but worse still, it seemed to have accelerated rather than reversed its declining vote share (Gundle 1996: 89). In 1976 the party therefore elected a new leader, Bettino Craxi, and within a few years he had fundamentally altered its strategic orientation. Instead of defining the PCI as the party's main competitor, Craxi now argued that the Socialists had to treat *both* the DC and the PCI as electoral threats. The PSI consequently began to construct a set of policies and an identity that would attract votes from both its rivals (Hine 1986: 110). After 1976 both the DC and the PCI were increasingly described in PSI literature as old parties, immersed in the compromise politics that were the hallmark of a weak executive and a fractious legislature. In contrast, the PSI claimed to offer a program of decisive government that would break with the traditions of compromise and enact radical reforms to modernize the ailing economy (Abse 1994: 211–2; Gundle 1996: 89–90). Lange (1986: 32–3) observed that Craxi's "rise to power had been partly built on his assertion that he was willing to make hard decisions (*decisionismo*) and to maintain the autonomy of the government's economic policy rather than always seeking intricate compromises with the Communist opposition."

The 1979 election saw little change in support for the PSI, which eventually joined the government in 1980 after six years in opposition. The June 1983 election, however, witnessed the DC vote drop by over 5 percentage points to less than 33 percent – its worst ever electoral performance – while the PSI vote rose to 11.4 percent and 73 seats. Craxi forcefully, and successfully, asserted his claim to be Prime Minister despite DC domination of the cabinet (Verzichelli and Cotta 2003: 465–7).

In January 1984 the government, unions, and employers were due to start negotiations on further revisions to the *scala mobile,* following on from the January 1983 pact. With unemployment a little higher than in January 1983 the government might well have been able to trade concessions on taxes and benefits for wage restraint. In addition the increase in the fragmentation of the legislature – the effective number of legislative parties rose from 3.4 to 4.0 – might also have been expected to push the government in the direction of a renewed social pact. On the other hand the new prime minister was highly critical of tripartism and the government wielded a significant and slightly increased majority in both houses of the legislature enabling it to pass legislation. With some factors pushing in the direction of pacts and others for legislation, the government did both. When its own far-reaching proposals for deep cuts in the *scala mobile* were rejected by the communist union confederation CGIL, though accepted by the other two confederations, Prime Minister Craxi quickly abandoned the idea of a pact and immediately resorted to legislation despite union criticism (Hine 1986: 112–3). No effective challenge to this policy was posed inside the legislature: many PSI deputies were loyal to their charismatic and successful leader and the DC did not want to undermine the government and risk another election after its poor showing only the previous summer (Gundle 1996: 91–2; Hine 1993: 206). Although Craxi's abandonment of social pacts was challenged by a national referendum initiated by the CGIL and the PCI, the electorate narrowly supported the government (Hine 1993: 154). Other poll evidence also indicated Craxi's abandonment of pacts had certainly not weakened his popularity nor that of his party and may even have strengthened them. In the 1987 national election the PSI boasted an all-time high vote share of 14.3 percent.

The governments of 1987–92 commanded comfortable majorities in both houses of the legislature and were dominated by the DC and the PSI, both of whom had seen their vote share increase in the 1987 election despite a continued rise in unemployment. Vote gains for the right as well as the majority status of government are often associated with a reduced willingness to offer pacts and an increased propensity to legislate. As we would expect, one of the governments formed in this period did propose legislation – on strikes in essential services in July 1988 – and secured its passage into law in May 1990. In June 1991 the government was weakened by the withdrawal of the Republican Party (PRI) and its 21 deputies and simultaneously transformed from a five-party connected coalition into a four-party unconnected coalition, increasing the likelihood of social pacts. Just a few months later the new cabinet offered a pact to the unions on wage indexation and the unions agreed in December 1991, in part because it preserved the status quo and postponed major decisions until the following year (Negrelli 2000: 93).

The reemergence of social pacts, 1992–93

In the wake of the April 1992 election the existing four-party coalition was resurrected but was now led by PSI deputy Amato. With the corruption scandal unfolding and plans for unpopular reforms, the government was compelled to search for allies outside the legislature to enhance its legitimacy. The economic crisis prompted the July 1992 tripartite agreement that abolished the *scala mobile* and froze wages for one year (Negrelli 2000: 93; Regini and Regalia 1997: 213–4). The government then proceeded to negotiate a far-reaching pension reform, which raised the retirement age and reduced the value of the final pension. In July 1993 the social partners signed another pact offer – the Ciampi Protocol – that confirmed the abolition of the *scala mobile* and also reorganized the structure of collective bargaining (Negrelli 2000: 95–9).

In the April 1992 election the main losers were the governing Christian Democrats, as their vote dropped below 30 percent, and the PCI, down almost 10 points to its lowest ever vote share while the Socialist vote fell by less than one point. The major gain was claimed by a conservative and regionalist party, the Northern League, increasing its vote share from just over one point in 1987 to 8.6 percent (55 seats) in 1992 (Donovan 1992: 174–5).

The vote and seat losses reduced the government's strength in both houses and therefore made pact offers more likely, in the same way that the increased government strength in 1987 had rendered pacts less likely (see also Baccaro and Lim 2007; Hellman 1993). In addition the fragmentation of the legislature increased significantly from 4.1 to 5.7 effective parties, the highest level in postwar Italian history. Consequently, the new Prime Minister Amato offered a social pact to the unions proposing the abolition of wage indexation. He advised the leaders of the union and employer organizations that unless they agreed he would abolish indexation by legislative action (Bufacchi and Burgess 2001: 75). He then informed the rest of the government and the opposition parties that if his legislation was blocked he would resign and call fresh elections. Within three days the main union confederations, the government, and the employers had signed the historic agreement to abolish the *scala mobile* (Bufacchi and Burgess 2001: 75; Daniels 1993: 190).

At first glance Amato's threat of legislation, normally the preserve of a strong, majority government of the right, appears to fly in the face of the governmental weakness that first led to the offer of a social pact. However, the factors that weakened the parties in the legislature and the government simultaneously strengthened the hands of the prime minister and the president. As Bufacchi and Burgess (2001: 69) observe, "Amato's weakness was also his strength. None of the coalition partners would want to do anything that might provoke a second election." Opinion polls during summer 1992 indicated that "new elections would see the Leagues and various reform lists make further inroads into the traditional parties ..." (Hellman 1993: 157). Electoral threats to the main parties continued into 1993. As the new caretaker Prime Minister Ciampi was assembling his cabinet in April 1993 following the Amato government's resignation, over 1,000 politicians including leading members of the PSI and DC, such as former Prime Ministers Craxi and Andreotti, were under investigation for corruption, further eroding the standing of these parties in opinion polls (Bufacchi and Burgess 2001: 120). These electoral threats weakened both governing and opposition parties in their dealings with Amato and Ciampi and allowed both prime ministers to pursue wage and pension pacts despite their critics.

Berlusconi's antagonism to pacts, 1994 and 2001–06

The two Berlusconi governments did not continue the series of social pacts. The first government was a right-center connected coalition that assumed office in May 1994. Two of its constituent parties, the Northern Leagues and the far-right MSI, recorded dramatic increases in votes and seats at the 1994 election while Berlusconi's new party Forza Italia became the third largest party in the legislature. Predictably the coalition displayed a strong predilection for legislation in preference to pacts. The second Berlusconi government (2001–06) was also a right-center connected coalition but Forza Italia now constituted the largest party in the legislature with a sizeable seat advantage of 42 over its nearest rival, the Democratic Left. Berlusconi was thus in a much stronger position than in 1994 to give vent to his hostility to social pacts.

According to the political economy hypothesis social pacts largely disappeared after 2000 because once Italy entered the EMU, pacts had served their purpose and were no longer required (Hancké and Rhodes 2005; Molina and Rhodes 2007b: 804, 806). A second, institutional hypothesis assumes pacts fell out of favor because Italy lacks the articulated bargaining structures required for effective concertation (Negrelli and Pulignano 2008: 64). Yet, the incidence of social pacts in Western Europe as a whole has not declined since the creation of EMU in 1998 (see Chapter 3). In Italy, for instance, the left-center government elected in 2006 signed a major tripartite pact on pension reform. Second, there is disagreement on the degree of articulation in Italian bargaining structures (Hancké and Herrmann 2007: 139–40) but either way, governments in other countries with degrees of bargaining coordination similar to Italy – notably Spain – have nonetheless offered social pacts (Calmfors *et al.* 2001: 73–4). Moreover, pacts were also present in Italy in the 1980s and early 1990s despite little variation over time in industrial relations institutions. The variables in our electoral model help illuminate the antipathy of the two Berlusconi governments to social pacts.

The 1994 election was marked by an unprecedented transformation of the party system: the dominant party of the postwar era, the DC, was dissolved just a few months prior to the election and three minor parties that had regularly participated in government, the Social Democrats, the Liberals, and the Republicans, split into numerous fragments (Leonardi and Alberti 2004: 117–8; Donovan 1994: 196–7). The PSI vote collapsed to just 2.2 percent, below the new 4-percent vote threshold, meaning the PSI was no longer represented in the legislature. Furthermore, one of the four parties that comprised the new government, Berlusconi's rightist Forza Italia (FI), had not even existed six months previously (Bufacchi and Burgess 2001: 182–4). In this exceptionally volatile election Forza Italia emerged as the party with the largest share of the vote – 21 percent – although it held fewer seats than the PDS and the Northern Leagues. Protracted negotiations resulted in a four-party connected, right-center coalition including two more right-wing parties, the Northern League and National Alliance (formerly the fascist MSI), whose seat totals had risen dramatically from 55 and 34 respectively to 117 and 109. The coalition was completed by the 27 seats of the Christian Democratic Center, a new party founded in January 1994 (Leonardi and Alberti 2004: 118).

The first Berlusconi government commanded a substantial majority in a more fragmented lower house with 58 percent of the seats (although it was two seats short of a majority in the upper house) and the policies of the right-center coalition reflected those of the dominant party, the conservative Forza Italia (Verzichelli and Cotta 2003: 451). Berlusconi himself was convinced he had an electoral mandate to implement the program set out in his manifesto through legislation (Pasquino 1996: 137–8). He was further encouraged by his party's showing in the June 1994 European elections, where it obtained 30.6 percent of the vote (Bufacchi and Burgess 2001: xvii). In June the government passed legislation easing restrictions on the use of part-time and fixed-term contracts and in September announced a package of tough spending cuts and pension reforms. Although some meetings took place with union leaders and employers over the summer, these represented no more than "a very loose kind of negotiation" and did not dissuade Berlusconi from pressing ahead with reforms through legislation (Ferrera and Jessoula 2007: 434). After a general strike in October and with a second strike threatened for December, Berlusconi was forced to rescind his legislative plans and enter talks with the unions. Just a few weeks later with his coalition in disarray following the withdrawal of the Northern League, he resigned (Bufacchi and Burgess 2001: 206–11).

The second Berlusconi government was in an even stronger position, with 59 percent of seats in the lower house and 56 percent in the upper house, following substantial vote gains. As before, the coalition was dominated by the three parties of the right, Forza Italia, National Alliance, and the Northern League and also included two small Christian Democratic parties, forming a surplus, connected coalition. In contrast to the 1994 government, the 2001 administration was unlikely to face effective opposition from its left and center critics in the upper house, a fact that would only increase its propensity to legislate rather than offer social pacts. At a conference shortly after the election one senior Forza Italia spokesperson declared that government policy was "legitimised by the people and therefore we did not need to search for the support of social partners" (Baglioni *et al.* 2008: 837). In October 2001, five months after assuming office, the government published a set of proposed labor law reforms that included a controversial proposal to reduce the degree of legal protection for workers unfairly dismissed. In December it issued a set of proposals to reform pensions by increasing the retirement age and transforming a defined-benefit scheme into a defined contribution scheme (Ferrera and Jessoula 2007: 443). As in 1994 the government threatened to enact these measures through legislation, and as before the unions responded with general strikes in December 2001 and April 2002. In July 2002 two of the three confederations finally reached agreement with the government and signed the Pact for Italy. The CGIL refused to sign and called another general strike in October 2002. Over the next three years the unions responded to their exclusion from pension discussions and from economic policymaking more generally with no less than six general strikes; the government, however, did not revert to social pacts (Kelly and Hamann 2009).

The temporary reemergence of social pacts, 1995–2000

Following the resignation of the first Berlusconi government in December 1994, the President appointed a new Prime Minister, Lamberto Dini, the former Finance Minister under Berlusconi and previously Director General of the Bank of Italy (Pasquino 1996). The Dini cabinet, like that of Carlo Ciampi, consisted primarily of independent "technocrats," who were not allied with any political party (Verzichelli and Cotta 2003: 455). The new government continued the reform agenda of Berlusconi but abandoned unilateralism and reverted to social pacts, opening talks with the unions on pensions and reaching agreement in June 1995. Shortly afterwards negotiations were opened on wage restraint, which, however, collapsed in January 1996, when the government resigned to make way for elections in April. The center-left "Olive Tree" alliance narrowly defeated Berlusconi's "Pole of Freedom" right-center coalition, governing Italy for two years under a four-party connected coalition headed by Christian Democrat Prime Minister Prodi. In 1998 this government was replaced by a seven-party connected coalition under a socialist prime minister until its defeat in 2001. Between 1996 and 1998 the government offered and signed four pacts with the unions and employers covering a wide range of issues: wages, job creation, training, investment in the South, and pensions.

The reemergence of pacts in 1995 cannot be attributed to a sharp and sudden deterioration in the economy in the aftermath of the first Berlusconi government: GDP growth was steady at around 2 percent throughout the 1990s, inflation was down to 2–3 percent over the same period and government borrowing continued to decline (Figure 7.2). Alternatively, it has been argued that as a "technical" government that lacked electoral or parliamentary legitimacy, the Dini administration (like the Ciampi government) was forced to secure legitimacy from the social partners for its potentially unpopular pension reforms (Bardi 2002: 61; Brown 1996).

Despite the absence of an electoral mandate, we argue that electoral and parliamentary competition played a critical role in the temporary reemergence of pacts. The Dini administration (January 1995–January 1996) was supported by a coalition of the Progressives' left alliance (Democratic Left, Greens, Communist Refoundation and others) as well as the main Christian Democrat party, the PPI, and the right-wing Northern League. Although this set of parties supported the government rather than comprising it, such broad and unconnected coalitions will typically be more favorable to pacts than legislation. In addition the vote gains for the Democratic Left and vote losses for the Christian Democrats also enhanced the likelihood of pacts. Thus, the government would therefore be expected to offer social pacts on unpopular reforms. Dini himself was anxious to avoid the industrial conflict associated with the exclusion of unions from discussion on pensions and made clear to the parties in parliament that failure to support his reforms would lead to his resignation and to fresh elections, a prospect that several parties were eager to avoid after their recent poor performances. Although the parties supporting Dini had narrow majorities in both houses of the legislature, the breadth of the coalition, ranging from the ex-communist PDS to the rightist Northern League, suggests this was a fragile and precarious foundation for government legislation. A pact on pensions was therefore offered to the unions and employers and the final agreement supported in both houses.

The left-center Olive Tree alliance government that assumed power after the April 1996 election was technically a minority administration holding 46 percent of seats, but with external support from the far-left Communist Refoundation its seat proportion rose to 51.4 percent. Dominated by the PDS and dependent on far-left support for its survival, the new government not surprisingly sought to reach agreement with the unions on further pension reforms and on wage increases and job creation in order to try and curb the growth in unemployment, then standing at 11.2 percent (Haddock 2002: 216). Following the change in Prime Minister in October 1998 the governing coalition was reconstructed, holding slightly more seats in the legislature but now comprising an unconnected coalition of seven political parties ranging from a small far-left party to an equally small center-right party, the UDR. Given its small majority and center-left party dominance and the apparent success of the 1996 and 1997 pacts, the government offered another social pact, covering wages, training, and investment, known as the Christmas Pact of December 1998.

Summing up the Italian case

Since the early 1980s Italy has displayed a complex cycle of decision making on labor market and welfare reforms, alternating between social pacts and legislation. Although most of the Italian pacts were in part responses to economic problems, the rise and fall of social pacts does not correspond neatly to trends in the main economic indicators. It does, however, correspond much more closely to fluctuations in electoral gains and losses for different party families. Pacts were repudiated by electorally successful connected coalition governments of the right, which used their parliamentary majorities to enact legislation and to exclude unions from involvement in policymaking. In contrast, center-left coalitions in Italy have tended to opt for pacts rather than legislation either because of recent vote losses (1992–96) or because they wielded small and precarious majorities (1996–98).

However, the Italian case shows that party family effects are complex and linked to party strategies for dealing with electoral competition. The center-left governments of 1983–92 made little use of pacts, in the belief that decisive legislative action was the most effective means for increasing their vote share. In contrast center-left governments in the 1990s acted on the assumption that union exclusion would be electorally damaging rather than beneficial. The impact of governmental strength is also complex. Although in general terms minority administrations are more likely to use pacts, and majority governments to legislate, most Italian governments since 1980 have held majorities in the lower house but many have still opted for social pacts (see Baccaro and Lim 2007).

Conclusion

The pattern of policy reform in Spain and Italy evinces some striking similarities. A relatively large number of social pact offers have been extended to unions in both countries, most of which have been accepted; the incidence of social pacts has fluctuated significantly over time; and the use of legislation and union exclusion has been comparatively rare. Although several government reforms and interventions have been triggered by either short-term or longer-run economic problems, the correlation between the patterns of social pact offers and the rhythms of the economy is weak. Developments in economic institutions might also seem to offer some insight into the patterns of social pacts because the level of bargaining coordination in Italian industrial relations increased through the 1990s, coincident with the reemergence of pacts. Yet, the limits of this explanation quickly become apparent given that the parallel reemergence of social pacts in Spain in the 1990s coincided with a decline in the level of bargaining coordination. Molina and Rhodes (2007a: 236) ascribe the government attempts to produce cross-class consensus through pacts to the existence of a "coordination deficit." While such a deficit may be present, this structural framework is not suited to explaining variation over time in governments' use of pacts and legislation to "resolve distributive conflict" (ibid.).

In turn, party competition, electoral pressures, and properties of governments offer more insight into the rise and fall of social pacts. Electorally successful majority governments in both countries made declining use of social pacts during the 1980s. Led by "modernizing" social democrats (González in Spain, Craxi in Italy) these strong governments found that the use of legislation in the face of union resistance to wage restraint or welfare reform did not create significant electoral problems. In the wake of these experiences governments relied less on unions in order to facilitate policy reform. It was the reemergence of electoral problems in conjunction with economic decline in the 1990s that was associated with the rediscovery of social pacts as the main governing parties lost votes and seats and government majorities were either significantly reduced or disappeared. Coupled with an increase in the effective number of parties in the legislature, this led governments to include trade unions in the process of policy formation and implementation through social pacts. In Italy, the meltdown of the party system in 1992–94 seriously eroded the legitimacy of all the main political parties and gave fresh impetus to the search for legitimacy outside the legislature. But issues of legitimacy were also present in Spain, albeit in a different form, where the conservative Popular Party, elected for the first time in 1996, had to convince voters it was a bona fide democratic party that had shaken off its Francoist past and could work effectively with the trade unions.

Two final points are worth noting concerning the role of electoral and governmental factors. Although our quantitative analysis suggested that leftist and center parties are more likely to offer pacts than their conservative rivals, the role of party family is more complex. For example, the Italian Socialists repudiated social pacts in the 1980s as they sought successfully to differentiate themselves from their Communist and Christian Democratic rivals, but embraced social pacts in the early 1990s as their popularity began to wane. Party family effects therefore are contingent on other factors. The second observation concerns the role of government strength. Much of the case study evidence is consistent with the quantitative finding that weaker governments are more likely to offer social pacts. However, government strength cannot always be accurately gauged by simply counting seat totals. The 1996–98 Olive Tree center-left coalition was technically a minority administration with just 46 percent of seats in the lower house but was able to rule as a majority government because of an agreement on policy and voting with Communist Refoundation despite the fact that the latter was not part of the executive. These observations, while confirming the broad patterns apparent in cross-national analysis, also point to the value of in-depth qualitative case studies.

8 Tripartism under duress in coordinated market economies

Germany and Austria

Germany and Austria are interesting cases in that no pacts (in Austria) or few pacts (in Germany) have surfaced. They share further similarities concerning their political-economic institutions and party systems: both are generally considered Coordinated Market Economies with fairly stable economies; they rank relatively high on the corporatism index with Germany positioned somewhat lower than its southern neighbor (Siaroff 1999); they have a conservative welfare state (Tálos 2004; Esping-Andersen 1990); and their party systems and governments have been dominated by two major parties, a Christian Democratic and a social democratic party. Moreover, in both countries, at least one of the two big parties was in office during the 1980–2006 period, though always in coalition (with the exception of 1980–83 in Austria). In addition, for both major parties in Germany and Austria "the building of a comprehensive welfare state was one of the most important policy goals" since the end of World War II (Busemeyer 2005: 571), and social spending was a major budget item in both countries – 26 percent of GDP in Austria in 2001 and 27.4 percent in Germany (Busemeyer 2005: 572).

Differences also exist, however: for instance, while Germany has been characterized as corporatist and as a "consensus" democracy (Carlin and Soskice 2009: 70), tripartism at the national level in Germany existed for only about a decade after 1967 during the Concerted Action (*Konzertierte Aktion*) (Leaman 2002: 142), and the links between the SPD and the union umbrella confederation DGB are less instutionalized than in Austria (Anderson and Meyer 2003).[1] In contrast, tripartism has been deeply engrained in Austrian policymaking structures since the late 1940s (Lewis 2002), granting "the trade unions a consultative role in all economic and social policy fields" (Blaschke *et al.* 2000: 81). Furthermore, extreme rightist parties have had little electoral success at the national level in Germany, but have recruited considerably more electoral support in Austria. Despite these differences, though, it is striking that in both cases near the turn of the century the tradition of union inclusion had been weakened or rejected for some important policy reforms, most notably, in the area of pensions but also for labor market policies.

Austria – and also Germany albeit to a more limited extent – thus present test cases for our argument. If the literature focusing on the economic pressures for producing pacts is correct in that pacts, or tripartism more generally, are widely preferred by governments facing the need for austerity policies, we should not witness a challenge to tripartism in countries where it has long been enshrined in the political structures. Instead, their encompassing wage bargaining structures and corporatist structures should favor tripartism over legislation. This is especially true during economic downturns and the build-up to the EMU; yet, neither of the two cases displays an increased presence of tripartism during those periods. In contrast, we draw attention to electoral dynamics, including popular perceptions of tripartism, to explain the shift away from tripartism and government reforms without union inclusion when the parties in government appear to consider this option a more viable electoral strategy. Thus, in both cases we look at variation within countries over time rather than contrasting the trajectories of pacts offers or legislation between them. The countries differ, however, in the way tripartism declined in the context of electoral dynamics.

Germany

The main issues of contention, much like in Austria, revolved around the reform of the social welfare system (especially pensions) rather than wages. In Germany, wages are legally exempt from government intervention due to *Tarifautonomie*, which guarantees the social partners, bargaining monopoly over wage setting. During the late 1970s and early 1980s, welfare retrenchment in Germany was "mild" (see Kitschelt 2001: 294) and reforms were implemented only infrequently. Apart from the legislative changes to social security (including pensions) in 1983, no major reform occurred until the pension changes in 1989. Reforms became more common during the 1990s following unification, mostly through legislation rather than tripartite negotiations. Unification increased the fiscal burden and extended the mounting problem load for the German economy to the pension system, health care, labor market policy, higher education, vocational training, industrial relations, and immigration policy (Kitschelt and Streeck 2004: 28; Streeck and Trampusch 2006; Wiesenthal 2004). To illustrate, unemployment had fallen below 5 percent just before unification but rose to over 9 percent by 1997, increasing the costs of unemployment benefits; and whereas inflation was low (apart from the early 1990s), the public deficit increased during the 1990s while real GDP growth declined from 5.7 percent in 1990 to 1.1 percent in 1993 and with few exceptions remained below 2 percent until 2006 (see Figure 8.1).

Reforms in the 1990s were primarily achieved through legislation rather than tripartite negotiations. As Dyson and Padgett (2006: 5; emphasis in the original) note, German "governments are faced with problems of managing the tensions and conflicts between *economic* and *electoral* incentives" when

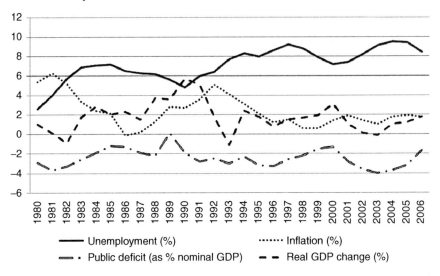

Figure 8.1 Main economic indicators, Germany, 1980–2006.
Source: OECD (June 2007; December 1999; December 1996).

engaging in economic adjustment, and successive governments have been unable to resolve this conflict as "[e]lectoral incentives are stacked against the welfare state" (Dyson and Padgett 2006: 8). That is, the public broadly supports both sound money and finance policies with near-balanced budgets and also employment protection and an expansive welfare state, which makes economic reform electorally risky. Since both major parties appeal to voters across classes, they gravitate towards the center, which makes it difficult to enact far-reaching reforms without risking punishment in elections (Kitschelt and Streeck 2004: 26). As governments take on the role of a broker in combining different interests concerning economic and policy reforms, one result has been "government by commission," a German variant of the social pact (Dyson and Padgett 2006: 5–7) where government-appointed commissions composed of experts in a particular area (and sometimes representatives of union and employer organizations) are charged with producing recommendations for policy reform. Furthermore, policy changes overall have been characterized by incrementalism and gradualism rather than radical reform (Seelaib-Kaiser 2003: 143), in part due to the complex system of negotiation necessitated by the federal system and the strong role of the upper house (Bundesrat), perhaps eliminating the need or desire for the government to engage in additional bargaining with unions and employers. In some ways, tripartite negotiations are thus substituted by negotiations with the opposition parties in the upper house and by government-appointed commissions. Thus, while tripartism has been infrequent, legislation is rarely unilateral, but instead subject to negotiations in other arenas and with other actors.

Industrial relations and economic context

The German economy is often featured as a paradigmatic case of a Coordinated Market Economy (e.g. Hall 2007; Hall and Soskice 2001b). Its industrial relations system is influenced by the bargaining autonomy of the social partners (*Tarifautonomie*), that is, the state is mandated to remain outside collective bargaining processes (Kitschelt and Streeck 2004: 6). This provision explains the absence of wage pacts. The "Modell Deutschland" developed during the postwar period of economic growth in West Germany and revolved around "labour market institutions facilitating sectoral and national wage-bargaining concertation, led by large companies, but compatible with the needs of most small and medium-sized enterprises" (Wiesenthal 2004: 44). The model produced tripartite consensus on economic policies to guide economic governance, resulting in social cohesion (Jeffrey and Paterson 2004: 60).

Germany's industrial relations are characterized by the existence of a dominant union confederation, the Deutsche Gewerkschaftsbund (DGB), which comprises approximately 80 percent of all union members. The metal workers' union IG Metall is the biggest of the DGB's eight industrial unions; other unions include the service sector union ver.di, formed in 2001. Collective bargaining coverage hovers around 80 percent; bargaining takes place at a sectoral level within regions. Unions face the encompassing sectoral employers' organizations, which are affiliated to the main national employers' organization BDA (Bundesvereinigung der Deutschen Arbeitgeberverbände). Union membership has steeply declined since the early 1990s, being almost halved from 12.4 million in 1991 to 6.8 million in 2005 (Behrens *et al.* 2007: 175), and the stability of the industrial relations system has been threatened by unification and employers' demands for more flexibility (see e.g. French 2000; Hassel 2007; Thelen 2001). Yet, overall, industrial relations have undergone few systemic changes.

Electoral and party systems

Since the creation of the Federal Republic of Germany in 1949, the German party system has been dominated by two major parties, the Social Democratic Party (SPD) and the Christian Democratic Union (CDU), which forms an electoral alliance and parliamentary party group (*Fraktion*) with its Bavarian sister party, the Christian Social Union (CSU). By the 1980s, the only other party that regularly gained seats in either house of parliament (the lower house, Bundestag, and the upper house, Bundesrat, representing the subnational Länder governments) was the small Free Democratic Party (FDP), a liberal party that wielded considerable political power as it regularly joined one of the larger parties in coalition governments. The Green Party first gained representation in the lower house in 1983, while the PDS (Party of Democratic Socialism) won seats starting with the 1990 "unification election." In 2005, the far-left Linkspartei (Left Party) also gained seats in the Bundestag (see Table 8.1). The Linke was constituted in 2007 after the PDS merged with the

Table 8.1 Election results, Germany (Bundestag), 1980–2005

	1980		1983		1987		1990		1994		1998		2002		2005	
	% votes	# seats (%seats)	% votes	# seats (%seats)	% votes	# seats (%seats)	% votes	# seats (%seats)	% votes	# seats (%seats)	% votes	# seats (%seats)	% votes	# seats (%seats)	% votes	# seats (%seats)
CDU/CSU	44.5	237 (45.7)	48.8	255 (49.0)	44.3	234 (45.1)	43.8	319 (48.2)	41.5	294 (43.8)	35.1	245 (36.6)	38.5	248 (41.1)	35.2	226 (36.8)
SPD	42.9	228 (43.9)	38.2	202 (38.9)	37.0	193 (37.2)	33.5	239 (36.1)	36.4	252 (37.5)	40.9	298 (44.5)	38.5	251 (41.6)	34.2	222 (36.2)
FDP	10.6	54 (10.4)	7.0	35 (6.7)	9.1	48 (9.3)	11.0	79 (11.9)	6.9	47 (7.0)	6.2	43 (6.4)	7.4	47 (7.8)	9.8	61 (9.9)
Greens/ Alliance 90	1.5	0 (0)	5.6	28 (5.4)	8.3	44 (8.5)	3.8	8 (1.2)	7.3	49 (7.3)	6.7	49 (7.0)	8.6	55 (9.1)	8.1	51 (8.3)
PDS/Linke							2.4	17 (2.6)	4.4	30 (4.5)	5.1	36 (5.4)	4.0	2 (0.3)	8.7	54 (8.8)
Others	0.5	0 (0)	0.4	0 (0)	1.3	0 (0)	5.5	0 (0)	3.5	0 (0)	6.0	0 (0)	3.0	0 (0)	4.0	0 (0)
Total	100	519 (100)	100	520 (100)	100	519 (100)	100	662 (100)	100	672 (100)	100	669 (100)	100	603 (100)	100	614 (100)

Source: See Appendix 1.

Note: % vote refers to the vote on the second ballot. CDU/CSU = Christlich Demokratische Union/Christlich Soziale Union (Christian Democratic Union/Christian Social Union); SPD = Sozialdemokratische Partei Deutschlands (Social Democratic Party of Germany); FDP = Freie Demokratische Partei Deutschlands (Free Democratic Party of Germany); Grüne/Allianz 90 = Greens/Alliance 90; PDS/Linke = Partei des Demokratischen Sozialismus (Party of Democratic Socialism) until 2007, then merged with WASG to form the Linke (Left Party).

small WASG (Election Alternative for Labor and Social Justice), a leftist splinter party of the SPD formed in opposition to the party's economic and social policies (Helms 2007: 224).

Germany's two-party dominant "restricted" party system (Smith 2003: 82) is a result of several factors, including the modified proportional representation system where half the seats in the Bundestag are decided by plurality vote in single-member districts. In addition, a party needs to reach at least 5 percent of the national vote or win three districts in the plurality ballot to gain seats through the proportional representation system. While this system has been characterized by its overall stability and the dominance of the two "core" parties, CDU and SPD, the entrance of new parties has rendered the system somewhat more fluid. This is reflected in the effective number of legislative parties, which has been relatively low and stable and stood between 2.2 and 2.5 from the late 1950s until 1983. Between 1983 and 2002, however, it ranged between 2.7 and 2.9 (Saalfeld 2003: 41; Saalfeld 2005: 217).

At the same time, the combined vote share of the two dominant parties declined from over 90 percent in the 1970s to just over 75 percent by 1998 and 2002 as new parties garnered support (Smith 2003: 83). In fact, Dalton (2003: 60) concludes that "Where once a stable basis of party competition seemed to determine electoral outcomes, the catchword for 2002 was the Weschelwähler [sic], or the changing voter." This is because voters' ties to social groups including class and religion have steadily eroded and affective ties between voters and parties have weakened; voters' electoral choices are thus increasingly driven by issues and candidates' campaign performance (Dalton 2003: 60). The percentage of West German voters reporting "very strong" or "strong" partisanship declined from 46 percent in 1980 to 37 percent in 2002, while the "no party; don't know" category increased from 19 percent in 1980 to 32 percent in 2002. Eastern voters who reported "no party; don't know" amounted to 45 percent in 2002, an increase of 8 percentage points compared to 1991 (Dalton 2003: 72). Electoral behavior in the new *Länder* in the eastern part of Germany is thus even more unstable since voters often lack the longstanding, traditional ties to political parties (Dalton 2003: 61). Whereas vote switching between elections was limited to 16 percent in the 1980 election, in the 1994 election almost one quarter (24 percent) of the electorate reported having switched their vote (Conradt 1996: 169; Scarrow 2002: 84).

Nonetheless, despite these changes in voting behavior, governments in Germany have a high propensity to finish out their legislative term and get reelected (Saalfeld 2003: 44), so much so that for half a century (1949–98) "no German federal government was completely replaced by the opposition as a direct result of elections" and near half of all governments incurred electoral gains in the next election (Saalfeld 2003: 78). However, losses for the main governing party have become more common in the post-1980 period (Saalfeld 2003: 78–9), coinciding with other changes in the party system, such as an increase in the number of parliamentary parties and a decline of the party members/electorate ratio from a peak of 4.7 percent in 1980 to 3.0 percent in 1998 (Scarrow 2002: 83).

Radical reforms are also relatively difficult to push through in Germany due to the role of the upper house, the Bundesrat. Germany is a federal state and it is in the Bundesrat that the interests of the *Länder* are represented at the national level. The Bundesrat is relatively powerful, possessing veto power for about half of all bills and suspensive veto power for all other bills (Lohmann *et al.* 1997: 426; Patzelt 1999: 61).[2] This existence of strong veto points, especially when combined with different parties dominating each house, has encouraged the German "negotiation" model of democracy, which places a premium on consensus-seeking (Dyson 2006: 111) in a system of cooperative federalism (Kitschelt and Streeck 2004: 27).

Reform through legislation: the Kohl era, 1982–98

The 1980 election returned the social-democratic/liberal coalition that had ruled since 1972, led by Chancellor Helmut Schmidt. Yet, differences between the coalition partners soon emerged, especially in the areas of economic and social policy as well as foreign policy. In addition, the SPD had become increasingly unpopular due to rising unemployment (2.6 percent in 1980 with a rising trend, see Figure 8.1) and was challenged by the new Green Party on issues of postmaterialism appealing to "new Left" citizens (Kaase 1983: 161). Despite the mounting discussions (and disagreements) concerning the economy, the SPD–FDP government attempted no major reforms during its two years in office (1980–82).

Chancellor Helmut Kohl came to office in 1982 not as the result of the SPD's declining electoral fortunes but due to the FDP's exit from the coalition based on policy disagreements with the SPD. Consequently, the SPD was left in a minority position and lost the resulting constructive vote of no-confidence, which simultaneously propelled Kohl into office as the new chancellor. Striving to enhance his government's legitimacy through new elections, Kohl then engineered a vote of confidence in the Bundestag the following year, which he lost as intended, leading to premature elections (Kaase 1983; Saalfeld 2003: 75–6). The election results reestablished the CDU/CSU–FDP coalition government, which had indicated a course of "change," or *Wende*, towards "less state, more market" (see Sturm 2007; Tálos 2004: 216). However, contrary to Kohl's slogan, few major reforms in labor market, social welfare, or wage policies were implemented. Streeck and Hassel (2004: 120) assert that absence of radical reform was due in part to the government's "fear of electoral retaliation," a fear that was borne out by Kohl's eventual loss to Schröder in 1998, and again by Schröder himself, whose reforms were met by an "unprecedented loss of government support in the opinion polls" (Streeck and Hassel 2004: 114, 119). Apart from confirming the position of the conservative-liberal coalition, the 1983 elections also ushered in the parliamentary presence of the Green Party, introducing new competition to the left of the SPD (see Table 8.1).

Some reforms were attempted, however. Between 1982 and 1984, the new government legislated cutbacks in the unemployment insurance program, active labor market policies, and social assistance (Leibfried and Obinger 2004: 209; Seelaib-Kaiser 2003: 149). These measures were facilitated by a change in public opinion, where the CDU/CSU was rated higher than its competitor parties in competency on all economic issues. Moreover, large proportions of the voters were willing to accept austerity measures in return for lower unemployment and economic recovery (Kaase 1983: 161). Given this support for cutbacks by the electorate, it comes as little surprise that the Kohl government refrained from tripartism after its first electoral victory: if voters backed reforms, the potential costs of negotiated adjustments could be avoided. Furthermore, the government enjoyed a solid majority in the Bundestag, which our cross-national analysis suggests is likely to reduce the odds of pact offers.

The 1987 election renewed the CDU/CSU–FDP coalition government, but both major parties (CDU and SPD) lost votes and seats while the FDP as well as the Greens recorded gains (see Table 8.1). Facing electoral decline, the CDU's reform attempts focused on the 1989 pension plan under the Minister for Social Affairs, Norbert Blüm. The "Blüm I" reform changed the wage indexation of pensions from gross to net income, increased the retirement age for women, the unemployed, and disabled people, and established deductions for early retirement (while also extending credit for child rearing from one to three years). Given the vote loss of the CDU in the federal election as well as in subsequent *Länder* elections, the party was keen to come to a consensus with the opposition SPD and both parties agreed not to make the overhaul of the pension system an issue for the 1990 election. Passed in late 1989 with a cross-party consensus in both houses of parliament, the reforms took effect in 1992 (Börsch-Supan and Wilke 2006: 575–7; Schulze and Jochem 2007: 676–82). The consensus was produced by "party strategies that referred to the imperatives of party competition" (Schulze and Jochem 2007: 682) rather than the institutional determinants of the veto power of the Bundesrat as the SPD did not hold the necessary majority in the upper house. The SPD was willing to support the pension reform in the middle of a recession, while the CDU was willing to make concessions to the SPD in order to keep the pension issue out of the 1990 election campaign (Schulze and Jochem 2007: 681–2).

The 1990 elections returned the CDU/CSU–FDP coalition back to government with just a small loss of votes for the CDU/CSU but a larger share of the seats, and also a 2-point gain for the FDP so that the governing coalition commanded 60 percent of the seats in the Bundestag (see Table 8.1). This first post-unification election contrasted the resounding victory of the governing coalition with the losses of the leftist opposition: the SPD lost 3.5 points compared to the 1987 election while the West German Greens failed to clear the 5 percent threshold.[3] Although the pressures of unification were particularly felt in social insurance, the immediate post-unification period witnessed few reforms and no pacts, contrary to our predictions, given that in cross-national comparison, parties further to the right are more likely to offer pacts if the vote gap increases. Legislation was initiated in 1993 concerning labor market programs and welfare (*EIRR* July 1993: 7; August 1993: 7–8; November 1993: 7), especially sick pay, old-age care, and unemployment compensation, the latter being a mounting concern in the face of unemployment rates reaching 7.7 percent (see Figure 8.1). However, the legislative proposals were for the most part vetoed in the Bundesrat (Clasen 2005: 69), where the government no longer commanded a majority.

Perhaps because of the absence of far-reaching reforms, the 1994 election again returned the Christian Democratic–Liberal coalition back to office, albeit with a reduced vote share (−2.3 percentage points) and 25 fewer seats for the CDU/CSU, the worst electoral result in their existence. The FDP suffered a vote loss of over 4 points and lost 32 seats, the party's worst performance since 1969 (see Statistisches Bundesamt 2005). In contrast, the SPD gained almost 3 percentage points compared to 1990. The election also established the far-left PDS as a serious and potentially permanent electoral competitor for the SPD, in effect dividing the left vote especially in Germany's new *Länder*, the stronghold of the PDS (Phillips 1995). At the same time, the PDS was not considered a potential coalition partner in the eyes of the other parties due to its extreme leftist leanings. The absence of a far left challenge to the SPD as a potential office-holding party helped strengthen the centrist tendencies among the Social Democrats. In sum, the governing parties were losing support as the economy was doing poorly while the far left and the Greens gained votes without, however, establishing themselves as potential office holders at the national level.

In this context of electoral shifts to the left and the consequent weaker parliamentary position of the government during a severe recession Kohl briefly revived tripartite neo-corporatism. He launched the Alliance for Jobs early in 1996 with the intention of combating rising unemployment (Bispinck and Schulten 2000: 190; Hassel 2001; Leaman 2002: 145), which had reached a new record high of 8.6 percent. The Alliance had first been proposed by the metal union's leader and the idea was then taken up by the government. Even though an agreement on part-time early retirement was reached, the Alliance was short-lived: the unions withdrew in April 1996 in protest over the government's plans on welfare retrenchment (Ebbinghaus and Hassel 2000: 50, 55) but continued to push for a fresh Alliance for Jobs (Leaman 2002: 145). In the meantime reforms such as cuts in sick pay were legislated. Lehmbruch (2003: 146) argues that this happened largely through pressure from the junior coalition partner, the FDP, which preferred concessions to business demands over negotiations with organized labor. With the decline in the Christian Democrats' electoral support it became more important for Kohl to appease the FDP in order to preserve the coalition government than to appease social groups such as organized labor. The sick pay cuts demonstrated to the FDP supporters that it remained the "indispensible guardian of free-market principles" (Lehmbruch 2003: 147). As Lehmbruch (2003: 147) concludes, "Competitive party politics, guided by a majoritarian logic, thus won the upper hand over the corporatist strategy of adjusting the welfare state."

The main area of reform at the end of the Kohl era concerned the social welfare system, in particular pensions. The crisis of the pension system was aggravated by the pressures of unification and the soaring unemployment rates especially in the east, worsening the contributor/recipient ratio. The government initiated a pension reform law in 1997 (Blüm II), based on recommendations of the Blüm Commission (including experts and politicians) set up in 1996. Once in the Bundestag, the bill was approved by the CDU/CSU deputies, while the SPD opposed and the PDS abstained. Perhaps most interestingly, the representatives of the coalition partner FDP were absent during the vote, together with the Green parliamentarians, thus making it possible for the bill to pass without the support of the junior coalition partner and to be moved on to the Bundesrat, where it was approved after a mediation process. In contrast to Blüm I, cross-party consensus was markedly absent not just with respect to the opposition SPD, which dominated the upper house, but also the governing FDP. Thus, again, "party competition" as well as intra-governmental dynamics produced the final reform plan (Schulze and Jochem 2007: 685–6) while "the Kohl government broke with the consensual pattern in pension policy that had characterized the Bonn Republic" (Leibfried and Obinger 2004: 211). The final bill reduced wage replacement rates, set a higher qualifying age, and defined tighter eligibility rules for full benefits. These cuts were highly unpopular with the electorate: in 1990 over one-third of survey respondents thought that a CDU government would best secure pensions, but by 1998 less than half (15.5 percent) thought so (Rohrschneider and Wolf 2004: 35). The SPD's candidate for chancellor, Gerhard Schröder, had promised to revoke the measures if elected. In the September 1998 election the CDU "paid a heavy price" for the pension reform and "lost control of the government" to the Social Democrats (Kitschelt 2001: 295; see also Helms 2004: 144; Schludi 2005: 143–4).

Reform through legislation via commission: the Schröder governments, 1998–2005

The 1998 election marked the first time in postwar German history that a complete turnover in government occurred; that is, none of the governing parties was returned to office as the SPD formed a coalition with the Green Party, which joined the national executive for the first time. Compared to the 1994 election, the SPD gained over 3 million additional votes, increased its vote share by 4.5 points to 40.9 percent, and occupied an additional 46 seats in the Bundestag (Statistisches Bundesamt 2005). As the cross-national analysis indicates (see Chapter 4), pacts are more likely when a new government takes office while having gained votes and furthermore, leftist governments tend to prefer pacts. At the same time, the new government boasted a relatively comfortable majority of 345 seats (a lead of 21 over the opposition), affording Schröder room for legislation if necessary. In fact, a combination of pact offers and legislation was the pattern that became evident in the way that reforms were introduced.

Although Schröder had promised to reverse Kohl's pension reforms, and did so for the most part, he also continued the path of welfare reform begun under Kohl. The first indication was presented by the April 1999 introduction of social insurance contributions payable by workers in the low-wage sector (Streeck and Trampusch 2006: 67). Soon after, in June 1999, Labor Minister Walter Riester announced a "major overhaul of the pension system" including a mandatory private pension, which became known as the "Riester Rente" (Streeck and Trampusch 2006: 67), and in the same yerar "no more than 18 percent of the voters regarded the SPD as the most credible party on pension policy" (Streeck and Trampusch 2006: 68). The DGB as well as the Association of German Pension Providers (VDR) opposed this mandatory third pillar of the pension system, which indicated a transformation of the fundamentals of the existing PAYG (pay-as-you-go) system. They forced the government into concessions (see Anderson and Meyer 2003), but the pension reform was enacted in 2001. Similarly, the new government suspended some of the health care reforms enacted by its predecessor. Subsequent health care reform bills were stalled by the opposition in the Bundesrat accompanied by "a large-scale campaign involving all the major actors in the health sector: doctors' associations, the pharmaceutical industries, and the health insurance funds, not to mention the voters" (Streeck and Trampusch 2006: 73–4). Chancellor Kohl then requested that all further health reforms be postponed until the next legislative period in an attempt to prevent potential voter backlash (Hartmann 2003: 276).

The new government also intervened in labor market policies and industrial relations by adopting a reform program to address the level of unemployment, which was falling from its 1997 peak but was still close to 8 percent. As we might expect from a leftist coalition, in an attempt to obtain union acquiescence for his policies, Chancellor Schröder offered a pact and revived the tripartite Alliance for Jobs (*Bündnis für Arbeit*) (Menz 2006: 84). First convening in December 1998, the Alliance was deadlocked almost from the outset and achieved very little in terms of actual reforms (Streeck and Trampusch 2006: 69; see also Dyson 2006). Padgett (2003: 141) concludes that the Alliance primarily had a symbolic function and provided a consensual environment for the government's tax and pension reforms while concessions to the unions included the tightening of some labor market regulations. Overall, the Alliance can be considered a failed effort at reviving tripartite concertation and represented the last government attempt to pursue reforms through negotiations with unions and employers.

With increasing pressures on the welfare state and rising unemployment, the government then took decisive action to reform through legislation. This shift was facilitated by the SPD's break with the unions after the collapse of the Alliance. Schröder reacted by concentrating on negotiations with the CDU instead, which was necessitated by the CDU's strong position in the upper house, and he declared that "from now on the government would be legislating the necessary reforms on its own" (Kitschelt and Streeck 2004: 29–30). This new approach was also facilitated by the Greens' shift to the right in the 1990s, as they began to advocate a lean state (Menz 2006: 85–6). Similar programmatic goals held by the SPD and the Greens, with both parties moving in the direction of the main competitor, the CDU/CSU, thus promoted legislative action rather than pacts.

However, the precursor to legislative reforms was the establishment of a commission of experts headed by Peter Hartz, personnel manager at VW (the Volkswagen company), tellingly named the Hartz Commission. It was appointed in February 2002 and charged to report on "modern services for the labor market" six months later. Hartz was authorized to select the members of the commission and had an important role in defining its agenda (Dyson 2006: 120). The Hartz Commission thus "represented a break with the tripartite philosophy of Bündnis für Arbeit [Alliance for Work] in that its 21 members included no more than two trade union representatives and only one official of a small-firm business association" (Streeck and Trampusch 2006: 70; see also Kemmerling and Bruttel 2006: 91). Some trade union "modernizers" were invited but official union representation from the umbrella organization DGB or the leadership of the largest unions, IG Metall and ver.di, was precluded, thus weakening the existing "tripartite principle in labour market administration" (Dyson 2006: 121). The official Hartz report was delivered on August 16, shortly before the September 2002 election, and reinforced Schröder's image as a "man of action" in an attempt to boost SPD standing in the opinion polls.[4]

The most important issue in the 2002 election campaign was unemployment, identified as such by 80 percent of respondents in a national poll. In the election month of September 2002, 36 percent of the electorate judged the Christian Democrats to possess the highest competency in labor market policy compared to 29 percent for the SPD (Helms 2004: 145). These ratings explain why Schröder was seeking decisive action to demonstrate his ability to deal with the crisis, and both his opposition to the U.S. led war in Iraq and the government's quick response to severe flooding in large areas of Germany during the summer boosted his popularity (Helms 2004: 145; Pulzer 2003). Nevertheless, the SPD vote share fell by 2.4 percentage points and it lost 47 seats placing it level with the CDU/CSU, which had gained 3.4 points to reach 38.5 percent. The SPD, however, nonetheless attained a three-seat advantage over its conservative competitor (251 compared to 248), and renewed its governing coalition with the Greens resulting in a slender majority of nine seats for the coalition.[5] The Greens had gained both votes and seats (1.9 percent and eight seats) compared to the 1998 election but the PDS had failed to clear the 5-percent hurdle and held just two seats (see Table 8.1). The rise in support for the Green Party has been explained as tactical voting by SPD supporters who desired a strong showing for the Greens to ensure a renewal of the Red–Green coalition (Helms 2004: 146). However, the opposition also won a *Land* election in Lower Saxony, resulting in the loss of the governing parties' majority in the Bundesrat (Streeck and Trampusch 2006: 71), effectively rendering the position of the government more fragile but still allowing for adjustment through legislation as the Christian Democrats were inclined to support welfare cuts.

Following the 2002 election and with the immediate threat of electoral backlash avoided, several health care reform Acts were passed (Streeck and Trampusch 2006: 73–4). While our cross-national comparison evinces that left governments that are weak and have lost votes are more likely to offer pacts, the case of the Red–Green coalition in Germany defies these findings as the SPD–Greens continued to pursue legislation based on commission recommendations rather than tripartism. The government's commitment to reform and the failed attempts at tripartism during the previous legislative period reinforced Schröder's policy course of legislation in conjunction with commissions, especially given the Christian Democrats' strong position in the upper house. For example, the Rürup Commission was established in late fall of 2002 and was charged with developing proposals to improve the sustainability of the social insurance systems. The commission's proposals, presented in August 2003, further challenged the fundamentals of the German PAYG pension system, and were put into law in spring 2004 (Börsch-Supan and Wilke 2006: 577). In 2003 Schröder announced the Agenda 2010, a program resulting from the recommendations of the Hartz Commission and aimed at rendering the German economy more flexible and competitive through reforms in pensions, health care, unemployment insurance, and taxation (Streeck and Trampusch 2006: 71). The first rounds of reforms (known as Hartz I and Hartz II) came into effect in early 2003 and included, for example, a provision to make it more difficult for job seekers to reject employment offers. Parts of Agenda 2010 were embodied in Hartz III and IV, which were to be implemented by 2006, resulting in less employment protection for workers in small firms, a shorter period of unemployment benefits coverage, and an amalgamation of unemployment assistance and social assistance (Streeck and Trampusch 2006: 70–1).

The electorate's reaction to the government's retrenchment policies soon became evident. Streeck and Trampusch (2006: 72) conclude that Agenda 2010 "scared the electorate and made it even more volatile. It caused devastating defeats for the SPD in state elections" (e.g. in Bavaria in 2003 and in Hamburg in 2004). Padgett (2005: 248) similarly points to an "electoral backlash against Agenda 2010 and the Hartz IV labour market reform" while Helms (2007: 223–4) observes that the SPD's unpopularity increased when it seemed that the 2002 campaign had been run on false promises. As a consequence, the SPD lost votes, seats, and office in *Länder* elections the following years, prompting the government to call for early elections in 2005, one year ahead of the regular election cycle. Unemployment had become the most pressing issue in the eyes of 85 percent of the voters. Interestingly, the CDU/CSU enjoyed considerably higher credibility on labor market policies than the SPD with 41 percent of the electorate judging the Christian Democrats to be best qualified for job creation, roughly twice as many as trusted the SPD (21 percent). Both parties were considered equally qualified in other areas, such as pensions, taxes, and health (Helms 2007: 224–5). In the 2005 election, the SPD lost votes to the Left Party while the CDU/CSU ceded votes to the FDP as conservative voters switched to the liberal party in an effort to avoid a grand coalition (Helms 2007: 226).

Yet, at the same time, Padgett (2005: 254) claims that the pressures on the German economy also seemed to have led to a change in voters' evaluation of the need or desirability of welfare reforms (see also Pico 2009). Public opinion shifted from an "exceptionally strong resistance to welfare retrenchment" to a more tolerant stance evident since 2000 and becoming "more pronounced in 2003–04, coinciding with the politicisation of the debate over the Hartz IV reform package" (Padgett 2005: 256). Furthermore, "*General* support for the government's reform course increased sharply from 35 percent to 46 percent in the first half of 2004. Increases in backing for retrenchment in *specific* areas of welfare are more modest" (Padgett 2005: 256; emphasis in the original; see Roller 1999 for earlier data). It is perhaps this reluctance to accept specific cutbacks that accounts for the electoral backlash against Agenda 2010 and Hartz IV. Even though 50 percent of the German adult population agreed in 2004 that the social insurance systems faced "significant problems" and another 44 percent believed they were "about to collapse," 50 percent were unwilling to retire later, 80 percent thought it was unnecessary to lower pensions, and 68 percent deemed it unnecessary for employees to pay higher contributions; 69 percent believed it was not necessary to cut health benefits, while 80 percent disagreed with gradually increasing the retirement age to 67 years (Streeck and Trampusch 2006: 78). Thus, while German voters appear to have developed a diffuse awareness of the general need to reform the welfare state, they were nonetheless unwilling to support policies that cut their benefits. These contradictions might help explain the simultaneous existence of the widening acceptance of retrenchment policies with electoral retributions for the party implementing reforms.

Summing up the German case

The analysis of the reform trajectory in Germany reveals two major points. First, the continuity in the preference for legislation over tripartism for both SPD and CDU-led governments is striking. Since 1980, party family appears to have made little difference in the governments' pursuit of welfare changes (Leibfried and Obinger 2004: 216). This is perhaps because both the SPD and the CDU/CSU "could take credit for crafting and extending the comprehensive welfare state" (Kitschelt 2004: 132), or because Germany exhibits a very weak pattern of partisan cleavage, meaning that "the relationship between CDU/CSU and SPD partisanship and preferences on income equality and welfare benefits is tenuous" (Padgett 2005: 268). Both major parties are cross-class catch-all parties that are in principle committed to the welfare state and depend on voters that are by and large averse to welfare cutbacks, and both points help explain the relative policy continuity. Based on our findings for other countries, we would not have expected pacts from majority governments dominated by a party of the right (CDU). While the SPD made an attempt to include unions once it was in office as we would expect for a party of the left with a parliamentary majority, it resorted to legislation when the Alliance for Jobs failed.

This leads to the second noteworthy point. It is equally striking that the absence of tripartism has not prevented negotiated or consensual reforms by other means, for instance with the opposition party or through the reports of government-appointed commissions. Dyson (2006: 110) observes that commissions were used to increase the legitimacy of the government in the face of enhanced electoral volatility. Furthermore, the strong role of the Bundesrat means that oftentimes policy reforms have to be negotiated with the opposition party rather than the social partners. While unions were traditionally more involved in policy making, especially with regards to labor market policies but also in the administration of the pension system, appointed commissions in some ways replaced them and were used to add "objectivity" to reform measures that aided the government in pursuing adjustment without negotiations with unions.

As a result of the patterns of party competition and the institutional mechanisms for policy reforms, such as the need to gain Bundesrat approval, radical changes have overall been rare. Instead, policy reforms have been gradual and incremental (Seelaib-Kaiser 2003: 143) in the face of a mounting problem load and constrained by the institutional environment in which German reform policies are negotiated even when attempting reform through tripartism (see also Hassel 2001). These constraints affect adjustment both through legislation and social pacts.

Austria

Austria has consistently ranked as one of the most corporatist countries in Western Europe. Yet, pacts have been conspicuously absent from Austrian politics since 1980. The political economy approach proposes that Austria's economy was not in need of pacts due to its encompassing corporatist bargaining institutions, which were able to provide wage adjustments or other policy measures without the need for formal pacts (Hassel 2006). Similarly, unions' regular consultative role in the policy-making process on economic and social policies rendered social pacts outside the regular institutionalized corporatist bargaining and legislative processes unnecessary. While pacts might thus not have been expected, union input into the policy-making process through regularized channels *was*. Nonetheless, after the 1999 election, the rightist governing coalition comprising the Christian Democratic Austrian People's Party (ÖVP) and the right-wing Austrian Freedom Party (FPÖ) pushed for welfare policy reforms unilaterally without consultation with the social partners and against union opposition, thus breaking with long-standing traditions of Austrian politics. Furthermore, the same government sought to dismantle existing corporatist practices and institutions and to weaken the institutionalized role of the social partners. Why was the government not interested in continuing to negotiate contentious reforms through corporatist procedures and institutions? This is particularly intriguing since tripartism had been upheld (though occasionally questioned) during the economic crisis of the early 1990s, but was undermined when the recession was less deep a decade later. We are thus interested in explaining change in governments' preferred policy-making strategy over time. We seek the answer by looking at changing electoral preferences, where voters became critical of tripartism. This enabled the extreme-right, anti-system FPÖ to make considerable inroads into voters previously supporting the major catch-all parties and to secure a strong position on the executive as a coalition partner.

Industrial relations institutions and economic context

Throughout the postwar period, both business associations and trade unions have been "part of the political decision-making structure" in Austrian corporatism, or social partnership (Tálos 1996: 103; see also Tomandl and Fuerboeck 1986). Labor is organized in a single confederation, the Österreichische Gewerkschaftsbund (ÖGB) and in the Federal Chamber of Labor, making it "exceptional in its centralization and unity" (Blaschke 2006: 150). Business is primarily represented by the Federal Chamber of Business (BWK), holding a legal monopoly of business representation (Tálos 1996: 105). Economic interest representation is thus both highly concentrated and centralized. The Austrian concept of "social partnership" is based on a "dense network of interactions" between political parties, the government, bureaucracy, and "highly monopolised, centralised, and politically privileged interest organisations" while sectoral wage bargaining is centrally coordinated (Kittel 2000: 109). Strikes have been rare in this system of interest moderation that puts the interests of the economy ahead of particularistic organizational interests and have occasionally been confined to single events per year – such as a "token strike of the employees in distributive trades" in 1981 (Tomandl and Fuerboeck 1986: 53; see also Blaschke *et al.* 2000).

At the same time, the interest organizations are closely linked to the two major parties: the ÖGB has strong ties to the SPÖ (Social Democratic Party; Socialist Party prior to 1991) and also contains informal factions linked to the ÖVP, which in turn is also tightly connected to the business chambers (see Blaschke *et al.* 2000: 82). In fact, in 1973, over half of all members of parliament were representatives of these interest associations (Tálos 1996: 106–8; see also Kittel 2000: 112). Corporatist interest associations, including labor and business, are "a part of the political decision-making structure" (Tálos 1996: 103). The policy-making influence of unions and business associations is high as "[s]ocial partnership negotiations settle all the decisive questions of a multitude of economic and social welfare laws before the bills even reach parliament," and the associations are further involved in formulating bills as they move through parliamentary procedure (Tálos 1996: 113).[6] Interest associations are particularly involved with the setting of incomes policy, some macroeconomic issues, and social welfare policy (Tálos 1996: 114–7). As Pelinka (2002: 326) summarizes, "Corporatism dominated all economic matters, including most aspects of social policy" with high involvement of the social partners (Tomandl and Fuerboeck 1986: 12).

However, the stability of Austrian corporatism has been the subject of discussion since the mid-1980s as the system "increasingly lost its ability to mobilize political loyalties within its traditional framework" (Pelinka 2002: 323; see also Gerlich *et al.* 1988; Kittel and Gröger 1997; Tálos 2005). Social partnership was threatened by declining union strength with union density decreasing from 60 percent in the 1950s to 52 percent in 1980 and 34 percent in 2003 (Blaschke 2006: 151), but also by economic challenges. The corporatist system was also weakened because the party system became more fragmented and competitive (Blaschke *et al.* 2000: 82), the role of parliament as a political actor was strengthened from a "rather irrelevant institution" during most of the postwar era to a "major political arena" by the late 1980s (Müller 1992: 105), and the state claimed a stronger role in policymaking, for example in issuing reforms on vocational training (1992–93) and working time (1995–97) (see Kittel 2000).[7] While criticisms of the corporatist system were signaled by the growing support for the smaller, anti-establishment "protest parties" (especially the FPÖ and the Greens), the two major parties responded by attempting adjustment within and through the system, rather than by dismantling it (Scott 1987) and corporatism overall proved resilient. For example, when the governing SPÖ–ÖVP coalition collapsed in 1995 over the debate on the austerity package (Sparpaket II), adopted to meet the EMU's fiscal requirements, the social partners assumed the role of a "preeminent arbiter" and were highly rated in opinion polls. In a 1995 poll on trustworthiness, the ÖGB ranked second, a strong position compared to the government, which ranked ninth, and political parties, ranked eleventh (Heinisch 2000: 91–2). Thus, Heinisch (2000: 67) concludes that for the 1990s, Austrian corporatism went through "a process of skilful adaptation" and was able "to strengthen its position relative to the 1980s."

From a different perspective, Schulze and Schludi (2007: 566) address the weakening influence of the social partners by pointing to the declining share of trade union functionaries represented in the Nationalrat (the lower house of parliament): For the SPÖ parliamentary party, this share declined by over half between 1987 and 2000, while the ÖVP had next to no trade union representation left in its ranks. By the mid-1990s, ties between the interest organizations and the parties had become looser, and the corporatist system began to encounter more criticism, while the role of parliament increased as it was less willing to automatically approve legislation previously agreed on with the interest associations (Tálos 1996: 117–8). This debate coincided with changes in the Austrian party system, as the next section discusses.

Tripartism was thus deeply rooted in Austrian policy making despite the fact that it was somewhat weakened and modified during the 1990s. This perhaps rendered social pacts unnecessary to reform welfare, labor market, and wage policies since negotiations were embedded in the routine policy-making process. However, it is all the more surprising that the government after 2000 actively sought to abandon corporatist policy making and instead produced legislation on welfare reforms without tripartite consultation.

Electoral and party systems in Austria

Austria employs a proportional representation electoral system resulting in a party system distinguished by a "remarkable degree of stability and concentration" until the mid-1980s (Müller 2003: 86). During the postwar period, the combined vote share of the two major parties – the SPÖ and the ÖVP – was extremely high and hovered around 95 percent but plummeted by 7.6 points to 85.8 percent in 1986 and then steadily declined to a low of 60 percent in 1995 (Müller 1996: 91; Table 8.2). The stability of the party system was shaken when the Green Party entered parliament in 1986, followed by the Liberal Forum in 1993, and perhaps most importantly by the growing electoral popularity of the far-right FPÖ, which increased its vote share from 5 percent (and 12 seats in the legislature) in 1983 to 26.9 percent of the vote and 52 seats (out of a total of 183) in 1994 (Müller 2003: 86–9; Table 8.2). The rise of the FPÖ coincided with a reform of the electoral law introducing a 4-percent threshold to prevent further fragmentation of the party system (see Müller 1996: 68–71; Ulram and Müller 1995: 13). The main political parties commanded the government either alone or in coalition with each other between 1947 and 2000 with the brief interlude of 1983–87, when the FPÖ joined the SPÖ to form the executive (Luther 2000: 29).[8] Again, in 2000 the Freedom Party was designated the ÖVP's new coalition partner, but this time with a much higher vote and seat share than in the mid-1980s. Mean aggregate electoral volatility increased substantially from 2.7 percent in the 1970s to 21.1 percent for the 2000–04 period (Gallagher *et al.* 2006: 294).

Simultaneously, Austria's traditionally high level of party membership (measured as a proportion of the electorate) shrank from near 28 percent in 1956 to just over 17 percent in 1994. Voter turnout had decreased from 92.2 percent in 1979 to 81.9 percent in 1994, while the proportion of floating voters almost tripled (from 7 to 19 percent) and the percentage

Table 8.2 Election results, Austria (Nationalrat), 1979–2006

| | 1979 | | 1983 | | 1986 | | 1990 | | 1994 | | 1995 | | 1999 | | 2002 | | 2006 | |
	% vote	# seats (%seats)	% vote	# seats (%seats)	% vote	# seats (%seats)	% vote	# seats (%seats)	% vote	# seats (%seats)	% vote	# seats (%seats)	% vote	# seats (%seats)	% vote	# seats (%seats)	% vote	# seats (%seats)
ÖVP	41.9	77 (42.1)	43.2	81 (44.3)	41.3	77 (42.1)	32.1	60 (32.8)	27.7	52 (28.4)	28.3	53 (29.0)	26.9	52 (28.4)	42.3	79 (43.2)	34.3	66 (36.1)
SPÖ	51.0	95 (51.9)	47.7	90 (49.2)	43.1	80 (43.7)	42.8	80 (43.7)	34.9	65 (35.5)	38.1	71 (38.8)	33.2	65 (35.5)	36.5	69 (37.7)	35.3	68 (37.2)
FPÖ	6.6	11 (6.0)	5.0	12 (6.6)	9.7	18 (9.8)	16.6	33 (18.0)	22.5	42 (23.0)	21.9	40 (21.9)	26.9	52 (28.4)	10.0	18 (9.8)	11.0	21 (11.5)
Grüne			1.9	0 (0.0)	4.8	8 (4.4)	4.8	10 (5.5)	7.3	13 (7.1)	4.8	9 (4.9)	7.4	14 (7.7)	9.5	17 (9.3)	11.1	21 (11.5)
LIF									6.0	11 (6.0)	5.5	10 (5.5)	3.7	0 (0.0)	1.0	0 (0.0)	0.0	0 (0.0)
KPÖ	1.0	0 (0.0)	0.7	0 (0.0)	0.7	0 (0.0)	0.5	0 (0.0)	0.5	0 (0.0)	0.3	0 (0.0)	0.5	0 (0.0)	0.6	0 (0.0)	1.1	0 (0.0)
BZÖ																	4.1	7 (3.8)
Others	0.5	0 (0.0)	1.5	0 (0.0)	0.4	0 (0.0)	3.2	0 (0.0)	3.2	0 (0.0)	1.1	0 (0.0)	1.4	0 (0.0)	0.1	0 (0.0)	3.1	0 (0.0)
Total	100	183 (100)	100	183 (100)	100	183 (100)	100	183 (100)	100	183 (100)	100	183 (100)	100	183 (100)	100	183 (100)	100	183 (100)

Source: See Appendix 1.

Note: ÖVP = Österreichische Volkspartei (Austrian People's Party); SPÖ = Sozialdemokratische Partei Österreichs (Social Democratic Party of Austria); FPÖ = Freiheitliche Partei Österreichs (Freedom Party of Austria); Grüne = Die Grüne Alternative (Greens – The Green Alternative); LIF = Liberales Forum (Liberal Forum); KPÖ = Kommunistische Partei Österreichs (Communist Party of Austria); BZÖ = Bündnis Zukunft Österreich – Liste Jörg Haider (Alliance for the Future of Austria – List Jörg Haider).

of "late deciders" doubled (from 9 to 18 percent) during the same time period (Müller 1996: 81; 75).

The FPÖ succeeded in consolidating most of its 1994 gains in the 1995 election – perhaps because Austria's system of social partnership "had served the country well but was beginning to look like political archaeology – unsuited to the challenges of a new age" (Sully 1996: 634). Nevertheless, tripartism persisted until the FPÖ joined the government in 2000.[9] Only then did the governing parties reject the tripartite corporatist structures and opt for legislation without prior negotiations to pass major policy reforms, especially in the area of pensions. While the system had been questioned previously, it was the rising power of the Freedom Party that led to a drastic change in the policy-making process.

Reforms through tripartism in a stable party system, 1980–2000

The general election of 1983 signaled the end of the "Kreisky Era," named after Bruno Kreisky, SPÖ Chancellor (1970–83), and also signaled the beginning of the end of the dominance of the SPÖ and ÖVP. This trend became more visible in the 1986 election, when the Greens entered the legislature and the FPÖ gained both votes and seats (see Table 8.2). The Freedom Party joined the SPÖ in the executive in the 1983 "Small Coalition" (Pelinka 2002: 321), which broke up when the SPÖ called an early election. It did so in response to the growing influence within the FPÖ of its far-right nationalist wing under Jörg Haider at the expense of its liberal wing (Scott 1987). The ensuing election resulted in vote and seat losses for both major parties, reflecting the rising electoral fortunes of the FPÖ and the Greens, and led to 14 years of a "Grand Coalition" between the SPÖ and ÖVP (1986–99) (Pelinka 2002: 321).

Since the 1980s, pension reform featured as a major issue as budget deficits began to grow. Schulze and Schludi (2007: 571–3) list eight pension reforms or reform attempts between 1984 and 2000, most of which were passed with the agreement of the unions and were relatively minor in scope. The ÖVP and SPÖ both faced electoral competition primarily from the right while also competing with each other to lead the coalition government. In addition the SPÖ still enjoyed close relations with the country's strong trade union movement. Together, these factors meant that the leaders of the major parties "feared electoral punishment from their core constituencies" if they enacted major pension reforms (Schulze and Schludi 2007: 556).

To illustrate, the increase in the budget deficit, from 2 percent in 1992 to almost 5 percent in 1995 (see Figure 8.2), prompted calls for pension reforms by the ÖVP–SPÖ government. After the coalition collapsed over the budget and an election was called for 1995, it was clear that voters' interests were crucially centered on pensions (Plasser and Ulram 1996: 15, 38). Campaigning on a platform of safe pensions, Chancellor Vranitsky and the SPÖ were the clear winners of the election with a vote gain of 3.2 percentage points and six additional seats, compared to a vote gain of less than one point and just one additional seat for the ÖVP. The coalition was renewed and began the process of pension reform. However, the ÖGB threatened to call a strike and union members in parliament warned they might break party discipline and vote against the Bill. In the end, the Bill submitted by Chancellor Vranitzky was watered down, reflecting concessions to the unions (Schulze and Schludi 2007: 580–1). In protest over the unions' capacity to influence policy, several government ministers resigned, signaling their criticism of Austrian corporatism. As Schulze and Schludi (2007: 581) conclude, it was the electoral pressures and the fear of the governing parties to abandon their core constituencies that led to the government's willingness to give in to union pressure and limit the amount of pension reform, thereby affirming the importance of the corporatist system.

Further pension reform plans in 1997 included suggestions based on a report issued by Bert Rürup, a German pension expert, who also played a pivotal role in Chancellor Schröder's plans for pension reforms in Germany. Again, SPÖ union members in parliament threatened to vote against the government under SPÖ Chancellor Klima[10] if the SPÖ proceeded unilaterally, without consensus with the unions, in reforming pensions. In the end, the reform was considerably watered down in an attempt to reach consensus between the two parties but also with the unions (Gächter 1997; Schulze and Schludi 2007: 584–7; Tálos and Kittel 2002: 47; see also Höll *et al.* 2003).

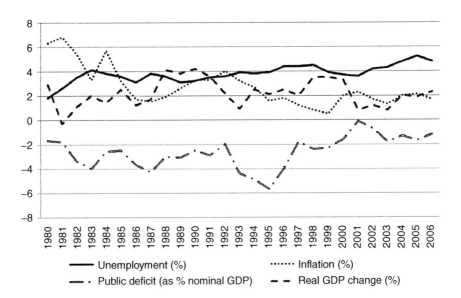

Figure 8.2 Main economic indicators, Austria, 1980–2006.

Source: OECD (June 2007; December 1999; December 1996).

The critique of corporatism in the decade prior to 2000 was linked to the political changes in Austria, where parties and interest groups became somewhat "uncoupled," that is, direct representation of interest groups within party and governmental leadership positions was reduced as new parties, as well as new interest groups, gained strength and emphasized non-economic issues, e.g. environmental issues. These new issues were not filtered through the corporatist system, resulting in an overall weakening of the role of the social partners in the policy-making process (Gerlich *et al.* 1988: 218–20). Only after the 2000 election and the rightist-populist FPÖ's reentry into government was social partnership "significantly devalued" (Fallend 2001: 252; Adam 2003b; Blaschke 2006: 152; Höll *et al.* 2003: 340; Tálos and Kittel 2002: 35).

Challenges to the tripartite model: the role of the FPÖ, 2000–06

The populist–right FPÖ and the Christian Democratic ÖVP formed a coalition government in February 2000 following protracted negotiations between the three major parties after the October 3, 1999 election, during which both the SPÖ and the ÖVP had incurred significant losses. In contrast, the FPÖ emerged as the net winner with a vote gain of 5 percentage points and an additional 12 seats to become the second-strongest party after the SPÖ, just 414 votes ahead of the ÖVP (see Figure 8.2). The FPÖ's success was driven by winning over many working class voters at the expense of the SPÖ: while just two decades earlier 63 percent of the SPÖ's voters were blue collar workers, in 1999 that proportion was almost halved to 35 percent. In contrast, while the FPÖ obtained just 4 percent of the blue collar vote in 1979, it secured a remarkable 47 percent in 1999 (Pelinka 2002: 335).

The ÖVP had announced that it would go into opposition if the election outcomes did not place it higher than third. However, the Austrian president still charged the SPÖ and ÖVP with forming a new coalition government. Coalition negotiations collapsed over portfolio allocation and the resistance of a leading SPÖ trade unionist to budget cuts. After a failed attempt to garner support for a SPÖ-led minority government, the ÖVP then formed a coalition with the FPÖ, which claimed 50 percent of the cabinet portfolios (Fallend 2001: 241–3; Müller 2004: 346; Schulze and Schludi 2007: 587–8).

Overall, the economy at that time was relatively stable: unemployment had declined to 3.9 percent in 1999 from about 4.4 percent over the previous three years; GDP growth was at 2.5 percent, and while inflation was up from 0.5 percent in 1999 to 2.0 percent in 2000, personal net income grew faster (by 2.7 percent and 2.3 percent in 1998 and 1999 respectively) (Müller 2000: 191–2; see also Figure 8.2). Thus, there was no obvious economic "need" to enact radical reforms and to do so outside the corporatist policy-making framework, but this is precisely what the new government did.

The ÖVP–FPÖ coalition: breaking with corporatism

As Rhodes (2003: 148) summarizes, the new ÖVP–FPÖ coalition broke "with the country's strong corporatist tradition, introducing unilaterally a series of pensions and social security reforms." The government also imposed a reform of the public social insurance system that benefits primarily the FA (Freiheitliche Arbeitnehmer) union, which is affiliated with the FPÖ (Rhodes 2003: 148). An attempt to negotiate the 2000–01 welfare spending reform resulted in failure. Furthermore, just half a year after taking office, the government "had passed a pension reform that significantly overhauled the existing system" after having made "few efforts" to negotiate with the social partners and instead opting for a "confrontational strategy" despite widespread demonstrations and strikes against the reform (Schulze and Schludi 2007: 589).

The party's opposition to social partnership was not just aimed at specific policies, though, but also targeted the corporatist institutions themselves. This became evident in the 2000–01 restructuring of the social insurance administration, a "center-piece of the Austrian consociational model" as it was "administered autonomously by the social partners" with the unions occupying a core position (Heinisch 2003: 105).[11] The FPÖ pushed for a change in the composition of the executive board of the 27 insurance funds against the opposition of the social partners. This signified a clear break with existing practices whereby the government generally refrained from intervening in negotiations between the social partners, but would subsequently adopt the outcomes of the negotiations into public policy (Heinisch 2000: 68; 2003: 105). When the unions resisted the government's proposed changes, Haider claimed he had information that "organised labour was planning a coup against the government" and generally attacked organized economic interests (Heinisch 2003: 108–9). Furthermore, the FPÖ wanted to reduce the "mandatory contributions of individuals to the Chamber of Labour" by 40 percent, and also proposed that leaders of corporatist organizations be barred from standing for parliament (Heinisch 2003: 105). Surprisingly, after the early election in 2002 – called after internal FPÖ disagreements leading to the resignation of the FPÖ vice chancellor and several FPÖ ministers – the ÖVP secured a landslide victory with an increase of 15 percentage points in its vote share and 27 additional seats, making it the largest party in parliament. The SPÖ vote also rose, though modestly (by 3 points) and it gained four seats, recapturing much of the working-class vote it had lost to the FPÖ in 1999 (Müller 2004: 351; see Table 8.2). In contrast, the FPÖ lost 17 percentage points of its vote share and 34 seats, the "worst defeat of any party" in the postwar period (Müller 2004: 350). A major problem for the FPÖ was that once in government and part of the "establishment," it faced increasing difficulties in continuing to portray itself as an anti-establishment protest party (see Luther 2000: 432). The party was also weakened because of its internal splits, illustrated by a succession of five leaders within a two-month period between September and November 2002

(Müller 2004: 347–9). Remarkably, controversial and "important issues such as pension reform, that emerged forcefully immediately after the election, were avoided by all parties" (Müller 2004: 350). The FPÖ succeeded in reentering the governing coalition with the ÖVP as the policy distances between the two parties were small compared to the policy distances between the ÖVP and the other parties. In addition, the small parliamentary size of the FPÖ made it a "much cheaper" coalition party for the ÖVP in terms of cabinet positions than a coalition with the considerably larger SPÖ (Müller 2004: 352).

The new government continued to pass controversial reforms unilaterally, perhaps unsurprising given its electoral success in 2002 following the turn away from tripartism. For instance, it introduced more flexible shop opening hours against the opposition of both unions and employer organizations (Adam 2003a). It was the ÖVP that initiated the proposal, while the FPÖ initially joined unions and employers in their opposition since the party was concerned about the electoral effects of this law given its decline in the 2002 election (Adam 2003a; Pernicka 2001; Stueckler 2001) – perhaps because the ÖVP had seen its electoral fortunes boosted after it had turned against tripartism in the previous legislative period, while the FPÖ suffered electoral decline in the 2002 election.

To balance the budget the coalition once more targeted pension reform and announced unilateral plans to harmonize all pensions, which were again met with widespread protests and demonstrations – over 1 million people demonstrated in Vienna on June 3, 2003 (Schulze and Schludi 2007: 592; see also Adam 2004). The government rejected the joint initiative of the ÖGB and the employers to develop an alternative plan, which marked the first time a government had rejected such an initiative in the postwar era. As a consequence, Austria experienced an almost unprecedented level of mobilizations and strikes. Over 60 percent of the Austrian population was reported to support the strike action (Adam 2003b), which is particularly remarkable given the overall absence of labor militancy and the country's comparatively low strike rates. The unions succeeded in achieving some modifications of the government's draft bill. After the mobilizations, the government announced plans to harmonize the pension systems for different groups of employees (private sector, public sector, farmers, and self-employed), but failed to reach an agreement with the social partners by summer 2004. In September 2004, the executive then presented a draft bill developed by government experts that was criticized by the unions as well as by the opposition parties.

Explaining the turn from tripartism to unilateral policymaking

As discussed earlier, fluctuations in the economy cannot explain the sudden shift from tripartism to unilateral policy formation. We therefore turn to electoral factors coupled with party ideology and government composition, especially the role of the FPÖ. The electoral performance of the Freedom Party during the 1990s was closely tied to the declining electoral fortunes of the ÖVP and the SPÖ. The SPÖ's vote share dropped from 43 percent in 1986 and 1990 to 33 percent in 1999, while the ÖVP's vote share fell from 41 percent in 1986 to a low of 27 percent in 1999. This decline was mirrored by the FPÖ's spectacular rise in electoral popularity from less than 10 percent in 1986 to 27 percent in 1999 (see Table 8.2).

The high electoral volatility of the 1990s, from which the FPÖ benefited, is rooted in several factors. First, voters were generally dissatisfied with the major political parties: Müller *et al.* (2004: 150) find that in "the late 1980s, disenchantment with parties and politicians was higher in Austria than in most other West European countries." This is reflected in the fact that traditional loyalties to the SPÖ and the ÖVP weakened in a context of austerity policies and international economic pressures, which diminished these parties' capacities to provide expected services to their support groups and led to loosening voter attachments. These attachments were then more easily transferred to the "third party," the FPÖ, rather than to the "other" main party (Luther 2000: 438–9), perhaps because the SPÖ and the ÖVP decreased their ideational distance during the 1980s, thus inducing voters to look for an alternative elsewhere (see Luther 1999: 51–2). Second, Luther (1999: 53) points to the declining potential for the traditional patronage policy as a consequence of EU regulations and Austria's economic downturn in the 1990s, which resulted in "substantial redundancies in public-sector enterprises, cuts in public subsidies and the abolition of various targeted tax concessions." Hence, the established parties were less well equipped to use "policy-based material rewards and individual patronage" to bolster their electoral support (Luther 1999: 54). While the clientelist system was beginning to erode, voters' disillusionment with the two main parties was strongly linked to the public's perception of clientelism and political corruption (Luther 1999: 55).

In surveys gauging the motives of FPÖ voters in 1995, "fighting corruption, privileges, uncovering scandals" was the most frequently mentioned reason, cited by 20 percent of respondents (Heinisch 2002: 219). Through his attacks on the "corrupt" SPÖ and ÖVP patronage system, especially since 1986 (Luther 1999: 53), Haider was able to use rising voter volatility to increase support for the Freedom Party (Luther 2000: 438–9; Méndez-Lago 1999: 192). Luther (2000: 437) proposes that it was in fact the party's attack on the influence of the two other major political parties and the neo-corporatist system that formed the core of the FPÖ's agenda.

The FPÖ's controversial party leader, Jörg Haider, attacked the "red-black" system, referring to the dominance of the SPÖ and ÖVP in the postwar period and the alleged resulting control of these parties over the state apparatus and public sector (Müller 2004: 347). In 1999, the most frequently cited motivation for voting for the Freedom Party was "Hope for Change/ Rejection of Coalition" with 22 percent, followed by "Foreigners in Austria" with a distant 14 percent (Heinisch 2002: 219), one of the core issues of the Freedom Party. It is this background that frames the Freedom Party's attacks on the corporatist system and the unions as part of the groups that enjoyed privileged access to policymaking. The party proposed to cut the power of the unions in collective bargaining as well as their rights for workers' representation (Minkenberg 2001), and in its party program, the FPÖ states with reference to the employer and union organizations:

> Through social partnership, the professional associations have developed into a shadow parliament and a "side government" without any lawful basis or democratic legitimacy for this and without being subject to any effective control. The professional associations should ... be restricted to their essential corporatist task.
>
> (FPÖ 2005: Kapitel 8, Art. 9(5); translation by the authors)

Similarly, in its plea for economic liberalization, the party emphasizes that the

> dominance of the party functionaries in the state sector should be abolished through real privatization, through the retreat of the political parties and associations from the economy, through the reduction of the influence of interest groups and through their limitation to their real tasks.
>
> (FPÖ 2005: Kapitel 10, Art. 3(6); translation by the authors)

In fact, one FPÖ leader with ministerial responsibility has been reported to have suggested "abolishing the trade unions" (Adams 2003b), and the FPÖ "has always been strongly opposed to social partnership" and created its own union, the Austrian Trade Union Federation, in an attempt to demolish the monopoly of the ÖGB (Guger 2001: 77). Blaschke (2006: 152) attributes the FPÖ's attacks on social partnership to the fact that the party was without influence in the tripartite system.

At the same time, the party was also interested in gaining enough votes to gain access to government power, which might explain its "ideological promiscuity" including Christian values, appeals to women (which had been severely underrepresented in the party's electoral profile) through child benefits, public housing, and job security (Luther 2000: 437), and nationalistic, anti-foreigner propaganda.[12] The FPÖ was successful especially in attracting blue-collar workers: in 1999, it was supported by 47 percent of skilled and 45 percent of unskilled blue-collar workers, compared to 35 percent of blue-collar voting for the SPÖ (Luther 2000: 431). At the same time, the relationship between the SPÖ and the unions weakened. For example, the leading unionists abandoned the SPÖ delegation negotiating the governing coalition after the 1995 election since they were unwilling to support the cuts in welfare programs that formed part of the coalition agreement. Again, four years later, the social-democratic metal workers union leader involved in the coalition negotiations in 1999–2000 announced that he would refuse to sign a SPÖ–ÖVP coalition agreement over budget cuts (Fallend 2001: 243). The SPÖ did not invite union leaders to its 2002 negotiating team (Müller *et al.* 2004: 171).

The FPÖ's election strategies and the attack on the existing party system are embedded in its ideology,[13] which combines economic liberalism, anti-statism, attacks on the privileges of the political class and party corruption, and economic nationalism attacking foreigners and liberal immigration policies. After 1986, the FPÖ went through a transformation into a "populist protest party with allegedly unclear boundaries to the extreme right" (Müller 2003: 94–5). To some extent, the FPÖ thus functioned as an opposition party targeting protest voters (Müller 2004: 347).

The FPÖ's attack on the corporatist institutions and practices is therefore coherent with its electoral strategy and ideology. It is less clear, though, why the ÖVP was willing to abandon tripartism. The party's electoral decline provides one explanation. Müller and Fallend (2004) argue that the coalition's "majoritarian" approach was driven by its weakness, and particularly the ÖVP's weakness. The ÖVP had incurred significant electoral losses in the 1999 elections, relegating it to third place for the first time in history, and in its campaign had promised to abandon government under these circumstances. With less than 20 percent of Austrian voters favoring an ÖVP–FPÖ coalition, the government suffered from low legitimacy (Müller and Fallend 2004: 807–9). In response, weakening the corporatist system, removing Social Democrats from power positions and in turn reforming the system and staffing it with ÖVP party loyalists were strategies directed at "strengthening the government parties' electoral chances" (Müller and Fallend 2004: 812). The 2006 election returned the SPÖ as the strongest party despite a small loss of votes (less than one percentage point) and one seat – probably linked to a massive financial scandal the unions, close to the SPÖ, were involved in – while the ÖVP incurred sizeable losses, over 8 percentage points of votes and 13 seats. This might be related to the fact that the pension "reforms themselves and the way they were introduced" by the ÖVP–FPÖ government had been highly unpopular – the reforms were rejected by almost 60 percent of the voters (cited in Müller 2008: 176) while the SPÖ was considered much more credible on social policy issues than the ÖVP (Müller 2008: 178). The FPÖ, for its part, had split the year prior to the election when its leader, Jörg Haider, had formed the Bündnis Zukunft Österreich (Union for the Future of Austria, BZÖ). After lengthy negotiations, the grand coalition between the SPÖ and ÖVP was revived (Müller 2008: 178).

Summing up the Austrian case

Social pacts in Austria were unlikely given that the deeply institutionalized corporatist system was built on tripartism, rendering pacts redundant. Hence, our focus in this chapter is not so much an attempt to explain the absence or presence of governmental pact offers. Rather, we centered on the reasons for the government's turn towards unilateral policy making instead of tripartism and the attack on corporatist bargaining itself. We have argued that the "pushing back of 'social partnership'" (Müller and Fallend 2004: 810) under the rightist coalition was neither due to the unresponsiveness of the bargaining institutions, nor to the unwillingness of the social partners to compromise, nor was it the only possible response to economic pressures. Instead, the FPÖ–ÖVP coalition (or at least a part thereof) targeted the corporatist institutions and actors themselves and questioned their legitimacy in participating in policy-making processes on non-wage issues. This theme resonated with voters' growing disillusionment with the system in a context of rising electoral volatility. The Freedom Party's impressive electoral returns and strong cabinet presence resulted in considerable policy influence in the ÖVP–FPÖ government. Electoral politics thus forms an integral part of the explanation of the absence of tripartism in non-wage policy reforms after 1999. Despite the popular and widespread protest against the unilateral pension reforms and other signs of weakening corporatism, the ÖVP succeeded in staying in office, while the FPÖ was considerably weakened, in part because of its internal problems and splits.

Conclusion

Tripartism, it seems, has come under fire in both Germany and Austria, as the consequence of governing parties' interests, electoral pressures, and popular perceptions of the desirability of reforms as well as of union inclusion in the process of negotiating reforms. However, the two countries also diverge in important ways. In Austria, the general but mostly latent popular dissatisfaction with corporatism did not lead to a change of the system until the far-right Freedom Party assumed a prominent role in government in 2000 and was able to exert significant influence over the government agenda. In turn, the entry of the FPÖ into the governing coalition meant that the SPÖ was relegated to opposition status, resulting in considerable loss of influence of the trade unions on the government agenda. Thus, a shift in the governing coalition preceded the frontal assault on tripartism.

Germany also experienced a change in governing coalition. However, in this case it was the turn to a leftist government – the Red–Green coalition under Chancellor Schröder – that led to the abandonment of tripartism after the failed Alliance for Jobs. In the German case, tripartism was not replaced by unilateralism, but rather by commissions that might or might not involve organized labor representatives. Commissions were appointed by the government and produced recommendations to support the governing agenda without generating the impression that the government was oblivious to outside advice. Furthermore, Bundesrat approval was not guaranteed even if the government had previously been able to agree with the unions. Thus, the government was often involved in negotiations with the opposition parties in preparing policy reforms rather than with the unions.

This chapter has highlighted the fact that social pacts were not an automatic solution for governments confronted with economic pressures and aiming at downsizing the welfare state, especially when popular support for reforms was modest. Where governing parties' attacks on tripartism resonated with voters, as in Austria, or where negotiations took place in different arenas, as in Germany, governments found incentives to turn their backs on negotiations with unions and explore other ways to implement reforms. Yet, the attack on tripartism evident in these two countries is by no means universal across the coordinated economies. Pacts have been signed with some regularity in Belgium and the Netherlands, for instance. Even in the Benelux countries, though, difficult tripartite negotiations have sometimes provoked general strikes, as in the Netherlands in 2004, illustrating the point that the offer of a pact does not necessarily promise voter approval of the measures under discussion.

9 Conclusion

The electoral politics of social pacts

Since the early 1980s, many governments in Western Europe have attempted to reform labor markets and welfare states through social pacts, national-level agreements with unions and sometimes employers. Other governments have opted for the unilateral route of legislation to reform, and yet others have resorted to both pacts and legislation. The emergence of social pacts is most commonly understood as a government response to severe economic problems whose precise form and content are shaped by industrial relations institutions. However, while economic problems may confront governments with the need to enact reforms, they fall short of explaining the incidence of social pacts as governments can also revert to legislation to implement policies. Whether, and when, governments choose one or the other is better explained by considering the political role of governments, in particular the interests of governing parties in the electoral arena. Thus, when governments (or governing parties) consider how to implement potentially unpopular labor and welfare reforms, their decision is heavily influenced by electoral considerations. Since approximately the 1980s, parties and governments in Western Europe have been facing growing electoral pressures because of the increasingly volatile and fluid electorate and the rise of new parties. Moreover, voters hold the government responsible for the state of economy. In addition, voters' dissatisfaction with welfare state performance "is becoming increasingly salient in real-world politics" and "matters for political orientations and behaviour" Kumlin (2007a: 366). Controlling for other factors (class, ideology, and retrospective economic evaluations), dissatisfaction with welfare state performance has a "significant negative impact on the probability of voting for a government party" (Kumlin 2007a: 366). These factors combine to shape governments' choices to privilege reforms either through social pacts or through legislative procedure. In subsequent sections we briefly summarize the main results of our analysis, reflect on the relationship between our quantitative and qualitative findings, consider the consequences for governing parties of pact offers and legislation, and set out some of the broader theoretical implications of our work.

Main findings

Both the quantitative data and the case studies lend considerable support to our main argument that the likelihood of governments choosing pacts or legislation is influenced by factors related to elections, in particular party competition, party family and position, and by attributes of the government and the legislature. While governments are obviously concerned with meeting economic targets, they are also concerned with the potential electoral costs of the welfare and labor market reforms and wage policies deemed necessary to meet these targets. Our quantitative analysis of 16 West European countries between 1980 and 2006 evinced that social pacts were more likely to be offered by governing parties that gained votes; center or leftist governing parties; unconnected coalitions (compared to single-party administrations); governments that were relatively weak; and in legislatures that were highly fragmented. At the same time parties responded to vote changes in different ways: vote losses, for example, were more likely to lead to pact offers from left parties but this was not the case for parties of the right. Legislation was more likely to be pursued by conservative parties with a high proportion of seats, particularly where the legislature contained only a small number of effective parties. While party politics matters, institutional variation provides relatively little insight into the cross-national and over-time differences in the incidence of social pacts. These findings echo other research on welfare state changes that provides evidence for the importance of party family in the extent of retrenchment (e.g. Allan and Scruggs 2004). Neither the level of bargaining coordination nor the type of welfare regime was associated with pact offers, although such offers were more likely in countries with low union density. Economic conditions are equally unhelpful in explaining variation in governments' choices of social pacts or legislation: our data provide no support for the role of EMU or for the impact of inflation, government deficits, or unemployment on the likelihood of governments offering social pacts in preference over legislation.

Pooled time-series analysis involves the construction of regression models to capture variation both between countries and over time. However, it is difficult to disentangle country effects and time effects. We set out to approximate the effects of types of countries by adding dummy variables for varieties of capitalism/welfare regime and for time periods; in both cases, the results were non-significant. Furthermore, while multivariate statistics point to associations between variables, we require more in-depth analysis of particular countries to understand the mechanisms behind these statistical associations. We therefore explored some of the processes of electoral and parliamentary competition that underpin these quantitative results through qualitative case studies.

Ireland and the UK are conventionally regarded as Liberal Market Economies that lack some, perhaps most, of the preconditions for sustained social pacts. Yet Ireland has experienced continuous social pacts since 1987 while the UK has resorted exclusively to legislation. Our qualitative analysis supports the reasoning that it was electoral competition that led Fianna Fáil and the conservative party respectively to effect a radical shift in their preferences between pacts and legislation and these shifts, in turn, influenced the policies of their electoral rivals. Fianna Fáil suffered two election defeats in quick succession (1981 and 1982) and as its main rival in government (Fine Gael) abandoned the tripartite experiments of the 1970s, Fianna Fáil adopted tripartism in order to differentiate itself from Fine Gael and compete more effectively for votes. Seat gains (despite vote losses) propelled Fianna Fail into power in 1987 and its position, first as a minority administration and subsequently as part of an unconnected coalition in an increasingly fragmented legislature, pushed in the direction of social pact offers. Parliamentary competition eventually led all the main Irish parties to switch from an anti-social pact to a pro-social pact position as they sought to gain office alongside the pivotal pro-pact party, Fianna Fáil. Similarly, in the UK it was also two election defeats – for the Conservatives in 1974 – that were integral to a shift in Conservative Party policy. While its main Labour rival pursued the tripartite experiment of the Social Contract in the 1970s, the Conservatives sought to differentiate themselves by repudiating tripartism. Vote gains secured Conservative electoral victory in 1979 but party family, party position, and the overwhelming strength in the legislature reinforced the policy of labor market legislation and union exclusion throughout the 1980s and 1990s. The recovery of the Labour vote in 1987 following its disastrous 1983 result might have been expected to reinforce the party's commitment to tripartism and to social pacts. In fact, the party underwent an even more radical shift in policy, moving close to the anti-pact policy of its successful Conservative rival (and lacking any opposition to its left). Consequently, despite a substantial vote gain in 1997, Labour's strength in the legislature and its conservative policy regarding trade unions ensured that pacts would not be offered during its period in office.

Our two Scandinavian cases also displayed profound differences in the incidence of social pacts: the mixture of pact offers and legislation in Sweden contrasts with the overwhelming preponderance of pacts in Finland. The similarities in the two countries' institutions and patterns of economic growth and contraction since 1980 are striking and therefore unable to account for the divergent preferences of the respective governments. Instead, differing patterns of electoral and parliamentary competition were critical in shaping government policies. The electorally successful Social Democrats ruled Sweden from 1932 until 1976 even though their vote share began to erode significantly from the 1970s, when the conservatives emerged as the main opposition party. Successive vote losses by minority Social Democratic governments in an increasingly fragmented legislature did not, however, lead to pacts but to an increased willingness by Social Democrats to legislate even at the price of union antagonism. Legislation in Sweden was also pursued, as we would predict from party family, by right-center coalitions in 1991–94 and after 2006. In contrast, Finnish policymaking, particularly on wages, was dominated by social pacts, a cross-party preference reinforced by a number of factors: the greater electoral strength of the center and the far left; the relative weakness of the conservatives compared to Sweden; the effective minority status of pre-1992 governments (most legislation required a two-thirds vote); the broad, unconnected character of the coalition governments typically found in Finland; and the high degree of party fragmentation in the legislature. In short, electoral and parliamentary competition in Sweden led to a cross-party consensus more favorable to legislation, but resulted in a consensus on social pacts in Finland.

Pacts have been very common in Spain and Italy and have alternated with legislation on wages, labor, and welfare reform. The interesting question in both countries is how to account for the pronounced cyclical pattern of pacts and legislation over time. The relative stability of industrial relations institutions means this type of variable cannot offer much insight into the ebbs and flows of pact offers. Similarly, fluctuations in economic indicators also provide little insight. Instead, patterns of electoral and parliamentary competition and properties of governments correspond better to the rise and fall of social pacts. Electorally successful majority governments in both countries made declining use of social pacts through the 1980s. Led by "modernizing" social democrats (González in Spain 1982–96, Craxi in Italy 1983–87), these governments in increasingly fragmented legislatures found that the use of legislation in the face of union resistance to wage restraint or welfare reform was either followed by a vote share increase (Italy 1987) or by only a limited decrease (Spain 1993). The reemergence of electoral problems in conjunction with economic decline in the early to mid-1990s was associated with the rediscovery of social pacts as government majorities were either significantly reduced or disappeared (as in Spain between 1993 and 2000). Yet when government strength changed, as in Spain 2000–04, the reelected Aznar administration made less use of pacts compared to the 1996–2000 administration.

In Germany and Austria tripartism has come under fire despite longstanding tripartite traditions and institutions in both countries. The attack on German tripartism followed a change in government from the CDU–CSU/FDP coalition government of Chancellor Kohl to the red–green coalition under Chancellor Schröder. Despite its leftist character and vote gain in 1998, the latter government responded to the failure of the Alliance for Jobs pact by reverting to a form of unilateralism based on commissions. These bodies were appointed by the government with minimal union involvement and produced recommendations to support the governing agenda on labor market and welfare reform, avoiding the impression that the government was oblivious to outside advice. At the same time, however, these commissions composed of experts did not afford any privileged role to the social partners. Moreover, the powerful role of the upper chamber compelled the government to engage in negotiations with the opposition parties in preparing policy reforms, further marginalizing the unions. In Austria, widespread voter dissatisfaction with corporatism did not lead to a repudiation of tripartism until the far-right Freedom Party, having pursued a campaign attacking tripartism, entered the government in 2000. The majority coalition with the Christian Democrats enabled the government to act on this preference and to pursue contentious pension reforms through legislation in a fragmented legislature.

Overall our country studies show that in all cases, electoral and party competition factors matter despite national variation in *which ones* matter and *how* they matter. The role of unconnected coalitions is highly important in some countries at some times, such as Ireland in the 1980s and 1990s or Finland in the 1990s, but is of very little importance in other countries, e.g. Spain, which has not had any formal coalition governments. Party family matters in some countries and helps explain fluctuations in pacts and legislation over time, e.g. Italy, but is less important in other countries, where parties have converged on a particular method of policy implementation, e.g. the UK or Ireland since the 1990s. Only through detailed case studies has it been possible to trace these national complexities.

The argument reassessed

All of these cases, in various ways, highlight the importance of electoral politics in shaping the decisions by governments as to whether they should include the unions in social pacts or instead exclude them and legislate contentious reforms. The combination of case studies and cross-national quantitative analysis allows us to reflect on several additional significant issues emerging from the data. First, electoral competition is heavily implicated in government choices; however, parties responding to past vote losses and coming to power with an increase in votes will not necessarily then opt for social pacts, as the quantitative data suggest is likely to be the case. Examples of vote-gaining parties that opted for pacts extend to the Spanish Socialists after their 1982 victory, the Finnish Social Democrats after 1995, the Italian left after 1996, and the centrist Fianna Fáil party in Ireland in 1997 and again in 2002. Exceptions, however, exist, and other parties that gained votes and assumed office were determined to legislate reforms and bypass unions: the Italian Socialists in 1983, British Conservatives in 1979, British Labour 1997, and the Austrian far-right in 1999.

This rather mixed evidence leads in the direction of a second, and more theoretical point, which is that parties can, and do, exercise strategic choice in response to electoral competition. Cross-national research indicates that parties are likely to shift their policies in the same direction as competing parties did in the previous election, and that they are particularly responsive to policy shifts of other parties within their ideological blocs (Adams and Somer-Topcu 2009). At the same time, these findings still leave room for party leaders to define their principal competitor (especially in cases where a governing party is the sole party in its ideological bloc or where new parties pose electoral threats), and they can also choose how to respond in terms of pacts and legislation. The Swedish Social Democrats provide a good illustration of the first point. Throughout the 1980s the party faced electoral threats on both its left and right flanks but the Carlsson party leadership defined the threat from the right as preeminent and concluded that the SAP should respond to this threat by considering the use of legislation to secure the passage of contentious reforms. The UK provides a fitting example of the second point concerning the different ways in which parties can respond to electoral threats. When Labour's adoption of a radical leftwing program led to a dramatic fall in its vote in 1983, the new post-election leader Neil Kinnock instituted a far-reaching policy review designed to shift the party towards the center ground, narrowing the policy space between itself and the electorally successful Conservatives. In Italy the new Socialist Party leader elected in 1976 (Bettino Craxi) began to shift the party away from the tripartism traditionally supported by all the main parties, from Communists to Christian Democrats, to differentiate the PSI from both of its main electoral rivals. In contrast, leaders of the left Olive Tree electoral alliance in the mid-1990s actively promoted tripartism as a viable alternative to the conflict associated with the first Berlusconi government's union exclusion and preference for legislation. While the strategic choices of party leaders appear highly significant as they respond to electoral pressures, it is extremely difficult to incorporate strategic choice and its determinants into a quantitative model. Our quantitative evidence suggests that center parties are most likely to pursue social pacts and conservative parties are least likely to do so, but we found no general tendency for social democratic parties to pursue pacts rather than legislation. The case study evidence illustrates that social democratic party leaderships have become highly pragmatic on the issue of including or excluding unions from policymaking. Perhaps this is why pacts are no longer contingent on the continuation of the "social-democratic model," which presupposed the existence of close ties and cooperation between social-democratic parties and trade unions. In recent years those ties have weakened considerably in several countries, including Germany, Spain, Sweden, and the UK (Aylott 2003; Burgess 2004; Piazza 2001; Upchurch *et al.* 2009).

Third, and related to the theme of strategic choice, party leaders may become publicly committed to their pact or legislation preferences, even in the face of adverse electoral results. Our analysis throughout the book has assumed that party leaders in government are willing to consider pacts or legislation for each reform issue that may arise and are not necessarily constrained by previous choices. This assumption was confirmed by our evidence, which showed that of the 49 cabinets that enacted legislation, 26 (53 percent) also offered social pacts to unions and employers while 23 did not offer pacts. However, it does appear that some governments retain a commitment to pacts (and sometimes to legislation) after being reelected despite losing votes in a post-pact (legislation) election. This was the case in Ireland, for example, when Fianna Fáil continued to offer social pacts despite vote losses in 1989 and 1992, and in Finland, when the Social Democrats persisted with social pacts despite vote losses in 1999. Likewise the Conservative government in the UK retained its hostility to tripartism despite modest vote losses in 1983 and 1987 and more significant losses in 1992.

Fourth, in analyzing particular countries we have drawn on different combinations of variables at different times and for different parties. For example, majority governments have in general been more willing to legislate than minority administrations, and leftist governments have generally been more willing to offer social pacts compared to conservative administrations. However, the case analyses point to interesting and important exceptions to these general associations. Some minority, social democratic governments in Sweden, for example, have been willing to try and build temporary coalitions in the legislature to secure the passage of contentious legislation. In Germany, the second Schröder government (2002–05) had a very narrow and precarious majority but was willing to pursue legislation despite its weakness in the legislature and despite union opposition. One lesson drawn from these examples is that the status of governments as "minority" or "majority" does not necessarily reveal the actual strength of these governments; consequently, we should avoid the easy but sometimes misleading equation of minority government with weak government (and the corollary that majority government equals strong government). Or to take another example, the role of party family varies between countries: in some cases, such as the UK, Ireland, and Germany, different parties eventually converged on a particular approach to policymaking (and often on particular measures of reform), thus weakening the impact of party family on the pacts/legislation choice. In other countries party family continues to distinguish party approaches very strongly: conservative and right parties in Italy remain fairly hostile to social pacts but the center and left parties continue to be favorable towards them.

Fifth, the case studies have also documented the impact of variables that would not be expected to be flagged up in pooled time-series analysis because of the infrequency of their occurrence. A good example is the role of the far right in government. Very few far-right parties have entered West European governments since 1980 but those that have, such as the Freedom Party in Austria (2000–06) or Forza Italia and the National Alliance in Italy (1994 and 2001–06), have been associated with an unusual degree of antagonism to tripartism and a preference for legislation. The continuing strength of the far right in countries such as Belgium (Vlaams Belang), Denmark (Danish People's Party), and France (National Front) may indicate that hostility to social pacts might increase throughout Western Europe. Although the far right has rarely been in government, it does pose an electoral threat to conservative and Christian Democratic parties. Its electoral presence may therefore be important in discouraging these more moderate parties from the pursuit of tripartism, as in Austria.

Sixth, although our analysis has demonstrated that "politics matters" and that industrial relations institutions provide little insight into government propensity to offer social pacts, our case studies demonstrate that in particular circumstances, institutions also matter. For example, the legislative powers of the German upper house provide governments with strong incentives to negotiate with opposition parties in the Bundesrat. This incentive, in turn, may reduce the likelihood of governments going outside the legislature to win the support of the social partners. In Finland, until 1992 the constitution contained a qualified majority voting rule under which most pieces of proposed legislation required at least a two-thirds majority to become law. One effect of this institutional arrangement was to facilitate the creation of surplus governing coalitions, often spanning a wide range of party families. The high degree of consensus that was required for the formation and maintenance of effective coalitions may well have increased the likelihood of consensual policymaking through social pacts.

Seventh, as the qualitative analyses reveal, sometimes governments have employed "functional equivalents" to pacts, as demonstrated by the use of commissions under the Schröder government in Germany. Here, the need to find legitimation for policy reforms outside the government was extended to an appointed group of experts rather than to the social partners. In contrast, in Italy pacts under the non-partisan technocratic governments of Ciampi (1993–94) and Dini (1995–96) played a similar legitimating role, bolstering the authority of governments that lacked an electoral mandate and that were supported in the legislature by broad and unconnected group of parties.

Finally, it is worth raising three methodological issues about the arguments presented in this book. We have deployed a mixture of quantitative analysis of pooled time-series data and qualitative case studies of individual countries. Our underlying assumption is that the mechanisms of electoral and parliamentary competition are likely to play out in broadly similar ways across a wide range of countries within Western Europe. The multivariate analysis reinforced that assumption because we found no effect of varieties of capitalism on pact offers. However, proponents of fuzzy sets analysis point out that multivariate analysis of cross-country pooled datasets can sometimes obscure different causal configurations in different groups of countries (Ragin 2008). For instance, Avdagic's (2010) fuzzy sets analysis has revealed different causal pathways to social pacts across different countries. Future research could therefore usefully explore the degree to which our findings can be replicated or refined using different methodologies.

Second, our analysis of electoral pressures has focused entirely around national elections for the legislature. Yet it emerged from the case studies that government behavior is also influenced by local, regional and European elections, as well as national elections. For example, poor results in regional elections in the early 2000s had a serious impact on the Social Democrats in Germany; conversely, good European election results strengthened the Italian Socialists in the mid-1980s. In addition poor local election results led to the resignation, and then the defeat, of the Portuguese Socialists in winter 2001–02. Additional research might therefore examine the impact of subnational and European, as well as national, elections on governments' choices for reform strategies.

Third, our model and much of our analysis is framed in terms of votes rather than seats. In highly proportional electoral systems such as Austria or Sweden, the two measures will often (though not always) be highly correlated, but this is not necessarily so for other cases. In several recent Irish elections, based on the STV form of PR, at least one party recorded an increase in seats despite a *decrease* in vote shares. In the UK's first-past-the-post system the disjuncture between votes and seats is even more pronounced. Further research might thus employ different measurements and methodological tools to enhance and refine our argument and test our findings.

The argument extended

Our case studies cover eight countries but we can extend the argument to the remaining eight members of the former EU-15 and Norway, which are included in our quantitative analysis in Chapter 4. Starting with the Scandinavian economies, Norway has a record of extensive pact offers rather like Finland, whereas governments in Denmark have shown a much greater proclivity for legislation (Dolvik and Martin 2000; Lind 2000).[1] In Norway, pacts have mostly been offered by minority social democratic administrations and more recently by an unconnected left-center majority coalition since 2005 and reelected in 2009). On those occasions when the country has been governed by conservative administrations (1981–86, 1989–90 and 2001–05) pact offers did emerge from two of these minority governments (on wages, welfare, and labor market reform in 1983, 2002, and 2005) but all three were rejected by trade unions. Denmark is a more puzzling case because in contrast to the rest of Scandinavia it has been governed by conservative and liberal governments for the majority of the period since 1980 (Bille and Pedersen 2004; Damgaard 2000). Despite their minority status these stable governments have nonetheless exhibited a propensity for legislation, irrespective of vote gains or losses for the main party. As in the UK, the commanding electoral position of the conservatives helped push the Danish Social Democrats towards the center despite the presence of a leftist party – the Socialist People's Party – polling around 12 percent of the vote in the 1980s. Social Democratic governments that ruled Denmark 1993–2001 offered several pacts but also pursued legislation on welfare and pension reforms in 1993 and 1995 (Green-Pedersen 2002).

Turning to Southern Europe, pact offers were rare in France and Greece (just four and two respectively), in contrast to Spain and Italy. The party systems of both countries are dominated by two main organizations, one on the left, the other on the right, as well as communist parties polling around 10 percent (Ioannou 2000; Knapp 2002; Zambarloukou 2006). Center, Christian Democrat, and liberal parties are either part of the conservative bloc (in France) or electorally insignificant (in Greece). Governments in both countries have typically comprised single-party, majority administrations in legislatures with a low level of fragmentation, conditions that our quantitative data indicate are not conducive to the emergence of pacts. On the few occasions they have been offered in France – July 1987, April 1993, February 2000, and February 2003 – three of these four offers originated from newly elected conservative governments that could instead have used their parliamentary majorities to legislate unpopular reforms. In France, however, conservative governments have frequently found that contentious reforms can elicit union protests in the form of general strikes: nine of the ten general strikes between 1980 and 2006 were in response to conservative government proposals (Kelly and Hamann 2009). Pact offers may therefore represent an attempt to reduce the likelihood of this type of discontent and its potential electoral consequences. In Greece the most comprehensive of the three social pacts – the 1997 Pact of Confidence – was offered, as we would predict, shortly after the ruling Socialist Party suffered one of its heaviest loss of votes at the 1996 election. The conservative New Democracy, in contrast, behaved in a similar fashion to Berlusconi's conservatives and used its parliamentary majorities to avoid social pacts (Tsakalotos 2001). Portugal, much like Spain, has a recent tradition of alternating single-party governments, comprising either the Socialists or the Social Democrats (a liberal party, despite its name), both of whom have offered social pacts on a variety of issues (Magone 2003). Legislation has rarely been attempted on labor market or welfare reform and then only by the liberals, but not the Socialists. The most intense period of pact offers came in the early 1990s following a significant reduction in the parliamentary strength of the ruling liberals (Campos Lima and Naumann 2000).

Finally, Belgium and the Netherlands have both witnessed substantial numbers of pact offers since 1980 (22 in Belgium, 13 in the Netherlands) (Arcq and Pochet 2000; Green-Pedersen 2002; Kuipers 2006; Visser and Hemerijck 1997). The majority of these (15 in Belgium, nine in the Netherlands) emanated from Christian Democrat-led unconnected coalition governments in fragmented legislatures. Christian Democrat parties in both countries have experienced substantial vote erosion since the 1950s although support for Dutch Christian Democrats has recovered since 2002 (Andeweg 1999; Andeweg and Irwin 2005). Their main electoral challenge has been posed by pro-market liberal parties and although the Christian Democrats have not generally responded with union exclusion, they have often proposed highly controversial reforms on wages or labor markets leading to relatively high levels of pact rejection: 9 out of 22 pact offers were rejected in Belgium and four out of nine in the Netherlands (Hamann and Kelly 2007b; Timmermans 2003). Luxembourg, in contrast, has witnessed very few social pact offers, which is not surprising in light of its tradition of large majority, broad coalition governments between the two main parties, the Social and Christian Democrats (Dumont and De Winter 2000).

Directions for future research: parties, varieties of capitalism, pact acceptance, and pact consequences

The core of our argument is that the government choice of pacts or legislation is not simply a technical decision about which type of policy instrument is best suited to achieve particular economic policy goals. Rather, we have conceptualized governments as political actors whose actions reflect their responses to electoral competition. We have also conceptualized political parties as unitary actors; yet it is clear that in a number of cases, party choices for pacts or legislation emerged from internal debates between rival factions. In Italy and Sweden the more "moderate" leaderships that emerged in the 1970s and 1980s respectively, willing to legislate unpopular reforms, were the products of factional debates inside the parties and their associated trade unions. This was also true in the British case: the left factions in the Labour Party were defeated by the center-right in the 1980s and the "corporatist" wing of the Conservative Party was defeated by the Thatcherite neoliberals once the Conservatives were in office. Further research on the internal dynamics of parties may evince that their choice between pacts and legislation was sometimes more finely balanced than might appear on the surface.

Given our focus on governments it is perhaps not surprising that we did not find any significant variation in pact offers between the different welfare regimes (or varieties of capitalism) of Scandinavia, Southern Europe, Germany and the Benelux countries, and the two LMEs (UK and Ireland). The Hall and Soskice (2001b) framework is centered around the firm and its coordination problems with the state having "no autonomous role to play" (Hancké *et al.* 2007b: 23; see also Crouch 2005 for similar points). In contrast, Amable's (2003) comparative framework incorporates the state and classifies countries on the basis of both employment and social protection policies. The clusters of countries that emerge from the empirical analyses often cut across the welfare regimes that informed our analysis and therefore help explain the absence of significant results. For example, under the heading of state employment policy, Greece, Spain, Norway, and the UK appear in one cluster while Germany, Finland, and Ireland end up in another. Or under the heading of social protection policy France appears in the same group as Belgium and Germany, while the UK is joined by Spain and the Netherlands in a second cluster (Amable 2003: 142, 155–6). Our evidence does not undermine or call into question the comparative analysis of Varieties of Capitalism or of welfare regimes. However, it does suggest that the types of categories that help make sense of national variations in economic and social institutions are far less useful in explaining variations in the behavior of governments in the electoral arena; these types of institutions may also be of limited use in explaining retrenchment dynamics (see also Allan and Scruggs 2004). Future research might explore the linkages between economic institutions, political institutions, and policy reform strategies in more detail. This line of research could also be extended to the economies in Eastern Europe, for instance, to see to what extent our argument travels and our findings hold in newer democracies that are distinguished by different histories of party politics, voter attachments, patterns of industrialization, and welfare state developments.

Returning to pact offers, we have largely ignored the question of whether or not pact offers by governments are accepted by the social partners. However, it is possible that pact offers are designed to signal to voters an impression of government's apparent willingness to negotiate, even if the likelihood of agreement is remote. We noted in Chapter 2 and in several case studies that a significant minority of social pact offers were rejected by the social partners, normally by the trade unions. In Sweden, unions rejected three pact offers out of six; in Spain, 6 out of 24; in Austria and Germany it was two out of three in each country. The determinants of pact acceptance or rejection by unions remain unclear. A cursory look at the raw data makes it apparent that while rejection rates are similar in Austria and Germany, for example, they differ radically between Sweden and Finland despite similar trade union structures and density levels. The Italian and Spanish cases are particularly interesting because the rejection of six pact offers in Spain and three in Italy does not appear to have deterred governments from continued attempts to include unions in policy making. While some governments might respond to union rejection by opting for legislation on future policy (as seems to have happened on several occasions in Sweden, for instance), other governments may perceive union rejection as costly and intensify future efforts at union inclusion (as in Finland and Italy in the 1990s, for example). Although work (e.g. Avdagic 2005; Avdagic *et al.* 2006) has begun to examine the determinants of pact acceptance and rejection, additional research is necessary to identify the factors that drive unions' decisions to accept or reject pact offers and, consequently, the varied responses of governments to pact rejection.

Finally, the question arises whether governments' strategic use of pacts or legislation as a means to guard their electoral fortunes bears out. In other words, are the odds of governments returning to office after the next election higher when they resort to pacts compared to those governments that reform contentious policies through legislation? Initial research confirms that governments extending pact offers are in fact more likely to govern for another term than those governments that pursue reforms through parliamentary channels. This finding is particularly true for single party majority governments whose pact offers are accepted (Hamann *et al.* 2010).

In conclusion, neither economic nor institutional variables alone are able to illuminate either between- or within-country differences in the governments' preferences for social pacts or legislation in their quest to reform the welfare state, labor markets, and wages. Instead, our analysis illustrates that electoral and parliamentary competition and the responses of political parties to this competition exert a significant influence on the willingness of governing parties to offer social pacts to unions and employers. In analyses of globalization it is now commonplace to assume that "institutions matter" (e.g. Swank 2002); we have argued that in the analysis of government modes of policy-making, strong theoretical and empirical grounds suggest that "politics matters."

Appendix 1

Data sources

Pacts and legislation including content and timing

European Industrial Relations Review, monthly, 1979–2006; European Industrial Relations Observatory, www.eiro.eurofound.ie *Annual Reviews* 1997–2006 and individual country entries. Additional material from Schludi (2005) and Immergut et al. (2007).

Vote and seat variables

Books

Budge *et al.* (2001); Klingemann *et al.* (2006); Mackie and Rose (1991; 1997).

Websites

Austria: Official Elections Authority Ministry of Interior www.bmi.gv.at/wahlen

Belgium: National Elections Authority www.elections.fgov.be

Finland: Official Elections Authority www.vaalit.fi
and National Statistics office www.stat.fi

France: Ministry of Interior www.interieur.gouv.fr

Germany: Official Elections Authority www.bundeswahlleiter.de
For Germany the party list data were used.

Greece: Ministry of Interior Public Administration and Decentralization www.ypes.gr/ekloges/content/gr/rthnik_fr.htm

Italy: Ministry of Interior http://elezionistorico.interno.it

Luxembourg: National Elections Authority www.elections.public.lu and 'Elections in Luxembourg' at the National Statistics Office www.statistiques.public.lu

Netherlands: National Elections Board www.nlverkiezingen.com

Norway: National Statistics office www.ssb.no

Portugal: Secretariado Técnico para Assuntos para o Processo Eleitoral (STAPE) www.stape.pt

Spain: Ministry of Interior www.mir.es
Sweden: Official Elections Authority www.val.se
UK: The Electoral Commission www.electoralcommission.co.uk

Party family

Names of all governing parties from Müller and Strøm (2003) for 13 countries 1980–98 and from national election sites for 1998–2006 and for Greece, Spain and the UK. Parties classified into families based on categories in Gallagher et al. (2006).

Coalition or single-party government, type of coalition, government strength, minority/majority status and cabinet duration

Data for 13 countries 1980–98 (excluding Greece, Spain, and the UK) from Müller and Strøm (2003). Additional data from Hirsh (2000) and from national election sites for 1998–2006 and for Greece, Spain, and the UK.

Effective number of parties in the legislature

Data for 13 countries 1980–98 (excluding Greece, Spain, and the UK) from Müller and Strøm (2003 [2000]). Others: authors' calculations.

Government deficit

General government financial balances as percent of nominal GDP from OECD *Economic Outlook* June 2007, Annex Table 27, and OECD *Economic Outlook* December 1996, Annex Table 30.

Government debt

General government net financial liabilities as percent of nominal GDP from OECD *Economic Outlook* June 2007, Annex Table 33 and OECD *Economic Outlook* December 1999, Annex Table 35.

Unemployment

Standardized unemployment rates, percent of civilian labor force from OECD *Economic Outlook* June 2007, Annex Table 14 and OECD *Economic Outlook* December 1999, Annex Table 22.

Inflation

Consumer price index, percentage change from previous year from OECD *Economic Outlook* June 2007, Annex Table 18 and OECD *Economic Outlook* December 1996, Annex Table 16.

Trade union density

Total union membership as a percentage of employed wage and salary earners. There is no single comprehensive time series for all 16 countries for the whole of our time frame. We therefore had to combine data from a number of different sources, as follows. Data for 1980–2001 for all 16 countries (also includes 2002 data for Germany, Italy, Netherlands, and the UK) from OECD *Unpublished Dataset* 1980–2001, compiled by Andrew Glyn and available from the authors on request. 2003 figures for 13 countries from Visser (2006) and based on the OECD dataset (the three exclusions are Greece, Luxembourg and Portugal). Data for the remaining countries and years were taken, or calculated, from EIRO *Annual Reviews* (see above) aiming, as far as possible, to use membership and employment definitions consistent with the OECD time series. Clearly data for the final years of our dataset, 2004–06, are less than ideal.

Bargaining centralization and coordination

Data from Driffil (2005) Tables 3 and 4 for 14 countries. Data for Greece and for 2005–06 inferred from EIRO *Annual Reviews* and from Kritsantonis (1998: 523); for Luxembourg from EIRO *Annual Reviews* 1997–2006 and from Tunsch (1998: 351).

Appendix 2

Variable names and measurements

Note: in all cases, "main party" and "main coalition party" refers to the party of the prime minister

Pact/legislation

Poffered	Pact offered 1 = yes, 0 = no
Legisl	Legislation instead of pact 1= yes, 0 = no

Content

Welfare	Dummy on content 1 = welfare content, 0 = non-welfare
Labor market	Dummy on content 1 = labor market content, 0 = non-labor market content
Wages	Dummy on content 1 = wage content, 0 = non-wage content

Electoral pressures: votes

Avote	Main coalition partner percentage of vote
Achngvote	Main coalition partner change in the vote percentage
Abschngv	Main coalition partner absolute change of votes
Directionv	Direction of change 1 = positive (increase), 0 = negative (decrease)
Distancev	Difference in % vote between the first and second strongest parties

Timing

Time1	Pact year 1992–1998
Time2	Pact year pre-1992 or post-1998

Party family

Party position	Left-right position of the main coalition partner
Socdem	Social Democrats or Labour 1 = yes, 0 = no
Center	Center Party 1 = yes, 0 = no

Liberals	Liberals 1 = yes, 0 = no
Conservatives	Conservatives 1 = yes, 0 = no
Christian	Christian Democrats 1 = yes, 0 = no

Type of government

Single	Dummy for single-party government 1 = yes, 0 = no
Connected	Dummy for connected coalition government 1 = yes, 0 = no
Unconnected	Dummy for unconnected coalition government 1 = yes, 0 = no
Strength	Percentage of seats in the lower house of the legislature held by the government

Legislative party fragmentation

| Effective | Effective number of parties in the legislature (lower house) |

Longevity of government

| Duration | Cabinet duration in days |

Control variables

Deficit	Government deficit as % of GDP for year prior to pact offer or legislation
Unemployment	Unemployment rate % for year prior to pact offer or legislation
Inflation	Inflation rate for year prior to pact offer or legislation
Density	Union density %
Coordination	Bargaining coordination
Previnflat	Inflation in the year before the election following a pact offer or legislation
Prevunemp	Unemployment in the year before the election following a pact offer or legislation

Economic institutions: welfare state categories

North	Northern Europe: Scandinavia 1 = yes, 0 = no
South	Southern Europe Mediterranean 1 = yes, 0 = no
Central	Central Europe (Austria, Germany and, Benelux) 1 = yes, 0 = no
UKEire	UK and Ireland 1 = yes, 0 = no

Notes

1 Introduction

1 We discuss this literature in detail in Chapter 2 (see, e.g. Avdagic 2006; Baccaro and Lim 2007; Fajertag and Pochet 2000; Hancké and Rhodes 2005; Hassel 2006).

2 Our focus is on national agreements, although we are aware of a growing interest in labor market regulation at regional level (Regalia 2005) as well as in company level "pacts for employment and competitiveness" (PECs) (Sisson *et al.* 1999; Seifert and Massa-Wirth 2005).

3 We thus reverse our earlier classification (Hamann and Kelly 2007b) that followed conventional practice and understood the Wassenaar agreement as a social pact. However, on a strict application of the definition used in this book it is not a social pact, however influential it may have been in stimulating pacts elsewhere (see Ahlquist 2008 for a similar view).

4 For alternative typologies, see e.g. Amable (2003) or Schmidt (2002).

5 For an excellent overview of the literature on attitudes towards the welfare state, see Kumlin (2007a).

6 Other studies, however, employing different measurements, data, and country cases, have found less systematic evidence of public support for the welfare state across types of welfare state regime (see, e.g. Papadakis and Bean 1993; Meier Jaeger 2006). Differences might also exist depending on whether the welfare state aims at increasing security or equality (for an overview, see Kumlin 2007a: 365). In addition, some results indicate that regime types vary in their support for specific welfare programs; for instance, support for the sick and the old varies little across regimes types, while support for the unemployed shows more variance across countries (Blekesaune and Quadagno 2003; see also Kumlin 2007a: 365). In contrast, Scheepers and Te Grotenhuis (2005) find that people in liberal welfare states are the most likely to donate money to the poor. Gelissen (2000) concludes that there is little difference across types of welfare states, and if any, citizens in the liberal welfare regimes are more supportive of the welfare state.

2 The institutional political economy of social pacts

1 While the remainder of the book looks at pact offers rather than signed pacts, here we only use data from pacts that were actually signed to make the data comparable with the existing literature.

2 The pseudo R-squared value was 0.03, LR Chi square was 8.99 and the p-value was 0.11.

3 The political logic of social pacts

1 To quote Pierson (1994: 17) with reference to governments' twin goals of advancing their policy agendas and get reelected, it is not necessary "to assume that governments consider only electoral implications in formulating policies; it is enough ... that such concerns are a central consideration, if only because failure to consider electoral consequences can jeopardize policymakers' long-term prospects for implementing their preferred policies." Similarly, Keman (2005: 223) concludes from an empirical study of 21 OECD countries that "parties – especially incumbent ones – appear to show both policy-seeking and office-seeking behavior."

2 There has been some debate in the literature as to the extent to which adjustment pressures and their political consequences have been real or objective, and to what extent governments have used them as rhetorical devices to justify unpopular policies that are not, or only partially, related to external pressures (e.g. Hay and Rosamond 2002; Schmidt 2002). This is not the issue here, however. The point of discussion is not governments' endogenous preference formation, but rather the different ways in which governments have attempted to implement these preferences. Furthermore, we do not argue that voters need to disagree with their country's joining the EMU – they might well support the outcome, without, however, embracing related policies that affect them negatively and personally, such as real wage loss, more expensive health care, or reduced pensions.

3 Some research discusses the lack of accountability through elections (see, e.g. Cheibub and Przeworski 1999) and the fact that overall, heads of governments in democracies often come to power through means other than elections. This was the case in 48 percent of the leaders in the cases of parliamentary democracies considered by Cheibub and Przeworski (1999: 232), who speculate that "governments are not accountable to voters, at least not for economic issues" (1999: 237). Similarly, Keman (2005) analyzes the duration and termination of administrations by government type and finds that just over half of postwar governments relinquished power because of elections; 30 percent did so because of internal political conflict, especially coalition governments.

4 See Lewis-Beck and Paldam (2000) for an overview of the literature on these two controversies in the economic voting literature.

5 The literature on economic voting is large and rapidly growing; therefore, we do not intend to report all detailed findings of this body of literature. In a summary article, Anderson (2007: 287) concludes that "the answer to the questions of whether and when the economy matters seems to be a resounding 'it depends.'"

6 Again, we are aware that this statement is a generalization and perhaps oversimplification, and that exceptions to this assumption exist at specific times, for specific issues, and in specific countries. However, as a general rule, we have found no evidence that by and large and all other things being equal, voters would generally prefer low wages rather than high wages, longer workweeks rather than shorter ones, or less employment protection rather than more.

7 Pierson (1994: 147–9) argues that the public's criticisms about taxation and declining popularity of specific welfare programs facilitated the initial electoral success of Margaret Thatcher in Britain and Ronald Reagan in the United States. In Britain, 34 percent of the electorate judged that welfare benefits were too generous (compared to 24 percent who thought they were too mean) in 1974, and 50 percent thought so in 1979. Similarly, public support for welfare programs

declined in the US in the 1970s. However, in both countries public opinion shifted back to a support for welfare programs once initial retrenchment policies were implemented.

8　The ten countries are Belgium, Denmark, Germany, Finland, Great Britain, Italy, the Netherlands, Norway, Austria, and Sweden. Scarrow (2000: 90) reports similar results, with only Germany showing a small increase (0.5 percent) in the member/electorate ratio; for data demonstrating overall party membership decline see also Mair and van Biezen (2001).

9　However, Scarrow (2000: 99) suggests that "although parties which were able to enroll large proportions of their voters may have been strong in terms of their ability to pursue a strategy of social encapsulation, they may have been comparatively weak in terms of their ability to contest elections in volatile electoral markets. Because of this, party strength does not necessarily decrease along with … drops in enrolment."

10　To cite Green-Pedersen (2002: 34–5), "Governments must be able to persuade voters that the welfare state is retrenched to save it or to remedy its policy failures … If retrenchment is politicised as a matter of being for or against the welfare state *per se*, the electoral changes are insurmountable." We argue that pacts may serve as one strategy to convince voters of welfare cutbacks as a superior alternative.

4　Governments, voters, and social pacts in Western Europe

1　We exclude legislation proposed by opposition parties or individual members of the legislature. Nor do we address here whether the bills got passed or not. We include only legislation that appears to be contentious, such as cuts in pension, longer workweek, etc., while excluding reforms that promise to generate little popular opposition, such as higher pensions, or a shorter workweek. We assume that in these cases, governments will see little point in offering pacts.

2　An alternative measure is the difference in parliamentary seats between the two largest parties (parliamentary competitiveness). However, we are here more directly concerned with voter behavior rather than the less direct measure of seats given the distorting effects of electoral institutions. Moreover, when checking correlations, seat totals and absolute and relative seat changes were highly correlated with the equivalent measures of votes. For example, the main coalition partner's changes in vote and seat share were correlated 0.59 ($p < 0.001$). We thus use only one measure, vote distance, between the two largest parties.

3　We are not aware of any literature that has systematically explored the relationship between party family and wage or labor market reform to any extent. We therefore concentrate our reasoning on welfare reform assuming that a parallel logic could be construed for the other two issues as well.

4　Given the substantial number of independent variables we ran diagnostic tests for multicollinearity. The Variance Inflation Factor (VIF) and the Tolerance scores were highly satisfactory for almost all of the independent variables: All but two of the VIF scores were well below the critical threshold of 10.0 and all but two of the Tolerance scores were well above 0.10. The problematic variables with evidence of multicollinearity were party position (based on the Manifesto Research Group data) and the interaction term between party position and government strength. In order to reduce these problems we centered the interval variables. Upon rerunning the regressions all of the VIF and Tolerance scores were satisfactory.

5 We assume that these reforms might still need to obtain subsequent legislative approval. However, it appears that it will be easier to pass reforms in the legislature if they are previously negotiated with unions and employers rather than being imposed in the face of social partner opposition.

6 We are conscious of the debate over the classification of France. Not all authors would agree with its placement alongside the Southern Europe cases as part of a "Mediterranean capitalism" (Hall and Soskice 2001b: 21). Schmidt (2002: 119) classifies France along with Italy and Spain as examples of a third variety of capitalism labeled "state capitalism." Amable (2003: 173) notes that France has features in common with both continental and Southern European economies but classifies it with the continental group. Hancké *et al.* (2007b: 25) class France in a separate category from Italy and Spain. There is also some debate as to whether the Irish case should be reclassified as a hybrid economy, comprising elements of both LMEs and CMEs (see Amable 2003: 173).

7 In the complicated case of Ireland we follow Gallagher *et al.* (2006: 242, 245) and classified Fine Gael as a Christian Democratic party but disagreed with their view of Fianna Fáil as a conservative party, labelling it instead as a center party.

8 We do not repeat here the z-scores and p-values reported in the tables. As a rule of thumb, and for one-tailed tests, z-scores of 1.65 or more are significant at the 5 percent level and scores of 1.30 or above are significant at the 10 percent level. For two-tailed tests, z-scores of 2.00 or more are significant at the 5 percent level and scores of 1.65 or above are significant at the 10 percent level.

9 We also estimated our model with an alternative measurement of executive strength, that of minority or majority status. Results showed that minority executives were significantly more likely to offer pacts than their majoritarian counterparts. Due to the high correlation between seat share and type of government, we include only one measure (seat share) in our models.

5 The divergent trajectories of social pacts in the Liberal Market Economies

1 We follow conventional practice in referring to the UK (England, Scotland, Wales, and Northern Ireland) rather than Great Britain (the UK excluding Northern Ireland). However, concerning industrial relations, Great Britain would make more sense as Northern Ireland is covered both by UK law but also by specific Northern Irish labor law. In contrast, Scotland and Wales do not have regionally specific industrial relations laws.

2 The reemergence of tripartism in 1987 has also been partly explained in terms of path dependency, in other words the government and the social partners recuperated and revised a tradition of centralized agreements present during the 1970s in responding to the economic problems of the 1980s (e.g. von Prondzynski 1998: 66). We do not find this analysis convincing because it cannot account for the case of the UK (see below), where a similar tradition of corporatism in the 1970s was repudiated by the Conservatives and later by Labour.

3 This is a contentious proposition and researchers have highlighted the role of other significant factors in the country's economic performance, such as the growth of foreign direct investment and of EU subsidies (e.g. Daly 2005).

4 During the first six years of Thatcher's leadership (1975–81), the Conservative Party was deeply divided between the older "corporatist" wing led by Shadow Employment Secretary Prior and the rising neoliberal wing formed around

Thatcher. Only when Prior and other corporatists were eventually removed from key ministerial posts and replaced by neoliberals in 1981 did Thatcher begin to consolidate the hegemony of the neoliberal program within her cabinet (Gamble 1994: 119).

5 The SDP was also in favor of incomes policy at this time but argued the case for government to have reserve powers of compulsion (SDP 1982a: 22).

6 This had been the position of the SDP since 1982 (SDP 1982b).

6 Social democracy between pacts and legislation in Scandinavia

1 Our measure of wage intervention was described earlier and centers on explicit and formal attempts by government, through pact offers and/or legislation, to moderate wage settlements. Clearly governments will also resort to informal exhortation and sometimes informal consultation in addition to, or instead of, more formal mechanisms.

2 In part the Swedish figure reflects a high unemployment benefit replacement ratio of 74 percent in 1995 (for workers on average wages) as well as a relatively high proportion of workers in the public sector of 22 percent (Fulcher 2002; Huber and Stephens 2001: 358, 360).

3 Under the Meidner Plan, first drafted by the union confederation LO in 1975 and then backed by the SAP, a proportion of company profits would be paid each year into a union-controlled "Wage Earner Fund," which would be used to buy up shares in companies. Over a long period of time the Funds would eventually give organized labor majority ownership in Swedish firms, in effect socializing Swedish capital (Sainsbury 1993: 44; Therborn 1991: 108–9).

7 Cycles of social pacts in the Mediterranean economies

1 Molina and Rhodes (2007a) also acknowledge that Italy bears some resemblance to CMEs especially with respect to its proportional electoral institutions (see also Thelen 2001). Spain, in contrast, displays some features that position it closer to the LMEs (e.g. Chari and Heywood 2008; Molina and Rhodes 2007a) while other authors assert that some aspects of economic institutions – specifically, industrial relations – position Spain closer to the CME cluster rather than the LMEs (e.g. Royo 2007).

2 However, it is important to note that party membership and the membership/ voter ratio has been on the rise in Spain since *c.* 1980 in contrast to many other West European countries. Around 1980, party membership was only 1.2 percent of the national electorate in the new democracy; in 1990, 2.1 percent of Spanish voters belonged to a party, and 3.4 percent another decade later (*c.* 1999). While in 1980 and 1990, Spain had the lowest membership/voter ratio out of 16 West European countries, by 1999, five other countries featured ratios even lower than that of Spain as Spanish party membership had increased by 250 percent between 1980 and 1999, by far the highest rate of increase in Western Europe (Katz 2005: 101–2).

3 Spain's mean effective number of legislative parties for 1979–2004 was 2.62 (authors' calculation based on Hopkin 2005a: 382, Table 18.4) compared to a mean of 3.6 in 27 democracies with proportional representation systems (1945–90) and 3.9 for 28 European countries 2000–04 (Gallagher 2005: 546).

4 See Gunther (1996) for an analysis of public policy and budgetary developments on social spending.

5 The Moncloa Pacts, signed by parliamentary parties, laid out economic reforms, such as inflation targets and wage ceilings, to stabilize the economy during the time that the constitutional assembly drafted the constitution. Gunther *et al.* (2004: 111) conclude that while "the economic consequences of the Pacts of Moncloa are debatable, the political impact of these negotiations was unambiguously positive." Here, we do not consider the Moncloa Pacts as a "pact" according to our definition since non-party actors were not directly included in the negotiations and did not sign the agreement.

6 Since this book is interested in governments' motivations to offer pacts rather than unions' or employers' motivation to engage in negotiations, we have excluded these bipartite, interconfederal pacts from our analysis in Chapter 4 and will not discuss them in detail in this chapter.

7 Electoral volatility is here measured in the aggregate "based upon net shifts in the total number of votes for each respective party" (Gunther *et al.* 2004: 415, note 4).

8 Spain's union density rate stood at about 15 percent (Jordana 1996: 215).

9 For a slightly different estimate, see Maurer (1999: 31).

10 This is true for the entire period from 1977–2004. While data on the reasons for which Bills were not passed are not available by legislative period, Field (2005: 1084) reports that 90 percent of Bills that did not become law expired due to parliamentary elections, 8 percent were withdrawn, and only 2 percent were rejected.

11 Astudillo Ruiz (2001) provides an alternative explanation, pointing to the patterns of inter-union competition in union elections.

12 In a 1996 sample, 34 percent of voters identified themselves as "center-left," and 37 percent as "center," while only 15 percent professed to be "center-right" and 4 percent claimed to be "right," with the average self-location being 4.7 on a 10-point scale, the same as in 1993 (Gunther *et al.* 2004: 236).

13 While we only consider developments until 2006 here, the government's cooperative stance continued beyond the 2006 period.

14 These figures are somewhat deceptive because approximately 50 percent of Italian union members are pensioners, not employed workers (Regalia and Regini 1998: 472).

15 Negrelli and Santi (1990: 164–70), however, reason that 1983 was not such a significant turning point because "talks" between government, unions, and employers continued well beyond this date. This argument seriously underplays the willingness of governments after 1983 to resort to unilateral implementation of labor market reforms. We therefore concur with the conventional view of 1983 as the turning point.

8 Tripartism under duress in coordinated market economies

1 Poguntke (2005b: 69) dates the beginning of the decline of tripartite agreements to 1977 following an employers' associations appeal to the Constitutional Court against the SPD–FDP's codetermination reform.

2 If the Bundesrat casts a suspensive veto, the Bundestag can either amend the bill until the Bundesrat accepts it, or it can overrule the veto if the entire Bundestag votes for the bill (Silvia 1999: 173).

3 The electoral laws were modified for this particular election to apply the 5 percent threshold separately for the former East and West German territories. Thus, the eastern Greens/Alliance 90 succeeded in gaining seats, but the western Greens – running on a separate ticket – failed to clear the threshold (James 1991).

4 On the role of electoral competition in the adoption of the Hartz reforms, see also Picot (2009).

5 This was because the SPD received four *Überhangmandate* (surplus seats) compared to the CDU/CSU's one, leading to a three-seat difference (Deutscher Bundestag 2007). *Überhangmandate* exist when a party receives more seats resulting from the first ballot (plurality ballot) than it is entitled to according to the second (proportional) ballot.

6 Kittel (2000: 112) provides a description of the policy-making process, including informal consultations with the ministry, the SPÖ and ÖVP, and interest organizations including labor and business; in a next step the Chambers (including the labor and employers' chamber) comment on the draft, which is then revised and discussed again in an iterative process; the resulting consensus document is then passed on to the executive and parliament, where the interest organizations have again input in modifying the draft as they are represented through their members who have parliamentary standing as elected party members. In a different approach from introducing legislation, parliamentary parties introduce Bills without prior negotiations with the interest organizations, which then act more as lobbying groups while the Bill is discussed; in yet other areas, interest groups are not consulted.

7 Concertation was not the prevalent decision-making mode in privatizing state-owned industries after 1985, where a weakening of the union influence in policy making was evident (Kittel 2000).

8 The FPÖ leadership then emphasized the party's move towards the center; moreover, the party obtained less than 5 percent of the vote in the elections, clearly relegating it to the position of a junior coalition partner and rendering it comparatively little influence on policies. The coalition fell apart when Jörg Haider assumed the party leadership in 1986, and early elections were called (Luther 2000: 29).

9 This mirrored the experience of a decade earlier, where Tálos (1996: 110) observes that the "clearly increasing divergence of interests brought on by growing economic and social problems at the end of the 1970s and the early 1980s" did not lead to "any fundamental doubts about social partnership."

10 Klima succeeded as chancellor when Vranitsky resigned in January 1997 as a result of the SPÖ's poor performance in the elections to the European parliament and Vienna state parliament (Schulze and Schludi 2007: 584).

11 The Constitutional Court ruled in 2003 that the government's reform had been unconstitutional (Adams 2003c).

12 See Minkenberg (2001) for a list of the Freedom Party's anti-immigrant and anti-foreigner policy proposals in the legislature and executive.

13 See Luther (2000) on changes in the FPÖ's ideology since its establishment.

9 Conclusion

1 Data on pact offers and legislation for all cases in this chapter from the Hamann-Kelly pacts dataset.

References

Abse, Tobias (1994) "Italy: A New Agenda," in Perry Anderson and Patrick Camiller (eds) *Mapping the West European Left*, London: Verso, pp. 189–232.

Adam, Georg (2003a) "Government Proposes Amendments to Shop Opening Hours Act," *European Industrial Relations Observatory*, July 8. Online. Available <http://www.eiro.eurofound.ie/2003/07/inbrief/at0307201n.html> (accessed November 22, 2009).

—— (2003b) "Government Challenges Social Partnership," *European Industrial Relations Observatory*, May 20. Online. Available <http://www.eiro.eurofound.ie/2003/05/feature/at0305202f.html> (accessed November 22, 2009).

—— (2003c) "Constitutional Court Overturns Reform of Social Security Body," *European Industrial Relations Observatory*, November 11. Online. Available <http://www.eiro.eurofound.ie/2003/11/inbrief/at0311201n.html> (accessed November 22, 2009).

—— (2004) "Controversy over Government's Pensions Harmonisation Plans," *European Industrial Relations Observatory*, 27 September. Online. Available <http://www.eiro.eurofound.ie/2004/09/feature/at0409203f.html> (accessed November 22, 2009).

Adams, James and Zeynep Somer-Topcu (2009) "Policy Adjustments by Parties in Response to Rival Parties' Policy Shifts: Spatial Theory and the Dynamics of Party Competition in Twenty-Five Post-War Democracies", *British Journal of Political Science*, 39(4): 825–46.

Aguar, María José, Alexandre Casademut, and Joaquim M. Molins (1999) "Las organizaciones empresariales en la etapa de la consolidación democrática (1986–1997). Unión Europea, desconcertación y diálogo social," in Faustino Miguélez and Carlos Prieto (eds) *Las relaciones del empleo en España*, Madrid: Siglo XXI, pp. 53–78.

Aguilar, Salvador and Jordi Roca (1991) *Sindicalisme i canvi social a Espanya, 1976–1988. Epíleg: la vaga general del 14–D*, Barcelona: Fundació Jaume Bofill/Fundació Volkswagen.

Ahlberg, Kerstin (1997) "1997 Annual Review for Sweden," *European Industrial Relations Observatory*, December 28. Online. Available <http://www.eurofound.europa.eu/eiro/1997/12/feature/se9712172f.htm> (accessed November 22, 2009).

Ahlquist, John (2007) "Policy by Contract: Social Pacts in Australia and New Zealand," Paper presented at Midwest Political Science Association Meeting, Chicago, April 12–15.

—— (2008) "Parties, Pacts, and Elections: The Determinants of Social Pacts, 1974–2000," University of Washington, Unpublished Manuscript.

Allan, James P. and Lyle Scruggs (2004) "Political Partisanship and Welfare State Reform in Advanced Industrial Societies," *American Journal of Political Science*, 48(3): 496–512.

Allern, Elin H., Nicholas Aylott and Flemming J. Christiansen (2007) "Social Democrats and Trade Unions in Scandinavia: The Decline and Persistence of Institutional Relationships," *European Journal of Political Research*, 46(5): 607–35.

Amable, Bruno (2003) *The Diversity of Modern Capitalism*, Oxford: Oxford University Press.

Anderson, Christopher J. (1995) "The Dynamics of Public Support for Coalition Governments," *Comparative Political Studies*, 28(3): 350–83.

—— (2000) "Economic Voting and Political Context: A Comparative Perspective," *Electoral Studies*, 19(2): 151–70.

—— (2007) "The End of Economic Voting? Contingency Dilemmas and the Limits of Democratic Accountability," *Annual Review of Political Science*, 10: 271–96.

Anderson, Karen M. and Traute Meyer (2003) "Social Democracy, Unions, and Pension Politics in Germany and Sweden," *Journal of Public Policy*, 23(1): 23–54.

Anderson, Karen M. and Ellen M. Immergut (2007) "Sweden: After Social Democratic Hegemony," in Ellen M. Immergut, Karen M. Anderson and Isabelle Schulze (eds) *The Handbook of West European Pension Politics*, Oxford: Oxford University Press, pp. 349–95.

Andeweg, Rudy B. (1999) "Parties, Pillars and the Politics of Accommodation: Weak or Weakening Linkages? The Case of Dutch Consociationalism," in Kurt R. Luther and Kris Deschouwer (eds) *Party Elites in Divided Societies: Political Parties in Consociational Democracy*, London: Routledge, pp.108–33.

—— and Galen A. Irwin (2005) *Governance and Politics of the Netherlands*, 2nd edn, Basingstoke: Palgrave Macmillan.

Anthonsen, Mette and Johannes Lindvall (2009) "Party Competition and the Resilience of Corporatism," *Government and Opposition*, 44(2): 167–87.

Arcq, Etienne and Philippe Pochet (2000) "Towards a New Social Pact in Belgium?," in Giuseppe Fajertag and Philippe Pochet (eds) *Social Pacts in Europe – New Dynamics*, 2nd edn, Brussels: European Trade Union Institute, pp. 113–34.

Arter, David (1987) "The 1987 Finnish Election: The Conservatives Out of the Wilderness," *West European Politics*, 10(4): 171–6.

—— (1991) "The Finnish Election of 17 March 1991: A Victory for Opposition," *West European Politics*, 14(4): 174–80.

—— (1994) "The War of the Roses': Conflict and Cohesion in the Swedish Social Democratic Party," in David S. Bell and Eric Shaw (eds) *Conflict and Cohesion in Western European Social Democratic Parties*, London: Pinter, pp. 70–95.

—— (1995) "The March 1995 Finnish Election: The Social Democrats Storm Back," *West European Politics*, 18(4): 194–204.

—— (1999a) *Scandinavian Politics Today*, Manchester: Manchester University Press.

—— (1999b) "The Swedish General Election of 20th September 1998: A Victory of Values over Policies?," *Electoral Studies*, 18(2): 296–300.

—— (2000) "The Finnish Election of 21 March 1999: Towards a Distinctive Model of Government," *West European Politics*, 23(1): 180–86.

—— (2003) "From the 'Rainbow Coalition' Back Down to Earth? The 2003 Finnish General Election," *West European Politics*, 26(3): 153–62.

—— (2006) *Democracy in Scandinavia: Consensual, Majoritarian or Mixed?*, Manchester: Manchester University Press.

Astudillo Ruiz, Javier (2001) "Without Unions, but Socialist: The Spanish Socialist Party and Its Divorce from Its Union Confederation (1982–96)," *Politics and Society*, 29(2): 273–96.

Avdagic, Sabina (2006) "Distributive Politics: Experimentation, Learning and Reform: National Social Pacts," New Modes of Governance Project (NEWGOV) No. CITI-2004-506392.

—— (2010) "When are Concerted Reforms Feasible? Explaining the Emergence of Social Pacts in Europe," *Comparative Political Studies*, 43(7):

—— Martin Rhodes and Jelle Visser (2005) The Emergence and Evolution of Social Pacts: A Provisional Framework for Comparative Analysis, European Governance Papers (EUROGOV) No. N-05-01. Online. Available <http://www.connex-network. org/eurogov/pdf/egp-newgov-N-05-01.pdf> (accessed November 22, 2009).

Aylott, Nicholas (2003) "After the Divorce: Social Democrats and Trade Unions in Sweden," *Party Politics*, 9(3): 369–90.

—— (2004) "From People's Movements to Electoral Machines? Interest Aggregation and the Social Democratic Parties of Scandinavia," in Kay Lawson and Thomas Poguntke (eds) *How Political Parties Respond: Interest Aggregation Revisited*, London: Routledge, pp. 61–85.

—— and Niklas Bolin (2007) "Toward a Two-Party System? The Swedish Parliamentary Election of September 2006," *West European Politics*, 30(3): 621–33.

Baccaro, Lucio (2002a) "Negotiating the Italian Pension Reform with Unions: Lessons for Corporatist Theory," *Industrial and Labor Relations Review*, 55(3): 413–31.

—— (2002b) "The Construction of 'Democratic' Corporatism in Italy," *Politics and Society*, 30(2): 327–57.

—— (2003) "What is Alive and What is Dead in the Theory of Corporatism," *British Journal of Industrial Relations*, 41(4): 683–706.

—— and Sang-Hoon Lim (2007) "Social Pacts as Coalitions of the Weak and Moderate: Ireland, Italy and South Korea in Comparative Perspective," *European Journal of Industrial Relations*, 13(1): 27–46.

—— and Marco Simoni (2007) "Centralized Wage Bargaining and the "Celtic Tiger" Phenomenon," *Industrial Relations*, 46(3): 426–55.

—— and Marco Simoni (2008) "Policy Concertation in Europe: Understanding Government Choice," *Comparative Political Studies*, 41(10): 1323–48.

Baglioni, Simone, Donatella Della Porta and Paolo Graziano (2008) "The Contentious Politics of Unemployment: The Italian Case in Comparative Perspective," *European Journal of Political Research*, 47(6): 826–51.

Bardi, Luciano (2002) "Italian Parties: Change and Functionality," in Paul Webb, David M. Farrell and Ian Holliday (eds) *Political Parties in Advanced Industrial Democracies*, Oxford: Oxford University Press, pp. 46–76.

—— (2004) "Party Responses to Electoral Dealignment in Italy," in Peter Mair, Wolfgang C. Müller and Fritz Plasser (eds) *Political Parties and Electoral Change*, London: Sage, pp. 111–44.

Bartolini, Stefano (2002) "Electoral and Party Competition: Analytical Dimensions and Empirical Problems," in Richard Gunther, José Ramón Montero and Juan J. Linz (eds) *Political Parties: Old Concepts and New Challenges*, Oxford: Oxford University Press, pp. 84–110.

—— and Peter Mair (2001) "Challenges to Contemporary Political Parties," in Larry Diamond and Richard Gunther (eds) *Political Parties and Democracy*, Baltimore, MD: Johns Hopkins University Press, pp. 327–44.

Becker, Uwe and Herman Schwartz (eds) (2005) *Employment "Miracles": A Critical Comparison of the Dutch, Scandinavian, Swiss, Australian and Irish Cases Versus Germany and the US*, Amsterdam: Amsterdam University Press.

Behrens, Martin, Michael Fichter and Carola M. Frege (2007) "Trade Union Revitalisation in Germany," in Craig Phelan (ed.) *Trade Union Revitalisation: Trends and Prospects in 34 Countries*, Oxford and Bern: Peter Lang, pp. 173–86.

Benner, Mats and Torben Bundgaard Vad (2000) "Sweden and Denmark: Defending the Welfare State," in Fritz W. Scharpf and Vivien Schmidt (eds) *Welfare and Work in the Open Economy Vol 2: Diverse Responses to Common Challenges*, New York: Oxford University Press, pp. 399–466.

Berg, Annika (1999) "1999 Annual Review for Sweden," *European Industrial Relations Observatory*, December 28. Online. Available <http://www.eurofound.europa.eu/eiro/1999/12/feature/se9912116f.htm> (accessed November 22, 2009).

Berglund, Sten (1991) "The Finnish Parliamentary Election of 1991," *Electoral Studies*, 10(3): 256–61.

—— (1995) "The Finnish Parliamentary Election of 1995," *Electoral Studies*, 14(4): 461–4.

Bergman, Torbjörn (2003) [2000] "Sweden: When Minority Cabinets are the Rule and Majority Coalitions the Exception," in Wolfgang C. Müller and Kaare Strøm (eds) *Coalition Governments in Western Europe*, New York: Cambridge University Press, pp. 192–230.

Bertram, Hans (1994) "Youth: Work and Unemployment – A European Perspective for Research," in Anne C. Petersen and Jeylan T. Mortimer (eds) *Youth Unemployment and Society*, New York: Cambridge University Press, pp. 273–94.

Bewley, Helen (2006) "Annual Review Article 2005: Raising the Standard? The Regulation of Employment, and Public Sector Pay Policy," *British Journal of Industrial Relations*, 44(2): 351–72.

Bille, Lars and Karina Pedersen (2004) "Electoral Fortunes of the Social Democratic Party and Liberal Party in Denmark: Ups and Downs," in Peter Mair, Wolfgang C. Müller and Fritz Plasser (eds) *Political Parties and Electoral Change: Party Responses to Electoral Markets*, London: Sage, pp. 207–33.

Bispinck, Reinhard and Thorsten Schulten (2000) "Alliance for Jobs – Is Germany Following the Path of 'Competitive Corporatism'?," in Giuseppe Fajertag and Philippe Pochet (eds) *Social Pacts in Europe – New Dynamics*, 2nd edn, Brussels: European Trade Union Institute, pp. 187–218.

Björklund, Anders (2000) "Going Different Ways: Labor Market Policy in Denmark and Sweden," in Gøsta Esping-Andersen and Marino Regini (eds) *Why Deregulate Labour Markets?*, Oxford: Oxford University Press, pp. 148–80.

Blaschke, Sabine (2006) "Restructuring as a Reaction to Growing Pressure on Trade Unionism: The Case of the Austrian ÖGB," *Industrial Relations Journal*, 37(2): 147–63.

—— Andrea Kirschner and Franz Traxler (2000) "Austrian Trade Unions: Between Continuity and Modernisation," in Jeremy Waddington and Reiner Hoffmann (eds) *Trade Unions in Europe: Facing Challenges and Searching for Solutions*, Brussels: European Trade Union Institute, pp. 81–103.

Blekesaune, Morten and Jill Quadagno (2003) "Public Attitudes toward Welfare State Policies: A Comparative Analysis of 24 Nations," *European Sociological Review*, 19(5): 415–27.

Board of Trade (1998) *Fairness at Work*, London: HMSO, Cm 3968.

Böckerman, Petri and Roope Uusitalo (2006) "Erosion of the Ghent System and Union Membership Decline: Lessons from Finland," *British Journal of Industrial Relations*, 44(2): 283–303.

Boreus, Kristina (1997) "The Shift to the Right: Neo-Liberalism in Argumentation and Language in the Swedish Public Debate since 1969," *European Journal of Political Research*, 31(3): 257–86.

Börsch-Supan, Axel H. and Christina B. Wilke (2006) "The German Public Pension System: How It Will Become an NDC System Look-Alike," in Robert Holzmann and Edward Palmer (eds) *Pension Reform: Issues and Prospects for Non-Financial Defined Contribution (NDC) Schemes*, Washington D.C.: The World Bank, pp. 573–610.

Brandl, Bernd and Fritz Traxler (2005) "Industrial Relations, Social Pacts and Welfare Expenditures: A Cross-National Comparison," *British Journal of Industrial Relations*, 43(4): 635–58.

Brooks, Clem and Jeff Manza (2007) *Why Welfare States Persist: The Importance of Public Opinion in Democracies*, Chicago: University of Chicago Press.

Brown, Michael (1996) "The Confederated Trade Unions and the Dini Government: 'The Grand Return to Neo-Corporatism?," in Mario Caciagli and David I. Kertzer (eds) *Italian Politics: The Stalled Transition*, Boulder, CO: Westview Press, pp. 205–21.

Budge, Ian, Hans-Dieter Klingemann, Andrea Volkens, Judith Bara and Eric Tanenbaum (2001) *Mapping Policy Preferences: Estimates for Parties, Electors, and Governments 1945–1998*, Oxford: Oxford University Press.

Bufacchi, Vittorio and Simon Burgess (2001) *Italy since 1989: Events and Interpretations*, rev. edn, Basingstoke: Macmillan.

Bundesministerium für Inneres (n.d.) "Nationalratswahlen," Online. Available <http://www.bmi.gv.at/wahlen/> (accessed November 22, 2009).

Burgess, Katrina (2004) *Parties and Unions in the New Global Economy*, Pittsburgh, PA: University of Pittsburgh Press.

Busemeyer, Marius R. (2005) "Pension Reform in Germany and Austria: System Change vs. Quantitative Retrenchment," *West European Politics*, 28(3): 569–91.

Butler, David and Dennis Kavanagh (1980) *The British General Election of 1979*, Basingstoke: Macmillan Press Ltd.

—— and Dennis Kavanagh (1984) *The British General Election of 1983*, Basingstoke: Macmillan Press Ltd.

—— and Dennis Kavanagh (1988) *The British General Election of 1987*, Basingstoke: Macmillan Press Ltd.

—— and Dennis Kavanagh (1992) *The British General Election of 1992*, Basingstoke: Macmillan Press Ltd.

—— and Dennis Kavanagh (2002) *The British General Election of 2001*, Basingstoke: Macmillan Press Ltd.

Callaghan, John (2000) *The Retreat of Social Democracy*, Manchester: Manchester University Press.

Calmfors, Lars, Alison Booth, Michael Burda, Danielle Chechi, Robin Naylor and Jelle Visser (2001) "The Future of Collective Bargaining in Europe," in Tito Boeri, Agar Brugiavini and Lars Calmfors (eds) *The Role of Unions in the Twenty-First Century*, Oxford: Oxford University Press, pp. 1–134.

Campos Lima, Maria da Paz and Reinhard Naumann (2000) "Social Pacts in Portugal: From Comprehensive Policy Programmes to the Negotiation of Concrete Industrial

Relations Reforms?," in Giuseppe Fajertag and Philippe Pochet (eds) *Social Pacts in Europe – New Dynamics*, 2nd edn, Brussels: European Trade Union Institute, pp. 321–42.

Carlin, Wendy and David Soskice (2009) "German Economic Performance: Disentangling the Role of Supply-Side Reforms, Macroeconomic Policy and Coordinated Economy Institutions," *Socio-Economic Review*, 7(1): 67–99.

Casey, Bernard and Michael Gold (2000) *Social Partnership and Economic Performance: The Case of Europe*, Cheltenham: Edward Elgar.

Chari, Raj (2004) "The 2004 Spanish Election: Terrorism as a Catalyst for Change?," *West European Politics*, 27(5): 954–63.

—— and Paul M. Heywood (2008) "Institutions, European Integration, and the Policy Process in Contemporary Spain," in Bonnie N. Field and Kerstin Hamann (eds) *Democracy and Institutional Development: Spain in Comparative Theoretical Perspective*, Basingstoke: Palgrave Macmillan, pp. 178–202.

Cheibub, José Antonio and Adam Przeworski (1999) "Democracy, Elections, and Accountability for Economic Outcomes," in Adam Przeworski, Susan C. Stokes and Bernard Manin (eds) *Democracy, Accountability, and Representation*, New York: Cambridge University Press, pp. 222–49.

Chubb, Basil (1987) "The Prospects for Democratic Politics in Ireland," in Howard R. Penniman and Brian Farrell (eds) *Ireland at the Polls 1981, 1982 and 1987: A Study of Four General Elections*, Durham, NC: Duke University Press, pp. 206–31.

Chuliá, Elisa (2007) "Spain: Between Majority Rule and Incrementalism," in Ellen M. Immergut, Karen M. Anderson and Isabelle Schulze (eds) *The Handbook of West European Pension Politics*, Oxford: Oxford University Press, pp. 499–554.

Clasen, Jochen (2005) *Reforming European Welfare States: Germany and the United Kingdom Compared*, Oxford: Oxford University Press.

Collins, Stephen (1992) *The Haughey File: The Unprecedented Career and Last Years of the Boss*, Dublin: The O'Brien Press.

—— (1993) *Spring and the Labour Story*, Dublin: The O'Brien Press.

—— (2000) *The Power Game: Fianna Fáil Since Lemass*, Dublin: The O'Brien Press.

—— (2005) *Breaking the Mould: How the PDs Changed Irish Politics*, Dublin: Gill and Macmillan.

Compston, Hugh (1995) "Union Participation in Economic Policymaking in France, Italy, Germany and Britain, 1970–1993," *West European Politics*, 18(2): 314–39.

—— (2002) "Policy Concertation in Western Europe: A Configurational Approach," in Stefan Berger and Hugh Compston (eds) *Policy Concertation and Social Partnership in Western Europe: Lessons for the 21st Century*, Oxford: Berghahn Books, pp. 353–73.

Conradt, David P. (1996) *The German Polity*, 6th edn, White Plains: Longman.

Crewe, Ivor and Anthony King (1995) *The Birth, Life and Death of the Social Democratic Party*, Oxford: Oxford University Press.

Cronin, James E. (2004) "Speaking for Whom? From 'Old' to 'New' Labour," in Kay Lawson and Thomas Poguntke (eds) *How Political Parties Respond: Interest Aggregation Revisited*, London: Routledge, pp. 15–40.

Crouch, Colin (1986) "Conservative Industrial Relations Policy: Towards Labour Exclusion?," in Otto Jacobi, Bob Jessop, Hans Kastendiek and Marino Regini (eds) *Economic Crisis, Trade Unions and the State*, London: Croom Helm, pp. 131–53.

—— (2005) *Capitalist Diversity and Change: Recombinant Governance and Institutional Entrepreneurs*, Oxford: Oxford University Press.

Culpepper, Pepper D. (2002) "Powering, Puzzling and 'Pacting': The Informational Logic of Negotiated Reforms," *Journal of European Public Policy*, 9(5): 744–90.

Dalton, Russell J. (2000) "The Decline of Partisan Identifications," in Russell J. Dalton and Martin P. Wattenberg (eds) *Parties without Partisans: Political Change in Advanced Industrial Democracies*, Oxford: Oxford University Press, pp. 19–36.

—— (2002) *Citizen Politics: Public Opinion and Political Parties in Advanced Industrial Democracies*, 3rd edn, New York: Chatham House.

—— (2003) "Voter Choice and Electoral Politics," in Stephen Padgett, William E. Paterson and Gordon Smith (eds) *Developments in German Politics*, 3rd edn, Durham, NC: Duke University Press, pp. 60–81.

—— (2006) *Citizen Politics: Public Opinion and Political Parties in Advanced Industrial Democracies*, 4th edn, Washington D.C.: CQ Press.

—— and Martin P. Wattenberg (2000) "Unthinkable Democracy: Political Change in Advanced Industrial Democracies," in Russell J. Dalton and Martin P. Wattenberg (eds) *Parties without Partisans: Political Change in Advanced Industrial Democracies*, Oxford: Oxford University Press, pp. 3–16.

—— Ian McAllister and Martin P. Wattenberg (2000) "The Consequences of Partisan Realignment," in Russell J. Dalton and Martin P. Wattenberg (eds) *Parties without Partisans: Political Change in Advanced Industrial Democracies*, Oxford: Oxford University Press, pp. 37–63.

Daly, Mary (2005) "Recasting the Story of Ireland's Miracle: Policy, Politics, or Profit?," in Uwe Becker and Herman Schwartz (eds) *Employment "Miracles": A Critical Comparison of the Dutch, Scandinavian, Swiss, Australian, and Irish Cases Versus Germany and the US*, Amsterdam: Amsterdam University Press, pp. 133–55.

Damgaard, Erik (2003) [2000] "Denmark: The Life and Death of Government Coalitions," in Wolfgang C. Müller and Kaare Strøm (eds) *Coalition Governments in Western Europe*, New York: Cambridge University Press, pp. 231–63.

Daniels, Philip (1993) "Italy and the Maastricht Treaty," in Stephen Hellman and Gianfranco Pasquino (eds) *Italian Politics: A Review, Vol 8*, London: Frances Pinter, pp. 178–91.

Davies, Robert J. (1983) "Incomes and Anti-Inflation Policy," in George Sayers Bain (ed.) *Industrial Relations in Britain*, Oxford: Blackwell, pp. 419–55.

Delaney, Paul (1988) "Seven Million Strike and Cripple Spain," *New York Times*, 15 December.

Denver, David (2007) *Elections and Voters in Britain*, 2nd edn, Basingstoke: Palgrave Macmillan.

Department of Trade and Industry (1996) *Industrial Action and Trade Unions*, London: HMSO, Cm 3470.

Deutscher Bundestag (2007) "Wahlergebnis 2002." Online. Available <http://webarchiv.bundestag.de/cgi/show.php?fileToLoad=137&id=1040> (accessed November 22, 2009).

Dølvik, Jon Erik and Andrew Martin (2000) "A Spanner in the Works and Oil on Troubled Water: The Divergent Fates of Social Pacts in Sweden and Norway," in Giuseppe Fajertag and Philippe Pochet (eds) *Social Pacts in Europe – New Dynamics*, 2nd edn, Brussels: European Trade Union Institute, pp. 279–319.

Donaghey, Jimmy and Paul Teague (2005) "The Persistence of Social Pacts in Western Europe," *Industrial Relations Journal*, 36(6): 478–93.

Donovan, Mark (1992) "A Party System in Transformation: The April 1992 Italian Election," *West European Politics*, 15(4): 170–77.

—— (1994) "The 1994 Election in Italy: Normalisation or Continuing Exceptionalism?," *West European Politics*, 17(4): 193–201.

Dorey, Peter (2001) *Wage Politics in Britain: The Rise and Fall of Incomes Policies Since 1945*, Brighton: Sussex Academic Press.

—— (2009) "Individual Liberty Versus Industrial Order: Conservatives and the Trade Union Closed Shop 1946–90," *Contemporary British History*, 23(2): 221–44.

Dorfman, Gerald A. (1983) *British Trade Unionism against the Trades Union Congress*, Basingstoke: Macmillan.

Downs, Anthony (1957) *An Economic Theory of Democracy*, Boston, MA: Addison-Wesley.

Driffil, John (2005) "The Centralization of Wage Bargaining Revisited. What Have We Learned?," London: Birkbeck College, World Economy and Finance Research Programme, Unpublished Report.

Dumont, Patrick and Lieven de Winter (2003) [2000] "Luxembourg: Stable Coalitions in a Pivotal Party System," in Wolfgang C. Müller and Kaare Strøm (eds) *Coalition Governments in Western Europe*, New York: Oxford University Press, pp. 399–432.

Dunphy, Richard (2004) *Contesting Capitalism: Left Parties and European Integration*, Manchester: Manchester University Press.

—— (2007) "In Search of an Identity: Finland's Left Alliance and the Experience of Coalition Government," *Contemporary Politics*, 13(1): 37–55.

Dyson, Kenneth (2006) "Binding Hands as a Strategy for Economic Reform: Government by Commission," in Kenneth Dyson and Stephen Padgett (eds) *The Politics of Economic Reform in Germany: Global, Rhineland, or Hybrid Capitalism?*, London: Routledge, pp. 110–33.

—— and Stephen Padgett (2006) "Introduction: Global, Rhineland or Hybrid Capitalism?," in Kenneth Dyson and Stephen Padgett (eds) *The Politics of Economic Reform in Germany: Global, Rhineland, or Hybrid Capitalism?*, London: Routledge, pp. 1–10.

Ebbinghaus, Bernhard and Anke Hassel (2000) "Striking Deals: Concertation in the Reform of Continental European Welfare States," *Journal of European Public Policy*, 7(1): 44–62.

Edlund, Jonas (2007) "Class Conflicts and Institutional Feedback Effects in Liberal and Social Democratic Welfare Regimes," in Stefan Svallfors (ed.) *The Political Sociology of the Welfare State: Institutions, Social Cleavages, and Orientations*, Stanford, CA: Stanford University Press, pp. 30–79.

EIRR (*European Industrial Relations Review and Report*) (1979–2006). Monthly. Various issues.

Elvander, Nils (2002) "The Labour Market Regimes in the Nordic Countries: A Comparative Analysis," *Scandinavian Political Studies*, 25(2): 117–37.

Employment Department (1991) *Industrial Relations in the 1990s: Proposals for Further Reform of Industrial Relations and Trade Union Law*, London: HMSO, Cm 1602.

Esping-Andersen, Gøsta (1990) *The Three Worlds of Welfare Capitalism*. Princeton, NJ: Princeton University Press.

Estivill, Jordi and Josep M. de la Hoz (1991) "Transition and Crisis: The Complexity of Spanish Industrial Relations," in Guido Baglioni and Colin Crouch (eds) *European Industrial Relations: The Challenge of Flexibility*, London: Sage, pp. 265–99.

European Commission (2003) *Employment in Europe 2003*, Luxembourg: Office for Official Publications of the European Communities.

Fajertag, Giuseppe and Philippe Pochet (eds) (2000) *Social Pacts in Europe – New Dynamics*, 2nd edn, Brussels: European Trade Union Institute.

Fallend, Franz (2001) "Austria," *European Journal of Political Research*, 40 (7/8): 238–53.

Farrell, David M. (1999) "Ireland: A Party System Transformed?," in David Broughton and Mark Donovan (eds) *Changing Party Systems in Western Europe*, London: Pinter, pp. 30–47.

Feigl-Heins, Monika (2004) "Why Do Social Democratic Parties Change Employment Policy Positions? A Comparison of Austria, Germany and the United Kingdom," in Giuliano Bonoli and Martin Powell (eds) *Social Democratic Party Policies in Contemporary Europe*, London: Routledge, pp. 161–79.

Ferner, Anthony (1988) *Governments, Managers and Industrial Relations: Public Enterprises and Their Political Environment*, Oxford: Blackwell.

Ferrera, Maurizio and Elisabetta Gualmini (2000) "Italy: Rescue From Without?," in Fritz W. Scharpf and Vivien A. Schmidt (eds) *Welfare and Work in the Open Economy Vol 2: Diverse Responses to Common Challenges*, New York: Oxford University Press, pp. 351–98.

—— (2004) *Rescued by Europe? Social and Labour Market Reforms in Italy from Maastricht to Berlusconi*, Amsterdam: Amsterdam University Press.

Ferrera, Maurizio and Matteo Jessoula (2007) "Italy: A Narrow Gate for Path-Shift," in Ellen M. Immergut, Karen M. Anderson and Isabelle Schulze (eds) *The Handbook of West European Pension Politics*, New York: Oxford University Press, pp. 396–453.

Field, Bonnie (2005) "De-thawing Democracy: The Decline of Political Party Collaboration in Spain (1977–2004)," *Comparative Political Studies*, 38(9): 1079–103.

—— (2008) "Interparty Politics in Spain: The Role of Informal Institutions," in Bonnie N. Field and Kerstin Hamann (eds) *Democracy and Institutional Development: Spain in Comparative Theoretical Perspective*, Basingstoke: Palgrave Macmillan, pp. 44–67.

—— and Kerstin Hamann (2008) "Introduction: The Institutionalization of Democracy in Spain," in Bonnie N. Field and Kerstin Hamann (eds) *Democracy and Institutional Development: Spain in Comparative Theoretical Perspective*, Basingstoke: Palgrave Macmillan, pp. 1–22.

Fielding, Steven (2003) *The Labour Party: Continuity and Change in the Making of 'New' Labour*, Basingstoke: Palgrave Macmillan.

Fishman, Robert M. (1990) *Working-Class Organization and the Return to Democracy in Spain*, Ithaca: Cornell University Press.

Fowler, Norman (1991) *Ministers Decide: A Memoir of the Thatcher Years*, London: Chapmans.

FPÖ (2005) *Das Parteiprogramm der Freiheitlichen Partei Österreichs*. Online. Available <http://www.fpoe.at/fileadmin/Content/portal/PDFs/09/fp_parteiprogramm_neu. pdf> (accessed November 22, 2009).

Franzese Jr., Robert and Peter Hall (2000) "Institutional Dimensions of Coordinating Wage Bargaining and Monetary Policy," in Torben Iversen, Jonas Pontusson and David Soskice (eds) *Unions, Employers and Central Banks: Macroeconomic Coordination and Institutional Change in Social Market Economies*, New York: Cambridge University Press, pp. 173–204.

French, Steve (2000) "The Impact of Unification on German Industrial Relations," *German Politics*, 9(2): 195–216.

Fulcher, James (2002) "Sweden in Historical Perspective: The Rise and Fall of the Swedish Model," in Stefan Berger and Hugh Compston (eds) *Policy Concertation and Social Partnership in Western Europe*, Oxford: Berghahn Books, pp. 279–93.

Gächter, August (1997) "Pension Reform Nears Completion," *European Industrial Relations Observatory*, November 28. Online. Available <http://www.eiro.eurofound. eu.int/1997/11/feature/at9711144f.html> (accessed November 22, 2009).

Gallagher, Michael (1982) *The Irish Labour Party in Transition 1957–1982*, Manchester: Manchester University Press.

—— (1985) *Political Parties in the Republic of Ireland*, Manchester: Manchester University Press.

—— (2005) "Conclusion," in Michael Gallagher and Paul Mitchell (eds) *The Politics of Electoral Systems*, Oxford: Oxford University Press, pp. 535–78.

—— Michael Laver and Peter Mair (2006) *Representative Government in Modern Europe*, 4th edn. New York: McGraw Hill.

Gamble, Andrew (1994) *The Free Economy and the Strong State: The Politics of Thatcherism*, 2nd edn, Basingstoke: Macmillan.

Gelissen, John (2000) "Popular Support for Institutionalised Solidarity: A Comparison between European Welfare States," *International Journal of Social Welfare*, 9(4): 285–300.

Gerlich, Peter, Edgar Grande and Wolfgang C. Müller (1988) "Corporatism in Crisis: Stability and Change of Social Partnership in Austria," *Political Studies*, 36(2): 209–23.

Gillespie, Richard (1990) "The Break-up of the 'Socialist Family': Party-Union Relations in Spain, 1982–89," *West European Studies*, 13(1): 47–62.

Girvin, Brian (1987) "The Campaign," in Michael Laver, Peter Mair and Richard Sinnott (eds) *How Ireland Voted: The Irish General Election 1987*, Dublin: Poolbeg, pp. 11–26.

—— (1990) "The Campaign," in Michael Gallagher and Richard Sinnott (eds) *How Ireland Voted 1989*, Galway: PSAI Centre for Study of Irish Elections, pp. 1–12.

—— (1993) "The Road to the General Election," in Michael Gallagher and Michael Laver (eds) *How Ireland Voted 1992*, Limerick: PSAI Press, pp. 1–20.

—— (1999) "Political Competition 1992–1997," in Michael Marsh and Paul Mitchell (eds) *How Ireland Voted 1997*, Boulder, CO: Westview Press, pp. 1–25.

Green-Pedersen, Christoffer (2002) *The Politics of Justification: Party Competition and Welfare-State Retrenchment in Denmark and the Netherlands from 1982 to 1998*, Amsterdam: Amsterdam University Press.

Guger, Alois (2001) "The Austrian Experience," in Andrew Glyn (ed.) *Social Democracy in Neoliberal Times*, Oxford: Oxford University Press, pp. 53–79.

Guillén, Ana, Santiago Alvárez and Pedro Adão e Silva (2003) "Redesigning the Spanish and Portuguese Welfare States: The Impact of Accession into the European Union," in Sebastián Royo and Paul Christopher Manuel (eds) *Spain and Portugal in the European Union: The First Fifteen Years*, London: Frank Cass, pp. 231–68.

Gundle, Stephen (1996) "The Rise and Fall of Craxi's Socialist Party," in Stephen Gundle and Simon Parker (eds) *The New Italian Republic: From The Fall of The Berlin Wall to Berlusconi*, London: Routledge, pp. 85–98.

Gunther, Richard (1992) "Spain: The Very Model of the Modem Elite Settlement," in John Higley and Richard Gunther (eds) *Elites and Democratic Consolidation in Latin America and Southern Europe*, Cambridge: Cambridge University Press, pp. 38–80.

—— (1996) "The Impact of Regime Change on Public Policy: The Case of Spain," *Journal of Public Policy*, 16(2): 157–201.

—— José Ramón Montero and Joan Botella (2004) *Democracy in Modern Spain*, New Haven, CN: Yale University Press.

Haddock, Bruce (2002) "Italy in the 1990s: Policy Concertation Resurgent," in Stefan Berger and Hugh Compston (eds) *Policy Concertation and Social Partnership in Western Europe: Lessons for the 21st Century*, Oxford: Berghahn Books, pp. 207–19.

Hale, Dominic (2008) "International Comparisons of Labour Disputes in 2006," *Economic and Labour Market Review*, 2(4): 32–9.

Hall, Peter (2007) "The Evolution of Varieties of Capitalism in Europe," in Bob Hancké, Martin Rhodes and Mark Thatcher (eds) *Beyond Varieties of Capitalism: Conflict, Contradictions, and Complementarities in the European Economy*, New York: Oxford University Press, pp. 39–85.

—— and David Soskice (eds) (2001a) *Varieties of Capitalism: The Institutional Foundations of Comparative Advantage*, New York: Oxford University Press.

—— and David Soskice (2001b) "An Introduction to Varieties of Capitalism," in Peter Hall and David Soskice (eds) *Varieties of Capitalism: The Institutional Foundations of Comparative Advantage*, New York: Oxford University Press, pp. 1–68.

Hamann, Kerstin (1993) "Afiliación, movilización y aliados políticos: las incógnitas del poder sindical español, 1970–1988," *Cuadernos de Relaciones Laborales*, 3: 107–25.

—— (2001) "The Resurgence of National-Level Bargaining: Union Strategies in Spain," *Industrial Relations Journal*, 32(2): 154–72.

—— and Miguel Martínez Lucio (2003) "Strategies of Labor Union Revitalization in Spain," *European Journal of Industrial Relations*, 9(1): 61–78.

—— and John Kelly (2007a) "Party Politics and the Re-emergence of Social Pacts in Western Europe," Paper presented at EUSA, Montreal, May 18.

—— and John Kelly (2007b) "Party Politics and the Re-emergence of Social Pacts in Western Europe," *Comparative Political Studies*, 40(8): 971–94.

—— and John Kelly (2008) "Varieties of Capitalism and Industrial Relations," in Paul Blyton, Nick Bacon, Jack Fiorito and Ed Heery (eds) *The Sage Handbook of Industrial Relations*, London: Sage, pp. 129–49.

——, Alexia Katsanidou, John Kelly and Philip H. Pollock (2010) "The Electoral Consequences of Policy Reform Strategies in Western Europe, 1980–2006," Presented at the Midwest Political Science Association Meeting, Chicago, IL, April 22–25.

Hancké, Bob (2002) "The Political Economy of Wage-Setting in the Eurozone," in Philippe Pochet (ed.) *Wage Policy in the Eurozone*, Brussels: Peter Lang, pp. 131–48.

—— and Martin Rhodes (2005) "EMU and Labour Market Institutions in Europe: The Rise and Fall of National Social Pacts," *Work and Occupations*, 32(2): 196–228.

—— and Andrea Herrmann (2007) "Wage Bargaining and Comparative Advantage in EMU," in Bob Hancké, Martin Rhodes and Mark Thatcher (eds) *Beyond Varieties of Capitalism: Conflict, Contradictions, and Complementarities in the European Economy*, Oxford: Oxford University Press, pp. 122–44.

—— Martin Rhodes and Mark Thatcher (eds) (2007a) *Beyond Varieties of Capitalism: Conflict, Contradictions, and Complementarities in the European Economy*, Oxford: Oxford University Press.

—— Martin Rhodes and Mark Thatcher (2007b) "Introduction: Beyond Varieties of Capitalism," in Bob Hancké, Martin Rhodes and Mark Thatcher (eds) *Beyond*

Varieties of Capitalism: Conflict, Contradictions, and Complementarities in the European Economy, Oxford: Oxford University Press, pp. 3–38.

Hardiman, Niamh (2002) "From Conflict to Coordination: Economic Governance and Political Innovation in Ireland," *West European Politics*, 25(4): 1–24.

Hartmann, Anja K. (2003) "Patientennah, Leistungsstark, Finanzbewusst? Die Gesundheitspolitik Der Rot-Grünen Bundesregierung 1998–2002," in Christoph Egle, Tobias Ostheim and Reimut Zohlnhöfer (eds) *Das Rot-Grüne Projekt: Eine Bilanz der Regierung Schröder 1998–2002*, Wiesbaden: Westdeutscher Verlag, pp. 259–82.

Hassel, Anke (2001) "The Problem of Political Exchange in Complex Governing Systems: The Case of Germany's Alliance for Jobs," *European Journal of Industrial Relations*, 7(3): 307–26.

—— (2003) "The Politics of Social Pacts," *British Journal of Industrial Relations*, 41(4): 707–26.

—— (2006) *Wage Setting, Social Pacts and the Euro: A New Role for the State*, Amsterdam: Amsterdam University Press.

—— (2007) "What Does Business Want? Labour Market Reforms in CMEs and its Problems," in Bob Hancké, Martin Rhodes and Mark Thatcher (eds) *Beyond Varieties of Capitalism: Conflicts, Contradictions, and Complementarities in the European Economy*, Oxford: Oxford University Press, pp. 253–77.

—— (2009) "Policies and Politics in Social Pacts in Europe," *European Journal of Industrial Relations*, 15(1): 7–26.

—— and Bernhard Ebbinghaus (2000) "From Means to Ends: Linking Wage Moderation and Social Policy Reform," in Giuseppe Fajertag and Philippe Pochet (eds) *Social Pacts in Europe – New Dynamics*, 2nd edn, Brussels: European Trade Union Institute, pp. 61–84.

Hastings, Tim, Brian Sheehan and Padraig Yeates (2007) *Saving the Future: How Social Partnership Shaped Ireland's Economic Success*, Dublin: Blackhall Publishing.

Hay, Colin (1999) *The Political Economy of New Labour: Labouring Under False Pretences?*, Manchester: Manchester University Press.

—— and Ben Rosamond (2002) "Globalization, European Integration and the Discursive Construction of Economic Imperatives," *Journal of European Public Policy*, 9(2): 147–67.

Heffernan, Richard (2000) *New Labour and Thatcherism: Political Change in Britain*, Basingstoke: Palgrave.

—— and Mike Marqusee (1992) *Defeat from the Jaws of Victory: Inside Kinnock's Labour Party*, London: Verso.

Heinisch, Reinhard (2000) "Coping with Economic Integration: Corporatist Strategies in Germany and Austria in the 1990s," *West European Politics*, 23(3): 67–96.

—— (2002) *Populism, Proporz, Pariah: Austria Turns Right: Austrian Political Change, its Causes and Repercussions*, New York: Nova Science Publishers.

—— (2003) "Success in Opposition – Failure in Government: Explaining the Performance of Right-Wing Populist Parties in Public Office," *West European Politics*, 26(3): 91–130.

Hellman, Stephen (1993) "Politics Almost as Usual: The Formation of the Amato Government," in Gianfranco Pasquino and Patrick McCarthy (eds) *The End of Post-War Politics in Italy: The Landmark 1992 Elections*, Boulder, CO: Westview Press, pp. 141–59.

Helms, Ludgar (2004) "The Federal Election in Germany, September 2002," *Electoral Studies*, 23(1): 143–49.

—— (2007) "The German Federal Election, September 2005," *Electoral Studies*, 26(1): 223–7.

Heywood, Paul (1995) "Sleaze in Spain," *Parliamentary Affairs*, 48(4): 726–37.

Hibbs Jr., Douglas, A. (2006) "Voting and the Macroeconomy," in Barry R. Weingast and Donald A. Wittman (eds) *The Oxford Handbook of Political Economy*, Oxford: Oxford University Press, pp. 565–86.

Hietanen, Juha (2000) "2000 Annual Review for Finland," *European Industrial Relations Observatory*, December 28. Online. Available <http://www.eurofound.europa.eu/eiro/2000/12/feature/fi0012171f.htm> (accessed November 22, 2009).

Hine, David (1986) "The Craxi Premiership," in Robert Leonardi and Raffaela Y. Nanetti (eds) *Italian Politics: A Review*, London: Frances Pinter, pp. 105–16.

—— (1993) *Governing Italy: The Politics of Bargained Pluralism*, Oxford: Oxford University Press.

Hirsh, Mario (2000) "Luxembourg," *European Journal of Political Research*, 38(3–4): 453–7.

Höll, Otmar, Johannes Pollack and Sonja Puntscher-Riekmann (2003) "Austria: Domestic Change through European Integration," in Wolfgang Wessels, Andreas Maurer and Jürgen Mittag (eds) *Fifteen into One? The European Union and Its Member States*, Manchester: Manchester University Press, pp. 337–54.

Holmberg, Sören (2000) "Issue Agreement,' in Peter Esaiasson and Knut Heidar (eds) *Beyond Westminster and Congress: The Nordic Experience*, Columbus, OH: Ohio State University Press, pp. 155–70.

Hopkin, Jonathan (2005a) "Spain: Proportional Representation with Majoritarian Outcomes," in Michael Gallagher and Paul Mitchell (eds) *The Politics of Electoral Systems*, Oxford: Oxford University Press, pp. 375–94.

—— (2005b) "From Consensus to Competition: The Changing Nature of Democracy in the Spanish Transition," in Sebastian Balfour (ed.) *The Politics of Contemporary Spain*, London: Routledge, pp. 6–26.

House, John D. and Kyla McGrath (2004) "Innovative Governance and Development in the New Ireland: Social Partnership and the Integrated Approach," *Governance*, 17(1): 29–58.

Howell, Chris (2001) "The End of the Relationship Between Social Democratic Parties and Trade Unions?," *Studies in Political Economy*, 65 (Summer): 7–37.

—— (2005) *Trade Unions and the State: The Construction of Industrial Relations Institutions in Britain, 1890–2000*, Princeton, NJ: Princeton University Press.

Huber, Evelyn and John D. Stephens (2001) *Development and Crisis of the Welfare State: Parties and Policies in Global Markets*, Chicago: University of Chicago Press.

Hughes, Colin and Patrick Wintour (1990) *Labour Rebuilt: The New Model Party*, London: Fourth Estate.

Hyman, Richard (1994) "Changing Trade Union Identities and Strategies," in Richard Hyman and Anthony Ferner (eds) *New Frontiers in European Industrial Relations*, Oxford: Blackwell, pp. 108–39.

Immergut, Ellen M. and Sven Jochem (2006) "The Political Frame for Negotiated Capitalism: Electoral Reform and the Politics of Crisis in Japan and Sweden," *Governance*, 19(1): 99–133.

Immergut, Ellen M., Karen M. Anderson and Isabelle Schultze (eds) (2007) *The Handbook of West European Pension Politics,* Oxford: Oxford University Press.

Ioannou, Christos A. (2000) "Social Pacts in Hellenic Industrial Relations: Odysseys or Sisyphus?," in Giuseppe Fajertag and Philippe Pochet (eds) *Social Pacts in Europe – New Dynamics*, 2nd edn, Brussels: European Trade Union Institute, pp. 219–36.

Isaakson, Guy-Erik (1994) "Party Behaviour in the Finnish Parliament," *Scandinavian Political Studies*, 17(2): 91–107.

Iversen, Torben (1999) *Contested Economic Institutions: The Politics of Macroeconomics and Wage Bargaining in Advanced Democracies*, New York: Cambridge University Press.

—— (2005) *Capitalism, Democracy, and Welfare*, New York: Cambridge University Press.

—— (2006) "Capitalism and Democracy," in Barry R. Weingast and Donald A. Wittman (eds) *The Oxford Handbook of Political Economy*, Oxford: Oxford University Press, pp. 601–23.

—— (2007) "Economic Shocks and Varieties of Government Responses," in Bob Hancké, Martin Rhodes and Mark Thatcher (eds) *Beyond Varieties of Capitalism: Conflict, Contradictions, and Complementarities in the European Economy*, New York: Oxford University Press, pp. 278–304.

James, Peter (1991) "Germany United: The 1990 All-German Elections," *West European Politics*, 14(3): 215–20.

Jeffrey, Charlie and William E. Paterson (2004) "Germany and European Integration: A Shifting of Tectonic Plates," in Herbert Kitschelt and Wolfgang Streeck (eds) *Germany: Beyond the Stable State*, London & Portland: Frank Cass, pp. 59–75.

Jenkins, Simon (2007) *Thatcher and Sons: A Revolution in Three Acts*, Harmondsworth: Penguin.

Jochem, Sven (2000) "Nordic Labour Market Policies in Transition," *West European Politics*, 23(3): 115–38.

—— (2003) "Nordic Corporatism and Welfare State Reforms: Denmark and Sweden Compared," in Frans van Waarden and Gerhard Lehmbruch (eds) *Renegotiating the Welfare State: Flexible Adjustment Through Corporatist Concertation*, London: Routledge, pp. 114–41.

Jones, Erik, Jeffry Frieden and Francisco Torres (eds) (1998) *Joining Europe's Monetary Club: the Challenges for Smaller Member States*, New York, NY: St Martin's Press.

Jordana, Jacint (1996) "Reconsidering Union Membership in Spain, 1977–1994: Halting Decline in a Context of Democratic Consolidation," *Industrial Relations Journal*, 27(3): 211–24.

Jungar, Ann-Cathrine (2002) "A Case of a Surplus Majority Government: The Finnish Rainbow Coalition," *Scandinavian Political Studies*, 25(1): 57–83.

Kaase, Max (1983) "The West German Election of 6 March 1983," *Electoral Studies*, 2(2): 158–66.

Kangas, Olli (2007) "Finland: Labor Markets Against Politics," in Ellen M. Immergut, Karen M. Anderson and Isabelle Schulze (eds) *The Handbook of West European Pension Politics*, Oxford: Oxford University Press, pp. 248–96.

Karl, Terri Lynn and Phillippe C. Schmitter (1991) "Modes of Transition in Latin America, Southern and Eastern Europe," *International Social Science Journal*, 43(2): 269–84.

Katz, Harry C., Wonduck Lee and Joohee Lee (eds) (2004) *The New Structure of Labor Relations: Tripartism and Decentralization*, Ithaca, NY: ILR Press.

Katz, Richard S. (2005) "The Internal Life of Parties," in Kurt Richard Luther and Ferdinand Müller-Rommel (eds) *Political Parties in the New Europe: Political and Analytical Challenges*, Oxford: Oxford University Press, pp. 87–118.

Katzenstein, Peter J. (1985) *Small States in World Markets: Industrial Policy in Europe*, Ithaca, NY: Cornell University Press.

Kauppinen, Timo (2000) "Social Pacts in Finland," in Giuseppe Fajertag and Philippe Pochet (eds) *Social Pacts in Europe – New Dynamics*, 2nd edn, Brussels: European Trade Union Institute, pp. 161–85.

—— and Jeremy Waddington (2000) "Finland: Adapting to Decentralisation," in Jeremy Waddington and Reiner Hoffmann (eds) *Trade Unions in Europe: Facing Challenges and Searching for Solutions*, Brussels: European Trade Union Institute, pp. 183–214.

Kavanagh, Dennis (1997) *The Reordering of British Politics: Politics after Thatcher*, Oxford: Oxford University Press.

Kavanagh, Ella, John Considine, Eleanor Doyle, Liam Gallagher, Catherine Kavanagh and Eoin O'Leary (1998) "The Political Economy of EMU in Ireland," in Erik Jones, Jeffery Frieden and Francisco Torres (eds) *Joining Europe's Monetary Club: The Challenges for Smaller Member States*, New York, NY: St Martin's Press, pp. 123–48.

Kelly, John (1998) *Rethinking Industrial Relations: Mobilization, Collectivism and Long Waves*, London: Routledge.

—— (2005) "Social Movement Theory and Union Revitalization in Britain," in Susan Fernie and David Metcalf (eds) *Trade Unions: Resurgence or Demise?*, London: Routledge, pp. 62–82.

—— and Kerstin Hamann (2009) "General Strikes in Western Europe, 1980–2006," Paper presented at CEACS, Instituto Juan March, Madrid, October 23.

Keman, Hans (2005) [2002] "Policy-Making Capacities of European Party Government," in Kurt Richard Luther and Ferdinand Müller-Rommel (eds) *Political Parties in the New Europe: Political and Analytical Challenges*, Oxford: Oxford University Press, pp. 207–45.

Kemmerling, Achim and Oliver Bruttel (2006) "'New Politics' in German Labour Market Policy? The Implications of the Recent Hartz Reforms for the German Welfare State," *West European Politics*, 29(1): 90–112.

Keune, Maarten (2008) "Introduction: Wage Moderation, Decentralisation of Collective Bargaining and Low Pay," in Maarten Keune and Béla Galgóczi (eds) *Wages and Wage Bargaining in Europe: Developments Since the 1990s*, Brussels: European Trade Union Institute, pp. 7–27.

Kiander, Jaakko (2005) "The Evolution of the Finnish Model in the 1990s: From Depression to High-Tech Boom," in Uwe Becker and Herman Schwartz (eds) *Employment 'Miracles': A Critical Comparison of the Dutch, Scandinavian, Swiss, Australian and Irish Cases Versus Germany and the US*, Amsterdam: Amsterdam University Press, pp. 87–110.

Kitschelt, Herbert (1994a) *The Transformation of European Social Democracy*, New York: Cambridge University Press.

—— (1994b) "Austrian and Swedish Social Democrats in Crisis: Party Strategy and Organization in Corporatist Regimes," *Comparative Political Studies*, 27(1): 3–39.

—— (1999) "European Social Democracy Between Political Economy and Electoral Competition," in Herbert Kitschelt, Peter Lange, Gary Marks and John D. Stephens (eds) *Continuity and Change in Contemporary Capitalism*, New York: Cambridge University Press, pp. 317–45.

—— (2001) "Partisan Competition and Welfare State Retrenchment: When Do Politicians Choose Unpopular Policies?," in Paul Pierson (ed.) *The New Politics of the Welfare State*, Oxford: Oxford University Press, pp. 265–302.

—— (2004) "Political-Economic Context and Partisan Strategies in the German Federal Elections, 1990–2002," in Herbert Kitschelt and Wolfgang Streeck (eds) *Germany: Beyond the Stable State*, London: Frank Cass, pp. 125–52.

—— and Wolfgang Streeck (2004) "From Stability to Stagnation: Germany at the Beginning of the Twenty-First Century," in Herbert Kitschelt and Wolfgang Streeck (eds) *Germany: Beyond the Stable State*, London: Frank Cass, pp. 1–34.

—— Peter Lange, Gary Marks and John D. Stephens (1999) "Convergence and Divergence in Advanced Capitalist Democracies," in Herbert Kitschelt, Peter Lange, Gary Marks and John D. Stephens (eds) *Continuity and Change in Contemporary Capitalism*, New York: Cambridge University Press, pp. 427–60.

Kittel, Bernhard (2000) "DeAustrification? The Policy-Area-Specific Evolution of Austrian Social Partnership," *West European Politics*, 23(1): 108–29.

—— and Herbert Gröger (1997) "Sozialpartnerschaft im Spiegel der Österreichischen Politikwissenschaft," *Österreichische Zeitschrift für Politikwissenschaft*, 26(2): 209–23.

Kjellberg, Anders (1998) "Sweden: Restoring the Model?," in Anthony Ferner and Richard Hyman (eds) *Changing Industrial Relations in Europe*, Oxford: Blackwell, pp. 74–117.

Klingemann, Hans-Dieter, Andrea Volkens, Judith Bara, Ian Budge and Michael McDonald (2006) *Mapping Policy Preferences II: Estimates for Parties, Electors, and Governments in Eastern Europe, European Union, and OECD 1990–2003, Vol 2*, Oxford: Oxford University Press.

Klitgaard, Michael Baggesen (2007) "Why Are They Doing It? Social Democracy and Market-Oriented Welfare State Reforms," *West European Politics*, 30(1): 172–94.

Knapp, Andrew (2002) "France: Never a Golden Age," in Paul Webb, David Farrell and Ian Holliday (eds) *Political Parties in Advanced Industrial Democracies*, Oxford: Oxford University Press, pp. 107–50.

Kritsantonis, Nicos D. (1998) "Greece: The Maturing of the System," in Anthony Ferner and Richard Hyman (eds) *Changing Industrial Relations in Europe*, Oxford: Blackwell, pp. 504–28.

Kuipers, Sanneke (2006) *The Crisis Imperative: Crisis Rhetoric and Welfare State Reform in Belgium and the Netherlands in the Early 1990s*, Amsterdam: Amsterdam University Press.

Kumlin, Staffan (2007a) "The Welfare State: Values, Policy Preferences, and Performance Evaluations," in Russell J. Dalton and Hans-Dieter Klingemann (eds) *The Oxford Handbook of Political Behavior*, Oxford: Oxford University Press, pp. 362–82.

—— (2007b) "Overloaded or Underdetermined? European Welfare States in the Face of Performance Dissatisfaction," in Stefan Svallfors (ed.) *The Political Sociology of the Welfare State: Institutions, Social Cleavages, and Orientations*, Stanford, CA: Stanford University Press, pp. 80–116.

Kunkel, Christoph and Jonas Pontusson (1998) "Corporatism Versus Social Democracy: Divergent Fortunes of the Austrian and Swedish Labour Movements," *West European Politics*, 21(2): 1–31.

Labour Party (1983) *The New Hope for Britain: Labour's Manifesto 1983*. London: Labour Party.

—— (1987) *Britain Will Win: Labour Manifesto June 1987*, London: Labour Party.

—— (1989) *Meet the Challenge, Make the Change: A New Agenda for Britain. Final Report of Labour's Policy Review for the 1990s*, London: Labour Party.

—— (1992) *It's Time to Get Britain Working Again*, London: Labour Party.

Lange, Peter (1986) "The End of an Era: The Wage Indexation Referendum of 1985," in Robert Leonardi and Raffaela Y. Nanetti (eds) *Italian Politics: A Review*, London: Frances Pinter, pp. 29–46.

Laver, Michael (1992) "Are Irish Parties Peculiar?," in John H. Goldthorpe and Christopher T. Whelan (eds) *The Development of Industrial Society in Ireland*, Oxford: Oxford University Press, pp. 359–81.

—— and Audrey Arkins (1990) "Coalition and Fianna Fail," in Michael Gallagher and Richard Sinnott (eds) *How Ireland Voted 1989*, Galway: PSAI Press, pp. 200–12.

—— Michael Marsh and Richard Sinnott (1987) "Patterns of Party Support," in Michael Laver, Peter Mair and Richard Sinnott (eds) *How Ireland Voted: The Irish General Election 1987*, Dublin: Poolbeg, pp. 99–140.

Lawson, Nigel (1993) *The View from No. 11: Memoirs of a Tory Radical*, London: Corgi Books.

Leaman, Jeremy (2002) "Germany in the 1990s: The Impact of Unification," in Stefan Berger and Hugh Compston (eds) *Policy Concertation and Social Partnership in Western Europe: Lessons for the 21st Century*, New York: Berghahn, pp. 139–54.

Lee, Wonduck and Joohee Lee (2004) "Will the Model of Uncoordinated Decentralization Persist? Changes in Korean Industrial Relations after the Financial Crisis," in Harry C. Katz, Wonduck Lee and Joohee Lee (eds) *The New Structure of Labor Relations: Tripartism and Decentralization*, Ithaca, NY: ILR Press, pp. 143–65.

Lehmbruch, Gerhard (2003) "Welfare State Adjustment between Consensual and Adversarial Politics: The Institutional Context of Reform in Germany," in Frans van Waarden and Gerhard Lehmbruch (eds) *Renegotiating the Welfare State: Flexible Adjustment through Corporatist Concertation*, London: Routledge, pp. 142–68.

Leibfried, Stephan and Herbert Obinger (2004) "The State of the Welfare State: German Social Policy between Macroeconomic Retrenchment and Microeconomic Recalibration," in Herbert Kitschelt and Wolfgang Streeck (eds) *Germany: Beyond the Stable State*, London: Frank Cass, pp. 199–218.

Leonardi, Robert and Paolo Alberti (2004) "From Dominance to Doom? Christian Democracy in Italy," in Steven van Hecke and Emmanuel Gerard (eds) *Christian Democratic Parties in Europe Since the End of the Cold War*, Leuven: Leuven University Press, pp. 105–31.

Lewis, Jill (2002) "Austria in Historical Perspective: From Civil War to Social Partnership," in Stefan Berger and Hugh Compston (eds) *Policy Concertation and Social Partnership in Western Europe: Lessons for the 21st Century*, New York: Berghahn, pp. 35–50.

Lewis-Beck, Michael S. and Martin Paldam (2000) "Economic Voting: An Introduction," *Electoral Studies*, 19(2): 113–21.

Lijphart, Arend (1999) *Patterns of Democracy: Government Forms and Performance in Thirty-Six Countries,* New Haven, CN: Yale University Press.

Lilja, Kari (1998) "Finland: Continuity and Modest Moves Towards Company-Level Corporatism," in Anthony Ferner and Richard Hyman (eds) *Changing Industrial Relations in Europe*, Oxford: Blackwell, pp. 171–89.

Lind, Jens (2000) "Recent Issues on the Social Pact in Denmark," in Giuseppe Fajertag and Philippe Pochet (eds) *Social Pacts in Europe – New Dynamics*, 2nd edn, Brussels: European Trade Union Institute, pp. 135–59.

Lindstrom, Ulf (1986) "The Swedish Elections of 1985," *Electoral Studies*, 5(1): 76–9.

Lindvall, Johannes and Joakim Sebring (2005) "Policy Reform and the Decline of Corporatism in Sweden," *West European Politics*, 28(5): 1057–74.

Linos, Katerina and Martin West (2003) "Self-Interest, Social Beliefs, and Attitudes to Redistribution," *European Sociological Review*, 19(4): 393–409.

Lipset, Seymor M. and Stein Rokkan (1967) *Party Systems and Voter Alignments: Cross-National Perspectives*, New York: The Free Press.

Lodovici, Manuel Samek (2000) "Italy: The Long Times of Consensual Re-regulation," in Gøsta Esping-Andersen and Marino Regini (eds) *Why Deregulate Labour Markets?*, Oxford: Oxford University Press, pp. 271–306.

Lohmann, Susanne, David W. Brady and Douglas Rivers (1997) "Party Identification, Retrospective Voting, and Moderating Elections in a Federal System: West Germany, 1961–1989," *Comparative Political Studies*, 30(4): 420–49.

Ludlam, Steve (2001) "New Labour and the Unions: The End of the Contentious Alliance?," in Steve Ludlam and Martin J. Smith (eds) *New Labour in Government*, Basingstoke: Palgrave Macmillan, pp. 111–29.

—— (2004) "New Labour, 'Vested Interests' and the Union Link," in Steve Ludlam and Martin J. Smith (eds) *Governing as New Labour: Policy and Politics Under Blair*, Basingstoke: Palgrave Macmillan, pp. 70–87.

Lundberg, Jenny (2007) "Industrial Relations Developments 2006 – Sweden," *European Industrial Relations Observatory*, 13 June. Online. Available <http://www.eurofound.europa.eu/eiro/studies/tn0703019s/se0703019q.htm> (accessed November 22, 2009).

Luther, Kurt Richard (1999) "Must What Goes Up Always Come Down? Of Pillars and Arches in Austria's Political Architecture," in Kurt Richard Luther and Kris Deschouwer (eds) *Party Elites in Divided Societies*, London: Routledge, pp. 43–73.

—— (2000) "Austria: A Democracy under Threat from the Freedom Party?," *Parliamentary Affairs*, 53(3): 426–42.

—— and Kris Deschouwer (1999) "Prudent Leadership' to Successful Adaptation?," in Kurt Richard Luther and Kris Deschouwer (eds) *Party Elites in Divided Societies*, London: Routledge, pp. 243–63.

McIlroy, John (1998) "The Enduring Alliance? Trade Unions and the Making of New Labour, 1994–1997," *British Journal of Industrial Relations*, 36(4): 537–64.

—— (2009) "Under Stress But Still Enduring: The Contentious Alliance in the Age of Tony Blair and Gordon Brown," in Gary Daniels and John McIlroy (eds) *Trade Unions in a Neoliberal World: British Trade Unions Under New Labour*, Abingdon: Routledge, pp. 165–201.

Mackie, Thomas T. and Richard Rose (1991) *The International Almanac of Electoral History*, 3rd edn, Basingstoke: Macmillan.

—— (1997) *A Decade of Election Results: Updating The International Almanac*, Glasgow: University of Strathclyde, Centre for the Study of Public Policy.

Madeley, John T. S. (1995) "The Return of Swedish Social Democracy: Phoenix or Ostrich?," *West European Politics*, 18(2): 422–8.

—— (1999) "The 1998 Riksdag Election: Hobson's Choice and Sweden's Voice," *West European Politics*, 22(1): 187–94.

Magone, José M. (2003) [2000] "Portugal: The Rationale of Democratic Regime Building," in Wolfgang C. Müller and Kaare Strøm (eds) *Coalition Governments in Western Europe*, New York: Oxford University Press, pp. 529–58.

Mahon, Rianne (1999) "'Yesterday's Modern Times Are No Longer Modern': Swedish Unions Confront the Double Shift," in Andrew Martin and George Ross (eds) *The Brave New World of European Labor*, New York: Berghahn, pp. 125–66.

Mair, Peter (1987a) *The Changing Irish Party System*, London: Frances Pinter.

—— (1987b) "Policy Competition," in Michael Laver, Peter Mair and Richard Sinnott (eds) *How Ireland Voted: The Irish General Election 1987*, Dublin: Poolbeg, pp. 32–44.

—— (2001) "The Freezing Hypothesis: An Evaluation," in Lauri Karvonen and Stein Kuhnle (eds) *Party Systems and Voter Alignments Revisited*, London: Routledge, pp. 27–45.

—— (2006) Personal communication, February 13.

—— and Ingrid van Biezen (2001) "Party Membership in Twenty European Democracies, 1980–2000," *Party Politics*, 7(1): 5–21.

—— and Michael Marsh (2004) "Political Parties in Electoral Markets in Postwar Ireland," in Peter Mair, Wolfgang C. Müller and Fritz Plasser (eds) *Political Parties and Electoral Change: Party Responses to Electoral Markets*, London: Sage, pp. 234–63.

Mandelson, Peter and Roger Liddle (1996) *The Blair Revolution. Can New Labour Deliver?*, London: Faber and Faber.

Manin, Bernard, Adam Przeworski and Susan Stokes (1999) "Elections and Representation," in Adam Przeworski, Susan C. Stokes and Bernard Manin (eds) *Democracy, Accountability, and Representation*, New York: Cambridge University Press, pp. 29–54.

Maravall, José María (1993) "Politics and Policy: Economic Reforms in Southern Europe," in Luis Carlos Bresser Pereira, José María Maravall and Adam Przeworski (eds) *Economic Reforms in New Democracies. A Social Democratic Approach*, Cambridge: Cambridge University Press, pp. 77–131.

Mares, Isabela (2006) *Taxation, Wage Bargaining, and Unemployment*, New York: Cambridge University Press.

Marginson, Paul and Keith Sisson (2004) *European Integration and Industrial Relations: Multi-Level Governance in the Making*, Basingstoke: Palgrave Macmillan.

Marsh, David (1992) *The New Politics of British Trade Unionism: Union Power and the Thatcher Legacy*, Basingstoke: Macmillan.

—— and Heather Savigny (2005) "Changes in Trade Union–Government Relations 1974–2002," *Politics*, 25(3): 165–74.

Marsh, Holly (2002) "Changing Pressure-Group Politics: The Case of the TUC 1994–2000," *Politics*, 22(3): 143–51.

Marsh, Michael and Richard Sinnott (1990) "How the Voters Decided," in Michael Gallagher and Richard Sinnott (eds) *How Ireland Voted 1989*, Galway: PSAI Press, pp. 94–132.

—— and Richard Sinnott and Richard Sinnott (1993) "The Voters: Stability and Change," in Michael Gallagher and Michael Laver (eds) *How Ireland Voted 1992*, Limerick: PSAI Press, pp. 93–114.

Marsh, Michael and Paul Mitchell (1999) "Office, Votes and Then Policy: Hard Choices for Political Parties in the Republic of Ireland, 1981–1992," in Wolfgang C. Müller and Kaare Strøm (eds) *Policy, Office or Votes? How Political Parties in Western Europe Make Hard Decisions*, New York: Cambridge University Press, pp. 36–62.

Martin, Roderick (1992) *Bargaining Power*, Oxford: Clarendon.

Martín Artiles, Antonio (2007) "Industrial Relations Developments 2006 – Spain," *European Industrial Relations Observatory*, June 13. Online. Available <http://www.eurofound.europa.eu/eiro/studies/tn0703019s/es0703019q.htm> (accessed November 22, 2009).

Martínez Lucio, Miguel (2002) "Spain in the 1990s: Strategic Concertation," in Stefan Berger and Hugh Compston (eds) *Policy Concertation and Social Partnership in Western Europe: Lessons for the 21st Century*, New York: Berghahn Books, pp. 265–78.

Maurer, Lynn M. (1999) "Parliamentary Influence in a New Democracy: The Spanish Congress," *Journal of Legislative Studies*, 5(2): 24–45.

Meardi, Guglielmo (2006) "Social Pacts on the Road to EMU: A Comparison of the Italian and Polish Experiences," *European Journal of Industrial Relations*, 27(2): 197–222.

Meier Jaeger, Mads (2006) "Welfare Regimes and Attitudes Toward Redistribution: The Regime Hypothesis Revisited," *European Sociological Review*, 22(2): 157–70.

Méndez-Lago, Mónica (1999) "Electoral Consequences of (De-)Pillarization: The Cases of Austria, Belgium and the Netherlands (1945–96)," in Kurt Richard Luther and Kris Deschouwer (eds) *Party Elites in Divided Societies: Political Parties in Consociational Democracy*, London: Routledge, pp. 191–223.

Menz, Georg (2006) "Old Bottles – New Wine: The New Dynamics of Industrial Relations," in Kenneth Dyson and Stephen Padgett (eds) *The Politics of Economic Reform in Germany: Global, Rhineland, or Hybrid Capitalism?*, London: Routledge, pp. 82–93.

Meredith, Stephen (2008) *Labours Old and New: The Parliamentary Right of the British Labour Party 1970–79 and the Roots of New Labour*, Manchester: Manchester University Press.

Mershon, Carol (2002) *The Costs of Coalition*, Stanford, CA: Stanford University Press.

Micheletti, Michele (1989) "The Swedish Elections of 1988," *Electoral Studies*, 8(2): 169–74.

Minkenberg, Michael (2001) "The Radical Right in Public Office: Agenda-Setting and Policy Effects," *West European Politics*, 24(4): 1–21.

Minkin, Lewis (1992) *The Contentious Alliance: Trade Unions and the Labour Party*, Edinburgh: Edinburgh University Press.

Mitchell, Paul (2003) [2000] "Ireland: From Single Party to Coalition Rule," in Wolfgang C. Müller and Kaare Strøm (eds) *Coalition Governments in Western Europe*, Oxford: Oxford University Press, pp. 126–57.

Molina Romo, Oscar (2005) "Political Exchange and Bargaining Reform in Italy and Spain," *European Journal of Industrial Relations*, 11(1): 7–26.

—— (2006) "Trade Union Strategies and Change in Neo-Corporatist Concertation: A New Century of Political Exchange?," *West European Politics*, 29(4): 640–64.

—— and Martin Rhodes (2002) "Corporatism: The Past, Present, and Future of a Concept," *Annual Review of Political Science*, 5: 305–31.

—— and Martin Rhodes (2007a) "The Political Economy of Adjustment in Mixed Market Economies: A Study of Spain and Italy," in Bob Hancké, Martin Rhodes and Mark Thatcher (eds) *Beyond Varieties of Capitalism: Conflict, Contradictions, and Complementarities in the European Economy*, Oxford: Oxford University Press, pp. 223–52.

—— and Martin Rhodes (2007b) "Industrial Relations and the Welfare State in Italy: Assessing the Potential of Negotiated Change," *West European Politics*, 30(4): 803–29.

Moses, Jonathan (1998a) "Sweden and EMU," in Erik Jones, Jeffry Frieden and Francisco Torres (eds) *Joining Europe's Monetary Club: the Challenges for Smaller Member-States*, New York: St Martin's Press, pp. 203–24.

—— (1998b) "Finland and EMU," in Erik Jones, Jeffry Frieden and Francisco Torres (eds) *Joining Europe's Monetary Club: the Challenges for Smaller Member-States*, New York: St Martin's Press, pp. 83–104.

Müller, Wolfgang C. (1992) "Austrian Governmental Institutions: Do They Matter?," *West European Politics*, 15(1) 99–131.

—— (1996) "Political Parties," in Volkmar Lauber (ed.) *Contemporary Austrian Politics*, Boulder, CO: Westview, pp. 59–102.

—— (2000) "The Austrian Election of October 1999: A Shift to the Right," *West European Politics*, 23(3): 191–200.

—— (2003) [2000] "Austria: Tight Coalitions and Stable Government," in Wolfgang C. Müller and Kaare Strøm (eds) *Coalition Governments in Western Europe*, Oxford: Oxford University Press, pp. 86–125.

—— (2004) "The Parliamentary Election in Austria, November 2002," *Electoral Studies*, 23(2): 346–53.

—— (2005) [2002] "Parties and the Institutional Framework," in Kurt Richard Luther and Ferdinand Muller-Rommel (eds) *Political Parties in the New Europe: Political and Analytical Challenges*, Oxford: Oxford University Press, pp. 249–92.

—— (2008) "The Surprising Election in Austria, October 2006," *Electoral Studies*, 27(1): 175–9.

—— and Franz Fallend (2004) "Changing Patters of Party Competition in Austria: From Multipolar to Bipolar System," *West European Politics*, 27(5): 801–35.

—— and Kaare Strøm (eds) (2003) [2000] *Coalition Governments in Western Europe*, Oxford: Oxford University Press.

——, Fritz Plasser and Peter A. Ulram (2004) "Party Responses to the Erosion of Voter Loyalties in Austria," in Peter Mair, Wolfgang C. Müller and Fritz Plasser (eds) *Political Parties and Electoral Change: Party Responses to Electoral Markets*, London: Sage, pp. 145–78.

Murphy, Gary (2003) "The Background to the Election," in Michael Gallagher, Michael Marsh and Paul Mitchell (eds) *How Ireland Voted 2002*, Basingstoke: Palgrave Macmillan, pp. 1–20.

Murphy, Ronan J., and David M. Farrell (2002) "Party Politics in Ireland: Regularizing a Volatile System," in Paul Webb, David Farrell and Ian Holliday (eds) *Political Parties in Advanced Industrial Democracies*, Oxford: Oxford University Press, pp. 217–47.

Myles, John and Paul Pierson (2001) "The Comparative Political Economy of Pension Reform," in Paul Pierson (ed.) *The New Politics of the Welfare State*, Oxford: Oxford University Press, pp. 305–33.

Natali, David and Philippe Pochet (2009) "The Evolution of Social Pacts in the EMU Era: What Type of Institutionalization?," *European Journal of Industrial Relations*, 15(2): 147–66.

Negrelli, Serafino (2000) "Social Pacts in Italy and Europe: Similar Strategies and Structures; Different Models and National Stories," in Giuseppe Fajertag and

Philippe Pochet (eds) *Social Pacts in Europe – New Dynamics*, 2nd edn, Brussels: European Trade Union Institute, pp. 85–112.

—— and Ettore Santi (1990) "Industrial Relations in Italy," in Guido Baglioni and Colin Crouch (eds) *European Industrial Relations: The Challenge of Flexibility*, London: Sage, pp. 154–98.

—— and Valeria Pulignano (2008) "Change in Contemporary Italy's Social Concertation," *Industrial Relations Journal*, 39(1): 63–77.

Newell, James L. and Martin Bull (1997) "Party Organizations and Alliances in Italy in the 1990s: A Revolution of Sorts," *West European Politics*, 20(1): 81–109.

Nousiainen, Jaakko (2003) [2000] "Finland: The Consolidation of Parliamentary Governance," in Wolfgang C. Müller and Kaare Strøm (eds), *Coalition Governments in Western Europe*, New York: Cambridge University Press, pp. 264–99.

Nurmi, Hannu and Lasse Nurmi (2001) "The 1999 Parliamentary Elections in Finland," *Electoral Studies*, 20(1): 147–57.

—— (2004) "The Parliamentary Election in Finland, March 2003," *Electoral Studies*, 23(3): 557–65.

Nygård, Mikael (2006) "Welfare-Ideological Change in Scandinavia: A Comparative Analysis of Partisan Welfare State Positions in Four Nordic Countries, 1970–2003," *Scandinavian Political Studies*, 29(4): 356–85.

Obinger, Herbert, Francis G. Castles, and Stephan Leibfried (2005) "Introduction: Federalism and the Welfare State," in Herbert Obinger, Stephan Leibfried and Francis G. Castles (eds) *Federalism and the Welfare State: New World and European Experiences*, Cambridge: Cambridge University Press. pp. 1–48.

O'Donnell, Rory and Damian Thomas (2002) "Ireland in the 1990s: Concertation Triumphant," in Stefan Berger and Hugh Compston (eds) *Policy Concertation and Social Partnership in Western Europe: Lessons for the 21st Century*, Oxford: Berghahn, pp. 167–89.

O'Donnell, Rory, Maura Adshead and Damian Thomas (2007) "The Emergence and Evolution of Social Pacts in Ireland," Florence: European University Institute, New Modes of Governance Project, Country Report.

OECD (1990) *Economic Outlook June 1990*, Paris: Organisation for Economic Cooperation and Development.

—— (1996) *Economic Outlook December 1996*, Paris: Organisation for Economic Cooperation and Development.

—— (1999) *Economic Outlook December 1999*, Paris: Organisation for Economic Cooperation and Development.

—— (2003) *Trade Union Membership Dataset 1980–2001*, Paris: Organisation for Economic Cooperation and Development.

—— (2004) *Employment Outlook 2004*, Paris: Organisation for Economic Cooperation and Development.

—— (2007) *Economic Outlook June 2007*, Paris: Organisation for Economic Cooperation and Development.

Padgett, Stephen (2003) "Political Economy: The German Model under Stress," in Stephen Padgett, William E. Paterson and Gordon Smith (eds) *Developments in German Politics*, 3rd edn, Durham, NC: Duke University Press, pp. 121–42.

—— (2005) "The Party Politics of Economic Reform: Public Opinion, Party Positions and Partisan Cleavage," *German Politics*, 14(2): 248–74.

Panitch, Leo and Colin Leys (2001) *The End of Parliamentary Socialism: From New Left to New Labour*, 2nd edn, London: Verso.

Papadakis, Elim and Clive Bean (1993) "Popular Support for the Welfare State: A Comparison Between Institutional Regimes," *Journal of Public Policy*, 13(3): 227–54.

Park, Sung Ho (2009) "Inter–Union Rivalry and the Modality of Political Exchange: The Experiences of Five Countries in Developed Europe," Paper presented at Midwest Political Science Association Meeting, Chicago, April.

Partido Popular (N.d.) "¿Quiénes Somos?," Online. Available <http://www.pp.es/partido_popular/qui_somos.asp> (accessed March 26, 2002).

—— (2000) "Programa 2000," Online. Available <http://www.pp.es/program_elect/program2000.asp> (accessed March 26, 2002).

Pasquino, Gianfranco (1996) "The Government of Lamberto Dini," in Mario Caciagli and David I. Kertzer (eds) *Italian Politics: The Stalled Transition*, Boulder, CO: Westview Press, pp. 137–52.

Patzelt, Werner J. (1999) "The Very Federal House: The German Bundesrat," in Samuel C. Patterson and Anthony Mughan (eds) *Senates: Bicameralism in the Contemporary World*, Columbus, OH: Ohio State University Press, pp. 59–92.

Pelinka, Anton (2002) "Austria Between 1983 and 2000," in Rolf Steininger, Günter Bischof and Michael Gehler (eds) *Austria in the Twentieth Century*, New Brunswick: Transaction, pp. 321–41.

Pérez, Sofía A. (2000a) "From Decentralization to Reorganization: Explaining the Return of National Bargaining in Italy and Spain," *Comparative Politics*, 32(4): 437–58.

—— (2000b) "Social Pacts in Spain," in Giuseppe Fajertag and Philippe Pochet (eds) *Social Pacts in Europe – New Dynamics*, 2nd edn, Brussels: European Trade Union Institute, pp. 343–64.

Pérez-Díaz, Victor (1999) *Spain at the Crossroads: Civil Society, Politics, and the Rule of Law*, Cambridge, MA: Harvard University Press.

Pernicka, Susanne (2001) "Negotiations Deadlocked Over More Flexible Shop Opening Hours," *European Industrial Relations Observatory*, July 28. Online. Available <http://www.eiro.eurofound.ie/2001/07/inbrief/at0107221n.html> (accessed November 22, 2009).

Pesthoff, Victor A. (2002) "Sweden in the 1990s: The Demise of Policy Concertation and Social Partnership and its Sudden Reappearance in 1998," in Stefan Berger and Hugh Compston (eds) *Policy Concertation and Social Partnership in Western Europe*, Oxford: Berghahn Books, pp. 295–308.

Pestieau, Pierre (2006) *The Welfare State in the European Union: Economic and Social Perspectives*, Oxford: Oxford University Press.

Phillips, Ann L. (1995) "An Island of Stability? The German Political Party System and the Elections of 1994," *West European Politics*, 18(3): 219–30.

Piazza, James (2001) "De-Linking Labour: Labour Unions and Social Democratic Parties Under Globalization," *Party Politics*, 7(4): 413–35.

Picot, Georg (2009) "Party Competition and Reforms of Unemployment Benefits in Germany: How a Small Change in Electoral Demand Can Make a Big Difference," *German Politics*, 18(2): 155–79.

Pierson, Paul (1994) *Dismantling the Welfare State? Reagan, Thatcher, and the Politics of Retrenchment*, New York: Cambridge University Press.

—— (1996) "The New Politics of the Welfare State," *World Politics*, 48(2): 143–79.

—— (2001) "Coping with Permanent Austerity: Welfare State Restructuring in Affluent Societies," in Paul Pierson (ed.) The *New Politics of the Welfare State*, Oxford: Oxford University Press, pp. 410–56.

Pizzorno, Alessandro (1978) "Political Exchange and Collective Identity in Industrial Conflict," in Colin Crouch and Alessandro Pizzorno (eds) *The Resurgence of Class Conflict in Western Europe since 1968, Vol 2*, London: Macmillan, pp. 277–98.

Plasser, Fritz and Peter A. Ulram (1996) "Kampagnedynamik: Strategischer und Thematischer Kontext der Wählerentscheidung," in Fritz Plasser, Peter A. Ulram and Günther Ogris (eds) *Wahlkampf und Wählerentscheidung: Analysen zur Nationalratswahl 1995*, Wien: Signum, pp. 13–46.

Pochet, Philippe (ed.) (2002) *Wage Policy in the Eurozone*, Brussels: Peter Lang.

—— and Giuseppe Fajertag (2000) "A New Era for Social Pacts in Europe," in Giuseppe Fajertag and Philippe Pochet (eds) *Social Pacts in Europe – New Dynamics*, 2nd edn, Brussels: European Trade Union Institute, pp. 9–40.

Poguntke, Thomas (2004) "Do Parties Respond? Challenges to Political Parties and Their Consequences," in Kay Lawson and Thomas Poguntke (eds) *How Political Parties Respond: Interest Aggregation Revisited*, London: Routledge, pp. 1–14.

—— (2005a) [2002] "Party Organizational Linkage: Parties Without Firm Social Roots?," in Kurt Richard Luther and Ferdinand Müller-Rommel (eds) *Political Parties in the New Europe: Political and Analytical Challenges*, Oxford: Oxford University Press, pp. 43–62.

—— (2005b) "A Presidentializing Party State? The Federal Republic of Germany," in Thomas Poguntke and Paul Webb (eds) *The Presidentialization of Politics: A Comparative Study of Modern Democracies*, Oxford: Oxford University Press, pp. 63–87.

Pontusson, Jonas (1994) "Sweden: After the Golden Age," in Perry Anderson and Patrick Camiller (eds) *Mapping the West European Left*, London: Verso, pp. 23–54.

Powell, G. Bingham and Guy D. Whitten (1993) "A Cross-National Analysis of Economic Voting: Taking Account of the Political Context," *American Journal of Political Science*, 37(2): 391–414.

Preston, Paul (1986) *The Triumph of Democracy in Spain*, London: Methuen.

Prior, Jim (1986) *A Balance of Power*, London: Hamish Hamilton.

Pulzer, Peter (2003) "The Devil They Know: The German Federal Election of 2002," *West European Politics*, 26(2): 153–64.

Ragin, Charles C. (2008) *Redesigning Social Inquiry: Fuzzy Sets and Beyond*, Chicago: University of Chicago Press.

Recio, Albert and Jordi Roca (2001) "The Spanish Socialists in Power: Thirteen Years of Economic Policy," in Andrew Glyn (ed.) *Social Democracy in Neoliberal Times*, Oxford: Oxford University Press, pp. 173–99.

Regalia, Ida (2005) *Regulating New Forms of Employment*, Abingdon: Routledge.

—— and Marino Regini (1998) "Italy: The Dual Character of Industrial Relations," in Anthony Ferner and Richard Hyman (eds) *Changing Industrial Relations in Europe*. Oxford, Blackwell, pp. 459–503.

Regini, Marino and Ida Regalia (1997) "Employers, Unions and the State: The Resurgence of Concertation in Italy?," *West European Politics*, 20(1): 210–30.

Rhodes, Martin (1996) "Globalization and the Welfare State: A Critical Review of Recent Debates," *European Journal of Social Policy*, 6(4): 305–27.

Rhodes, Martin (1997) "Spain," in Hugh Compston (ed.) *The New Politics of Unemployment: Radical Policy Initiatives in Western Europe*, New York: Routledge, pp. 103–24.

—— (2001) "The Political Economy of Social Pacts: 'Competitive Corporatism' and European Welfare Reform," in Paul Pierson (ed.) *The New Politics of the Welfare State*, Oxford: Oxford University Press, pp. 165–94.

—— (2003) "National 'Pacts' and EU Governance in Social Policy and the Labor Market," in Jonathan Zeitlin and David Trubek (eds) *Governing Work and Welfare in a New Economy*, Oxford: Oxford University Press, pp. 129–57.

Rigby, Mike and Mari Luz Marco Aledo (2001) "The Worst Record in Europe?: A Comparative Analysis of Industrial Conflict in Spain," *European Journal of Industrial Relations*, 7(3): 287–305.

Roche, William (1997a) "Pay Determination, the State and the Politics of Industrial Relations," in Thomas V. Murphy and William K. Roche (eds) *Irish Industrial Relations in Practice*, 2nd edn, Dublin: Oak Tree Press, pp. 145–226.

—— (1997b) "Between Regime Fragmentation and Realignment: Irish Industrial Relations in the 1990s," *Industrial Relations Journal*, 29(2): 112–25.

—— (2007) "Social Partnership in Ireland and New Social Pacts," *Industrial Relations Journal*, 46(3): 395–425.

Rohrschneider, Robert and Michael Wolf (2004) "One Electorate? Social Policy Views and Voters' Choice in Unified Germany Since 1990," in Werner Reutter (ed.) *Germany on the Road to "Normalcy": Policies and Politics of the Red-Green Federal Government, 1998–2002*, New York: Palgrave Macmillan, pp. 21–46.

Roller, Edeltraud (1999) "Shrinking the Welfare State: Citizens' Attitudes Towards Cuts in Social Spending in Germany in the 1990s," *German Politics*, 8(1): 21–39.

Ross, Fiona (2000a) "'Beyond Left and Right': The New Partisan Politics of Welfare," *Governance*, 13(2): 155–83.

—— (2000b) "Framing Welfare Reform in Affluent Societies: Rendering Restructuring More Palatable?," *Journal of Public Policy*, 20(3): 169–93.

Rothstein, Bo (2000) "The Future of the Universal Welfare State: An Institutional Approach," in Stein Kuhnle (ed.) *Survival of the European Welfare State*, London: Routledge, pp. 217–34.

Royo, Sebastián (2002) "A New Century of Corporatism? Corporatism in Spain and Portugal," *West European Politics*, 25(3): 77–104.

—— (2006) "Beyond Confrontation: The Resurgence of Social Bargaining in Spain in the 1990s," *Comparative Political Studies*, 39(8): 969–95.

—— (2007) "Varieties of Capitalism in Spain: Business and the Politics of Coordination," *European Journal of Industrial Relations*, 13(1): 47–65.

Rueda, David (2007) *Social Democracy Inside Out: Partisanship and Labor Market Policy in Industrialized Democracies*, New York: Oxford University Press.

Ruin, Olof (1983) "The 1982 Swedish Election: The Re-Emergence of an Old Pattern in a New Situation," *Electoral Studies*, 2(2):166–71.

Saalfeld, Thomas (2003) [2000] "Germany: Stable Parties, Chancellor Democracy, and the Art of Informal Settlement," in Wolfgang C. Müller and Kaare Strøm (eds) *Coalition Governments in Western Europe*, Oxford: Oxford University Press, pp. 32–85.

—— (2005) "Germany: Stability and Strategy in a Mixed-Member Proportional System," in Michael Gallagher and Paul Mitchell (eds) *The Politics of Electoral Systems*, Oxford: Oxford University Press, pp. 209–30.

Sainsbury, Diane (1991) "Swedish Social Democracy in Transition: The Party's Record in the 1980s and the Challenge of the 1990s," *West European Politics*, 14(3): 31–57.

—— (1992) "The 1991 Swedish Election: Protest, Fragmentation, and a Shift to the Right," *West European Politics*, 15(2): 160–66.

—— (1993) "The Swedish Social Democrats and the Legacy of Continuous Reform: Asset or Dilemma?," *West European Politics*, 16(1): 39–61.

Sassoon, Donald (1996) *One Hundred Years of Socialism: The West European Left in the Twentieth Century*, London: I.B.Tauris.

Scarrow, Susan (2000) "Parties Without Members? Party Organization in a Changing Electoral Environment," in Russell J. Dalton and Martin P. Wattenberg (eds) *Parties Without Partisans: Political Change in Advanced Industrial Democracies*, Oxford: Oxford University Press, pp. 79–101.

—— (2002) "Party Decline in the Parties State? The Changing Environment of German Politics," in Paul Webb, David M. Farrell and Ian Holliday (eds) *Political Parties in Advanced Industrial Democracies*, Oxford: Oxford University Press, pp. 77–106.

Scheepers, Peer and Manfred te Grotenhuis (2005) "Who Cares for the Poor? Micro and Macro Determinants for Alleviating Poverty in 15 European Countries," *European Sociological Review*, 21(5): 453–65.

Schludi, Martin (2005) *The Reform of Bismarckian Pension Systems: A Comparison of Pension Politics in Austria, France, Germany, Italy and Sweden*, Amsterdam: Amsterdam University Press.

Schmidt, Vivien A. (2002) *The Futures of European Capitalism*, New York: Oxford University Press.

Schmitter, Philippe and Gerhard Lehmbruch (eds) (1979) *Trends Towards Corporatist Intermediation*, Beverly Hills, CA: Sage.

Schulze, Isabelle and Sven Jochem (2007) "Germany: Beyond Policy Gridlock," in Ellen M. Immergut, Karen M. Anderson and Isabelle Schulze (eds) *The Handbook of West European Pension Politics*, Oxford: Oxford University Press, pp. 660–706.

——, Sven Jochem and Michael Moran (2007) "United Kingdom: Pension Politics in an Adversarial System," in Ellen M. Immergut, Karen M. Anderson and Isabelle Schulze (eds) *The Handbook of West European Pension Politics*, Oxford: Oxford University Press, pp. 49–96.

——, Sven Jochem and Martin Schludi (2007) "Austria: From Electoral Cartels to Competitive Coalition Building," in Ellen M. Immergut, Karen M. Anderson and Isabelle Schulze (eds) *The Handbook of West European Pension Politics*, Oxford: Oxford University Press, pp. 555–604.

Scott, Alan (1987) "The Austrian General Election of 1986," *Electoral Studies*, 6(2): 154–60.

SDP (1982a) "Towards Full Employment: A Common-Sense Approach to Economic Policy," London: Social Democratic Party, Green Paper No. 1.

—— (1982b) "Industrial Relations 1. Trade Union Reform," London: Social Democratic Party, Policy Document No. 3.

Seeleib-Kaiser, Martin (2003) "The Welfare State: Incremental Transformation," in Stephen Padgett, William E. Paterson and Gordon Smith (eds) *Developments in German Politics*, 3rd edn, Durham, NC: Duke University Press, pp. 143–60.

Seifert, Hartmut and Heiko Massa-Wirth (2005) "Pacts for Employment and Competitiveness in Germany," *Industrial Relations Journal*, 36(3): 217–40.

Seyd, Patrick and Paul Whiteley (2004) "From Disaster to Landslide: The Case of the British Labour Party," in Kay Lawson and Thomas Poguntke (eds) *How Political Parties Respond: Interest Aggregation Revisited*, London: Routledge, pp. 41–60.

Share, Donald (1986) *The Making of Spanish Democracy*, New York: Praeger.

Shaw, Eric (1996) *The Labour Party Since 1945: Old Labour, New Labour*, Oxford: Blackwell.

Siaroff, Alan (1999) "Corporatism in 24 Industrial Democracies: Meaning and Measurement," *European Journal of Political Research*, 36(2): 175–205.

Silvia, Stephen J. (1999) "Reform Gridlock and the Role of the Bundesrat in German Politics," in Joanne B. Brzinski, Thomas D. Lancaster and Christian Tuschhoff (eds) *Compounded Representation in Western Federations*, London: Routledge, pp. 167–81.

Sisson, Keith, Jacques Freyssinet, Hubert Krieger, Kevin O'Kelly, Claus Schnabel and Hartmut Seifert (1999) *Pacts for Employment and Competitiveness: Concepts and Issues*, Dublin: European Foundation for the Improvement of Living and Working Conditions.

Smith, Gordon (2003) "The 'New Model' Party System," in Stephen Padgett, William E. Paterson and Gordon Smith (eds) *Developments in German Politics*, 3rd edn, Durham, NC: Duke University Press, pp. 82–100.

Statistisches Bundesamt (2005) "Wahlberechtigte, Wähler, Stimmabgabe und Sitzverteilung bei den Bundestagswahlen seit 1949," Online. Available <http://www.bundeswahlleiter.de/de/bundestagswahlen/downloads/bundestagswahlergebnisse/btw_ab49_ergebnisse.pdf> (accessed November 22, 2009).

Stokes, Susan (2001) "Introduction: Public Opinion of Market Reforms: A Framework," in Susan Stokes (ed.) *Public Support for Market Reforms in New Democracies*, New York: Cambridge University Press, pp. 1–32.

Streeck, Wolfgang and Anke Hassel (2004) "The Crumbling Pillars of Social Partnership," in Herbert Kitschelt and Wolfgang Streeck (eds) *Germany: Beyond the Stable State*, London: Frank Cass, pp. 101–24.

Streeck, Wolfgang and Christine Trampusch (2006) "Economic Reform and the Political Economy of the German Welfare State," in Kenneth Dyson and Stephen Padgett (eds) *The Politics of Economic Reform in Germany: Global, Rhineland, or Hybrid Capitalism?*, London: Routledge, pp. 60–81.

Strøm, Kaare (1990) *Minority Government and Majority Rule*, New York: Cambridge University Press.

—— and Wolfgang C. Müller (1999) "Political Parties and Hard Choices," in Wolfgang C. Müller and Kaare Strøm (eds) *Policy, Office, or Votes? How Political Parties in Western Europe Make Hard Decisions*, New York: Cambridge University Press, pp. 1–35.

Stueckler, Angelika (2001) "New Controversy Over Shop Opening Hours," *European Industrial Relations Observatory*, February 28. Online. Available <http://www.eiro.eurofound.ie/2001/01/inbrief/at0101239n.html> (accessed November 22, 2009).

Sturm, Daniel Friedrich (2007) "Wie es zur Bonner Wende Kam," *Die Welt*, October 1. Online. Available <http://www.welt.de/die-welt/article1225579/Wie_es_zur_Bonner_Wende_kam.html> (accessed November 22, 2009).

Sully, Melanie A. (1996) "The 1995 Austrian Election: Winter of Discontent," *West European Politics*, 19(3): 633–40.

Sundberg, Jan (2002) "The Scandinavian Party Model at the Crossroads," in Paul Webb, David Farrell and Ian Holliday (eds) *Political Parties in Advanced Industrial Democracies*, Oxford: Oxford University Press, pp. 181–216.

Suzuki, Akira (2004) "The Rise and Fall of Interunion Wage Coordination and Tripartite Dialogue in Japan," in Harry C. Katz, Wonduck Lee and Joohee Lee (eds) *The New Structure of Labor Relations: Tripartism and Decentralization*, Ithaca, NY: ILR Press, pp. 119–42.

Svallfors, Stefan (1997) "Worlds of Welfare and Attitudes to Redistribution: A Comparison of Eight Western Nations," *European Sociological Review*, 13(3): 283–304.

Swank, Duane (2001) "Political Institutions and Welfare State Restructuring: The Impact of Institutions on Social Policy Change in Developed Democracies," in Paul Pierson (ed.) *The New Politics of the Welfare State*, Oxford: Oxford University Press, pp. 197–237.

—— (2002) *Global Capital, Political Institutions, and Policy Change in Developed Welfare States*, New York: Cambridge University Press.

Sweeney, Kate and Jackie Davies (1996) "International Comparisons of Labour Disputes in 1994," *Labour Market Trends*, 104(4): 153–59.

Taagepera, Rein and Matthew Soberg Shugart (1989) *Seats and Votes: The Effects and Determinants of Electoral Systems*, New Haven CN: Yale University Press.

Tálos, Emmerich (1996) "Corporatism – the Austrian Model," in Volkmar Lauber (ed.) *Contemporary Austrian Politics*, Boulder, CO: Westview, pp. 103–23.

—— (2004) "Umbau des Sozialstaates? Österreich und Deutschland im Vergleich," *Politische Vierteljahresschrift*, 45(2): 213–36.

—— (2005) "Vom Vorzeige- zum Auslaufmodell? Österreichs Sozialpartnerschaft 1945–2005," in Ferdinand Karlhofer and Emmerich Tálos (eds) *Sozialpartnerschaft: Österreichische und Europäische Perspektiven*, Wien: LIT Verlag, pp. 185–216.

—— and Bernhard Kittel (2002) "Austria in the 1990s: The Routine of Social Partnership in Question?," in Stefan Berger and Hugh Compston (eds) *Policy Concertation and Social Partnership in Western Europe: Lessons for the 21st Century*, New York: Berghahn, pp. 35–50.

Tarrow, Sidney (2004) "Bridging the Qantitative-Qualitative Divide," in Henry E. Brady and David Collier (eds) *Rethinking Social Inquiry: Diverse Tools, Shared Standards*, Lanham, MD: Rowman and Littlefield, pp. 171–80.

Taylor, Andrew (2001) "The 'Stepping Stones' Programme: Conservative Party Thinking on Trade Unions, 1975–9," *Historical Studies in Industrial Relations*, 11: 109–33.

Taylor, Robert (1993) *The Trade Union Question in British Politics: Government and Unions Since 1945*, Oxford: Blackwell.

—— (2000) *The TUC: From the General Strike to New Unionism*, Basingstoke: Palgrave.

Teague, Paul and Jimmy Donaghey (2004) "The Irish Experiment in Social Partnership," in Harry C. Katz, Wonduck Lee and Joohee Lee (eds) *The New Structure of Labor Relations: Tripartism and Decentralization*, Ithaca, NY: ILR Press, pp. 10–36.

—— (2009) "Why Has Irish Social Partnership Survived?," *British Journal of Industrial Relations*, 47(1): 55–78.

Tebbit, Norman (1989) *Upwardly Mobile*, London: Futura Publications.

Thatcher, Margaret (1993) *The Downing Street Years*, London: Harper Collins.

Thelen, Kathleen (2001) "Varieties of Labor Politics in the Developed Democracies," in Peter Hall and David Soskice (eds) *Varieties of Capitalism: The Institutional Foundations of Comparative Advantage*, New York: Oxford University Press, pp. 71–103.

Therborn, Goran (1991) "Swedish Social Democracy and the Transition from Industrial to Post-Industrial Politics," in Frances Fox Piven (ed.) *Labor Parties in Post-Industrial Societies*, Cambridge: Polity Press, pp. 101–23.

Thompson, Noel (2006) *Political Economy and the Labour Party: The Economics of Democratic Socialism, 1884–Present*, 2nd edn, London: Routledge.

—— (2008) "Hollowing out the State: Public Choice Theory and the Critique of Keynesian Social Democracy," *Contemporary British History*, 22(3): 355–82.

Thomsen, Jens and Peter Frølund (1996) *British Politics and Trade Unions in the 1980s: Governing Against Pressure*, Aldershot: Dartmouth.

Thorpe, Andrew (2001) *A History of the British Labour Party*, 2nd edn, Basingstoke: Palgrave Macmillan.

Timmermans, Arco I. (2003) *High Politics in the Low Countries: An Empirical Study of Coalition Agreements in Belgium and the Netherlands*, Aldershot: Ashgate.

Timonen, Virpi (2003) *Restructuring the Welfare State: Globalisation and Social Policy Reform in Finland and Sweden*, Cheltenham: Edward Elgar.

Tomandl, Theodor and Karl Fuerboeck (1986) *Social Partnership: The Austrian System of Industrial Relations and Social Insurance*, Ithaca, NY: ILR Press.

Torcal, Mariano and Guillem Rico (2004) "The 2004 Spanish General Election: In the Shadow of Al-Qaeda?," *South European Society & Politics*, 9(3): 107–21.

Traxler, Franz (2000) "National Pacts and Wage Regulation in Europe," in Giuseppe Fajertag and Philippe Pochet (eds) *Social Pacts in Europe – New Dynamics*, 2nd edn, Brussels: European Trade Union Institute, pp. 401–17.

—— and Bernd Brandl (2009) "Preconditions for Pacts on Income Policy: Bringing Structures Back In. A Comparison of Western Europe, 1980–2003," Paper presented at ESPAnet Conference, Urbino, Italy, September 17–19.

—— Sabine Blaschke and Bernhard Kittel (2001) *National Labour Relations in Internationalized Markets: A Comparative Study of Institutions, Changes, and Performance*, Oxford: Oxford University Press.

Tsakalotos, Euclid (2001) "The Political Economy of Social Democratic Economic Policies: The PASOK Experiment in Greece," in Andrew Glyn (ed.) *Social Democracy in Neoliberal Times*, Oxford: Oxford University Press, pp. 138–72.

Tunsch, Gary (1998) "Luxembourg: A Small Success Story," in Anthony Ferner and Richard Hyman (eds) *Changing Industrial Relations in Europe*, 2nd edn, Oxford: Blackwell, pp. 348–56.

Turnbull, Peter, Charles Woolfson and John Kelly (1992) *Dock Strike: Conflict and Restructuring in Britain's Ports*, Aldershot: Avebury.

Ulram, Peter A. and Wolfgang C. Müller (1995) "Die Ausgangslage für die Nationalratswahl 1994: Indikatoren und Trends," in Wolfgang C. Müller, Fritz Plasser and Peter A. Ulram (eds) *Wählerverhalten und Parteienwettbewerb: Analysen zur Nationalratswahl 1994*, Vienna: Signum, pp. 13–40.

Upchurch, Martin, Graham Taylor and Andrew Mathers (2009) *The Crisis of Social Democratic Trade Unionism in Western Europe: The Search for Alternatives*, Farnham: Ashgate.

van der Brug, Wouter, Cees van der Eijk and Mark Franklin (2007) *The Economy and the Vote: Economic Conditions and Elections in Fifteen Countries*, Cambridge: Cambridge University Press.

van Kersbergen, Kees (1999) "Contemporary Christian Democracy and the Demise of the Politics of Mediation," in Herbert Kitschelt, Gary Marks, Peter Lange and John D. Stephens (eds) *Continuity and Change in Contemporary Capitalism*, Cambridge: Cambridge University Press, pp. 346–70.

van Waarden, Frans and Gerhard Lehmbruch (eds) (2003) *Renegotiating the Welfare State: Flexible Adjustment Through Corporatist Concertation*, London: Routledge.

Verzichelli, Luca and Maurizio Cotta (2003) [2000] "Italy: From Constrained Coalitions to Alternating Governments?," in Wolfgang C. Müller and Kaare Strøm (eds) *Coalition Governments in Western Europe*, New York: Oxford University Press, pp. 433–97.

Vis, Barbara (2009) "Governments and Unpopular Social Policy Reform: Biting the Bullet or Steering Clear?," *European Journal of Political Research*, 48(1): 31–57.

Visser, Jelle (2006) "Union Membership Statistics in 24 Countries," *Monthly Labor Review*, 129(1): 38–49.

—— and Anton Hemerijck (1997) *"A Dutch Miracle." Job Growth, Welfare Reform and Corporatism in the Netherlands*, Amsterdam: Amsterdam University Press.

Volkens, Andrea and Hans-Dieter Klingemann (2005) [2002] "Parties, Ideologies, and Issues. Stability and Change in Fifteen European Party Systems 1945–1998," in Kurt Richard Luther and Ferdinand Müller-Rommel (eds) *Political Parties in the New Europe: Political and Analytical Challenges*, Oxford: Oxford University Press, pp. 143–67.

Von Prondzynski, Ferdinand (1998) "Ireland: Corporatism Revived," in Anthony Ferner and Richard Hyman (eds) *Changing Industrial Relations in Europe*, 2nd edn, Oxford: Blackwell Publishers, pp. 55–73.

Waddington, Jeremy (2000) "United Kingdom: Recovering from the Neo-liberal Assault?," in Jeremy Waddington and Reiner Hoffman (eds) *Trade Unions in Europe: Facing Challenges and Searching for Solutions*, Brussels: European Trade Union Institute, pp. 575–626.

Wallace, Joseph, Patrick Gunnigle and Gerard McMahon (2004) *Industrial Relations in Ireland*, 3rd edn, Dublin: Gill and Macmillan.

Webb, Paul (2004) "Party Responses to the Changing Electoral Market in Britain," in Peter Mair, Wolfgang C. Müller and Fritz Plasser (eds) *Political Parties and Electoral Change: Party Responses to Electoral Markets*, London: Sage, pp. 20–48.

Weiss, Linda (2003) "Introduction: Bringing Domestic Institutions Back In," in Linda Weiss (ed.) *States in the Global Economy: Bringing Domestic Institutions Back In*, Cambridge: Cambridge University Press, pp. 1–33.

Western, Bruce (1997) *Between Class and Market: Postwar Unionization in the Capitalist Democracies*, Princeton, NJ: Princeton University Press.

Wickham-Jones, Mark (1995) "Anticipating Social Democracy, Preempting Anticipations: Economic Policy-Making in the British Labor Party, 1987–1992," *Politics and Society*, 23(4): 465–94.

—— (1996) *Economic Strategy and the Labour Party: Politics and Policy-Making, 1970–83*, Basingstoke: Macmillan.

—— (2000) "New Labour in the Global Economy: Partisan Politics and the Social Democratic Model," *British Journal of Politics and International Relations*, 2(1): 1–25.

Widfeldt, Anders (1992) "The Swedish Parliamentary Election of 1991," *Electoral Studies*, 11(1): 72–77.

—— (1995) "The Swedish Parliamentary Election of 1994," *Electoral Studies*, 14(2): 206–12.

—— (2001) "Sweden: Weakening Links Between Political Parties and Interest Organizations," in Clive S. Thomas (ed) *Political Parties and Interest Groups: Shaping Democratic Governance*, Boulder, CO: Lynne Rienner.

—— (2003) "The Parliamentary Election in Sweden, 2002," *Electoral Studies*, 22(4): 778–84.

Wiesenthal, Helmut (2004) "German Unification and 'Model Germany': An Adventure in Institutional Conservatism," in Herbert Kitschelt and Wolfgang Streeck (eds) *Germany: Beyond the Stable State*, London: Frank Cass, pp. 37–58.

Wilensky, Harold L. (2002) *Rich Democracies: Political Economy, Public Policy, and Performance*, Berkeley, CA: University of California Press.

Young, Hugo (1990) *One of Us: A Biography of Margaret Thatcher*, London: Pan Macmillan.

Young, Lord (1990) *The Enterprise Years: A Businessman in the Cabinet*, London: Headline.

Zambarloukou, Stella (2006) "Collective Bargaining and Social Pacts: Greece in Comparative Perspective," *European Journal of Industrial Relations*, 12(2): 211–29.

Index